Contents at a Glance

Google™
Search and
Tools

P.186 onwards.

Preston Gralla

SAMS
**Teach
Yourself**

Sams Publishing, 800 East 96th Street, Indianapolis, Indiana 46240 USA

Google™ Search and Tools in a Snap

International Standard Book Number: 0-672-32869-0

Library of Congress Catalog Card Number: 2005934934

Printed in the United States of America

First Printing: April 2006

09   08   07   06   4   3   2   1

Trademarks

All terms mentioned in this book that are known to be trademarks or service marks have been appropriately capitalized. Sams Publishing cannot attest to the accuracy of this information. Use of a term in this book should not be regarded as affecting the validity of any trademark or service mark.

Google is a trademark of Google, Inc.

Warning and Disclaimer

Every effort has been made to make this book as complete and as accurate as possible, but no warranty or fitness is implied. The information provided is on an "as is" basis. The author and the publisher shall have neither liability nor responsibility to any person or entity with respect to any loss or damages arising from the information contained in this book.

Bulk Sales

Sams Publishing offers excellent discounts on this book when ordered in quantity for bulk purchases or special sales. For more information, please contact

> **U.S. Corporate and Government Sales**
> 1-800-382-3419
> corpsales@pearsontechgroup.com

For sales outside the United States, please contact

> **International Sales**
> international@pearsoned.com

Acquisitions Editor
Betsy Brown

Development Editor
Alice Martina Smith

Managing Editor
Charlotte Clapp

Project Editor
Tonya Simpson

Production Editor
Heather Wilkins

Indexer
Erika Millen

Proofreader
Heather Waye Arle

Technical Editor
Greg Perry

Publishing Coordinator
Vanessa Evans

Book Designer
Gary Adair

About the Author

Preston Gralla has been using Google since the days when it was an obscure, little-known website that claimed to have better search tools than anyone else. He quickly concluded that they were right. Preston is a best-selling author of more than 30 books that have been translated into 20 languages, including *How the Internet Works*, *How to Expand and Upgrade PCs*, *How Wireless Works*, and many others. A well-known technology guru, he has made many television and radio appearances including the *CBS Early Show*, CNN, MSNBC, and *ABC World News Now*. He has also done occasional commentaries about technology for National Public Radio's *All Things Considered*.

Gralla has published articles about technology for many national newspapers and magazines, including *USA Today*, the *Los Angeles Times*, the *Dallas Morning News* (for which he was a technology columnist), and *PC Magazine*. He was the founding managing editor of *PC Week* and founding editor, editor, and editorial director of *PC/Computing*. He also received the award for the Best Feature in a Computer Publication from the Computer Press Association.

Gralla is editor-in-chief of the Case Study Forum, which specializes in writing case studies for technology companies. He lives in Cambridge, Massachusetts, with his wife Lydia, son Gabe, and daughter Mia, who occasionally visits from college.

Dedication

To Google users everywhere, whose thirst for truth and bizarre, little-known facts knows no bounds.

Acknowledgments

Thanks, as always, to my wife Lydia, son Gabe, and daughter Mia. Thanks to Betsy Brown for entrusting me with the project; to Alice Martina Smith for focused, heads-up editing; to Tonya Simpson for keeping the project on track; and to Heather Wilkins for eagle-eyed attention to conventions. Thanks also to Greg Perry, Erika Millen, and Heather Waye Arle for their input in improving all aspects of this book.

We Want to Hear from You!

As the reader of this book, *you* are our most important critic and commentator. We value your opinion and want to know what we're doing right, what we could do better, what areas you'd like to see us publish in, and any other words of wisdom you're willing to pass our way.

You can email or write me directly to let me know what you did or didn't like about this book—as well as what we can do to make our books stronger.

Please note that I cannot help you with technical problems related to the topic of this book, and that due to the high volume of mail I receive, I might not be able to reply to every message.

When you write, please be sure to include this book's title and author as well as your name and phone or email address. I will carefully review your comments and share them with the author and editors who worked on the book.

Email: consumer@samspublishing.com

Mail: Mark Taber
         Associate Publisher
         Sams Publishing
         800 East 96th Street
         Indianapolis, IN 46240 USA

Reader Services

Visit our website and register this book at www.samspublishing.com/register for convenient access to any updates, downloads, or errata that might be available for this book.

PART I

Find Anything with Google

IN THIS PART:

1

✔ Start Here

Was the Internet searchable before there was Google?

Sometimes it seems as if it wasn't. True, there were other search sites, such as www.altavista.com, www.askjeeves.com, and www.yahoo.com. But anyone who used those sites remembers that, although they made it easy to *search* for something, they made it very difficult to actually *find* anything.

Then Google came along, and suddenly the world changed. It applied its "special sauce" to searching, and the rest is history. Put simply, no search site on the planet comes near to Google in the speed and accuracy of its searches.

But if you think searching is all that Google is about, you're missing a lot. Google offers loads of services in addition to searching, such as maps, email, personalized home pages, free blogging, image-editing software...the list is long and getting longer every day.

This book will help you get the most out of using Google and all of its tools. Whether you want to blog, send and receive mail, take a virtual trip around the world, find a long-lost high school sweetheart, get a great deal online, or a lot more, you've come to the right place.

Why Use Google?

Let's start off with the most basic question: Why bother to use Google? After all, there are other search sites out there.

It's true that there are other search sites, but none are as fast or effective as Google. Google doesn't necessarily scan more of the Web and index more websites than any other search engine. That's not really what's important. What it does better than any other site is deliver more accurate results. At times, the results seem so uncanny that you almost feel as if Google is reading your mind. (You'll learn more details about why Google is so accurate in the next section, "How Google Works.")

▶ **NOTE**

You might have heard that a child has been named after Google, but did you know that an ant has been named after the site as well? The entomologist Brian Fisher discovered a new species of ant and named it *Proceratium google*, to honor the mapping program **Google Earth**. Fisher received help from the **Google Earth** team when he needed to combine an online repository of ant data (called AntWeb) with **Google Earth**. Thanks to the work, scientists can search for ant species by location and plot ant habitats in three dimensions. By the way, here's a tidbit about the *Proceratium google* species: It lives in Madagascar and eats only one kind of food—spider eggs. If you don't believe me, do a Google search.

Google does something else exceptionally well—presenting its search results and enabling you to quickly go to the page you want. Its search results pages load fast—they're not weighted down with unnecessary graphics and ads—and they're easy to scan at a glance. Before the days of Google, this wasn't how search sites displayed their results. They were heavy with graphic-rich ads, they were slow to load, and you often had to wade through a great deal of advertising and unnecessary material until you got what you wanted.

With Google, your results are front and center.

There are reasons beyond accuracy and presentation to use Google as well. Google is constantly coming up with new tools to integrate searching and other Web services into your life. **Google Desktop**, for example, can search your hard disk in the same way that Google searches the Web, and you can even see both sets of results at the same time—what's on your PC as well as what's on the Web. And there are plenty of other examples like this.

How Google Works

Before you can understand how Google works, you probably should have a basic idea of how the Web works. When you visit a website, your browser is actually contacting a web *server*, a computer whose job is to deliver web pages. So when you click a link, your browser contacts the server and says, "Send me this page." The server takes the request and then sends the page to the browser, which displays it on your computer.

▶ KEY TERM

Server—A computer whose job is to perform a specialized task and deliver information. For example, a web server serves up websites, while an email server sends or receives email.

Okay, now that you have that basic background down, let's see how Google works.

In some very basic ways, Google works just like other *search engines*. Its basic operations are exactly the same. Like all search engines, Google is composed of three parts:

- **A spider, also called a crawler**—This spider "crawls" the Web and finds content on web pages.

- **An indexer**—This software takes all the information the spider gives it and creates a giant index that can be searched.

- **A query engine**—This is what takes your search request, sends it to the indexer, and reports the results to you.

▶ KEY TERM

Search engine—A site that allows you to search the Web.

The Spider

The spider part of the Google search engine is an automated piece of software, also called a *robot*, that requests many thousands of pages from hundreds of websites simultaneously. When it finds links on pages, it follows those, and requests those as well.

The main Google spider is the **GoogleBot**, and it essentially crawls the Web once a month. Obviously, many sites change more than once a month, and so Google also has a crawler named **FreshBot** that crawls pages constantly.

The Indexer

The spiders send information about all the pages they find to the indexer part of the search engine. The indexer then does a pretty amazing job—it creates an index of every word on every page sent to it by the Google spider. Not only does it index every word and every URL, it also keeps a record of where every word is on every page.

Multiple copies of this index are kept on various Google servers. A single server wouldn't be able to keep up with all the search requests that are done.

The Query Engine

The only part of Google that you see is the query engine, and you only see *part* of that. It's the public face of Google—that inviting search box at the top of Google pages.

When you type a search term, a Google web server sends your request to the indexer, which is housed on multiple indexing servers. The index servers look through the index and match what they find with your request. The index server then sends that information to document servers, which retrieve the correct information and format it so your browser can understand it. That formatted information is then sent to your browser.

And it all happens in a fraction of a second.

Google's Special Sauce

All this search engine logic is nothing new or revolutionary. This technology has been around for years, long before Google was a glimmer in its founders' eyes.

So why is Google so good at what it does?

Google uses better *algorithms* than any other search engine, and constantly refines them. Algorithms are sets of rules for performing a particular task. In Google's case, its algorithms are responsible for taking your search request and deciding which results to show you.

▶ KEY TERM

Algorithm—A set of rules for performing a task. In Google's case, algorithms are what determines which pages it says match your search requests.

Google's algorithms aren't particularly easy for mere mortals to understand, they're changing all the time, and they're not made public. Google uses more than 100 factors in its algorithms. For every search you do, it considers all of those factors and then calculates a score for every possible matching page. The page with the highest score is the first search result. The page with the second-highest score is the second search result, and so on.

Some of the metrics are fairly obvious—the search term needs to appear on a page, for example. Google's algorithms also factor in the number of times the term appears on a page, whether the term appears on a prominent part of a page, whether it appears in the title of a page, and many other factors.

None of this is particularly revolutionary, either. Many search engines do the same thing.

Google's real brilliance is in harnessing the collective intelligence of the Web to figure out what was truly relevant, instead of merely relying on these kinds of rules. Google also gives a great deal of weight to the number and kinds of pages that link to a web page. For example, Google figures that if a web page has many sites linking to it, the odds are very good that the page is an important one. And if important sites are linking to that page, it's even more important.

So Google calculates a page rank for each page, and that page rank becomes a very important part of the calculation as well. For example, you do a search, and Google finds your search term five times on a page to which hardly any pages link, but three times on a page (such as on the *New York Times* website) that has many sites linking to it. The more important page (the *New York Times* page) appears higher on the search results list, even though the search term appears on it less frequently.

Why Use Google Tools?

Google, as mentioned previously, is more than a search engine. It provides a whole complex of sites and services that this book refers to as Google tools. These tools include things such as **Gmail** web service, **Google Local** (previously called **Google Maps**) search service, and **Google Desktop** for searching your computer.

Google is such a great search site, but why bother using Google tools? These tools are in many ways as remarkable as the Google search engine itself. Some of these tools are specialized versions of the search engine. For example, **Froogle** is the Google service for finding online bargains, and **Google News** is the service that delivers the latest news.

Other tools are extensions of Google. The **Google Desktop** extends Google's power to your PC, for example. And the **Google Toolbar** enables you to search Google no matter where you are on the Web.

Still other tools are great services for the Internet, such as **Blogger**, which enables you to create your own blogs; **Gmail**, its email service; or **Google Talk**, which enables you to chat with friends.

So if you're a Google user and haven't used any of its tools, this book will be your guide. And even if you have used its tools, you'll learn inside tips and secrets you didn't know before.

How to Download and Install Google Tools

Many Google tools live on the Web and don't require you to install any special software. For example, **Gmail**, **Froogle**, and **Blogger** are all websites; to use them, you only need to point your browser to the right page.

But other tools are software programs that live on your PC, and they require that you download and install them before you can use them. (The Appendix, "Google Tools and Services," lists all the Google tools available to you.) All are installed in the same basic way, as outlined in the following steps. The **Google Toolbar** is used as an example of how to install software. (To see other download-able tools, go to www.google.com, click the **More** link at the top of the page, and then click the **Google Downloads** link on the left side of the page.)

1. Go to the web page that hosts the software. When you get there, you see a link for downloading the software. The nearby figure shows the download page for the **Google Toolbar**, at http://toolbar.google.com.

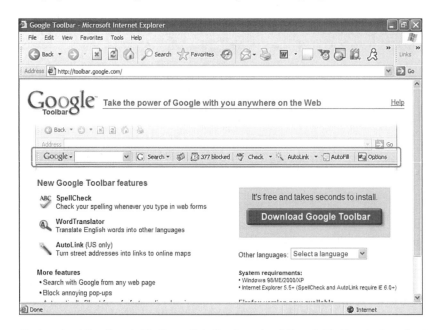

*To download the **Google Toolbar**, click the **Download Google Toolbar** button. Pretty simple, huh?*

2. When you're prompted to save the file to disk, save it to a location. Remember where it's located.

3. Double-click the file you downloaded. This action begins the installation process.

4. Follow the installation instructions. These instructions vary greatly depending on the tool you're installing. Google is very good at giving instructions, so just follow what you find onscreen. But for all installations, you are asked to read a **Terms and Conditions** statement that outlines how you're allowed to use the software, as you can see in the nearby figure. It's written in a language that only lawyers could love. Read it, click **Agree & Continue**, and then follow the instructions onscreen.

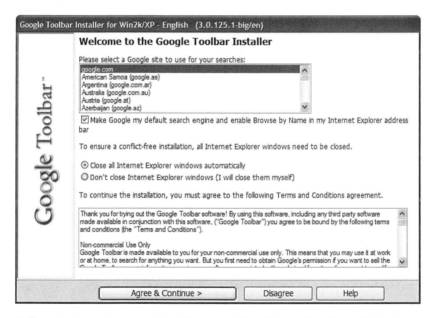

*Follow the instructions, read the **Terms and Conditions**, click **Agree & Continue**, and you are ready to go.*

5. At the end, click **Finish**. Restart your computer if you're told to do so. If you have to restart your computer, save all your open files and close all your open programs before you restart.

6. Begin using the program. The nearby figure shows the **Google Toolbar**, installed.

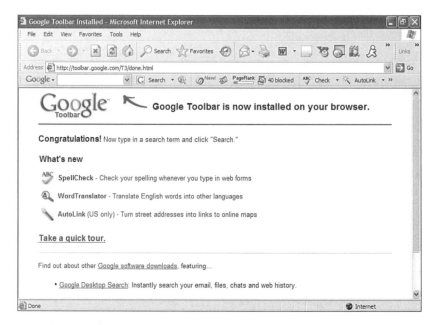

*You're locked and loaded—time to start using the **Google Toolbar**.*

Sign Up and Manage Your Google Account

Many of the Google tools or services that are websites, such as **Gmail**, require that you sign up for a Google account. After you have set up an account, you won't have to set it up again. You can use your single Google account as the centerpiece for all of Google's services.

To sign up, head to **www.google.com** and click **Sign In**. On the right side of the page that appears, click the **Create an account now** link. The page shown in the nearby figure appears.

Fill in an email address, enter a password and retype it, choose your location, type what you see as the weird-looking text in the **Word Verification** area, read the **Terms of Service**, and then click **I accept. Create my account**. That's all it takes; you're signed up and ready to go. When you need to use a Google service from now on, type your email address and password when prompted.

After you have an account, click the **My Account** link if you want to change your personal information, such as your password and name. From your account page, you also see a list of services for which you've signed up, and you can look for other services that you might want to try.

Google Accounts — Create a Google Account

Create an Account

Your Google Account gives you access to many Google services.

Required information for Google account

Your current email address: [   ]
e.g. myname@example.com. This will be your username and sign-in.

Choose a password: [   ]   Password strength: Too short
Minimum of 6 characters in length.

Re-enter password: [   ]

Creating a Google Account activates Personalized Search, which tailors your Google search based on your search history and more.
☐ Check here to disable Personalized Search.

Location: [United States   ▾]

Word Verification: Type the characters you see in the picture below.

                    essiangs

[   ] ♿
characters are not case-sensitive

Terms of Service: Please check the Google Account information you've entered above (feel free to change any like), and review the Terms of Service below.

                                                          Printab

Google Terms of Service for Your Personal Use

Welcome! By using Google's search engine or other Google services ("Google Services"), you agree to be bound by the following terms and conditions (the "Terms of Service"). As used in this

By clicking on 'I accept' below you are agreeing to the Terms of Service above and the Priva Policy.

[I accept. Create my account.]

©2005 Google · Google Home - Terms of Service · Privacy Policy - About Google Accounts

*Fill out this page and click **I accept. Create my account**. Then you are ready to use all of Google's services.*

▶ NOTE

Even if you don't sign up for a Google account, many of Google's services and tools are still available to you. For example, you can still use **Froogle**, the **Google Toolbar**, **Picasa**, and several other services and tools. And if you only want to search the Web, you don't need to sign up for an account, either.

Google and Your Privacy

If people fear one thing about Google, it's that Google might invade their privacy in some way. That's a natural fear. As Google creates more and more services, it can gather an increasing amount of information about you. And there are also worries that Google tracks all of your searches, and it could then easily create a personal profile of you and sell the results to the highest bidder.

If you want the whole story of Google's privacy policy, head to the Google Privacy Center at www.google.com/privacy.html. It spells out in a good deal of detail what information Google finds out about you and what it does with that information.

But here, in a nutshell, is the scoop: When you create a Google account, you need to enter basic information—your email address and password. Google doesn't share that information with any other website.

When someone visits a Google site or does a search using Google, Google servers record information about that visit, including the *IP address* of the visitor, the URLs, and the date and time of the request.

▶ KEY TERM

IP address—A unique number, such as 233.23.234.22, that identifies each computer that uses the Internet. The IP address of your computer is typically assigned by your ISP when you connect to the Internet. Your ISP changes your IP address each time you connect, and if you have an always-on connection (such as with a cable or DSL modem), your ISP also changes the IP address occasionally.

Google doesn't use that information to build a profile of you or track the searches you do; this information stays on Google's servers. By itself, that information doesn't identify you because Google, by itself, can't match an IP address to an individual. Law enforcement officials, however, can subpoena that information, and they can use it to identify you and the searches you do. They can subpoena your ISP and find out the subscriber name of the person with the IP address at a given time. So based on Google logs and information provided by your ISP, law enforcement officials can identify you and what you do on Google. Google complies with subpoenas.

Google also uses *cookies*, which are small bits of data placed on your computer that Google uses to recognize you when you log in. Cookies can store your personal preferences and other information. For example, Google uses a cookie to recognize that you have a Google account, so you don't have to log in every time to use some Google services.

▶ KEY TERM

Cookie—A small bit of data put on a computer that identifies a person and can store personal preferences and other information.

In addition, Google shares what it calls "aggregated non-personal information" with other companies. This aggregated information is information that Google records but that isn't tied to an individual. So, for example, it might collect information about what pages are most popular among Google visitors. It aggregates information from many people's Web-surfing activities to get this information. But it doesn't track any single individual's use.

A Quick Tour of Google

Google is far more than a search site—it has grown to be a sizable collection of services and tools, and the collection is getting larger all the time. No longer is Google a single search site; instead, it's a conglomeration of multiple sites. And no longer can you even call it Web-based because Google now includes software that you download and run on your PC.

This book often refers to tools and services. Although there is a lot of gray area in the definitions of these two terms, generally a service is a website run by Google. So, for example, the bargain-finding site **Froogle** (www.froogle.com) is a service because it's a Google-run website; you have to visit it on the Web to use it. Google's image-management software **Picasa** (www.picasa.com), on the other hand, is software that you download to your PC, and so it considered a tool.

So where are the gray areas? **Google Earth** is an example of something you could consider both a tool and a service: You have to download it and run it on your PC, but you also have to be connected to the Internet to use it because it gets all its information from Google online. The same holds true for the **Google Toolbar**, which you download and use on your PC, but also use to search Google.

This book covers all of the major tools and services—or at least those that were available during the writing of the book. Google introduces new tools and services all the time—and changes or updates its existing ones—so what you see when you head to Google might be slightly different from what you read in this book.

Because of that, before reading the rest of the book, it's a good idea to take a quick tour of Google so you can find the newest tools and services on your own.

▶ **NOTE**

When you use Google's tools and services, you'll notice that many of them are labeled as being **Beta**. Traditionally, beta software is software that is still in the testing phase, is still being worked on, might have bugs in it, and might have features that will change. But Google is extremely liberal in applying the term beta. In fact, for Google, the term is essentially meaningless. A Google tool or service might be labeled beta for a year or more, even if it has no bugs and doesn't change.

The nearby figure shows Google's familiar main page. To do a search, type your search terms in the search box. But look beyond the familiar search box. Across the top-right side of the page is a series of links. The links show that I've already signed into Google because the links include **Personalized Home**, **Search History**, **My Account**, and **Sign Out**. If I hadn't been logged in, only two links would be there: **Sign In** and **Personalized Home**. (And when I clicked the **Personalized Home** link, I'd first have to sign in before I could get to my **Personalized Home** page.)

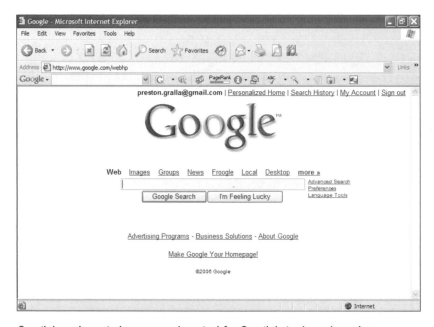

Google's main page is command central for Google's tools and services.

The links do exactly what they say. Click the **Personalized Home** link to go to a personalized, customizable home page that includes news stories, information feeds, stock and weather information, and more. (For details on how to set it up, start with **46 About Google Personalized Home**.) Click the **Search History** link and you come to a page that includes all the searches you've done while you've been logged into your Google account. (See **48 Add Bookmarks and Your Search History to Google Personalized Home**.) The **My Account** link enables you to change your Google account settings, which were covered earlier in this chapter. And the **Sign Out** link, obviously, allows you to sign out of your Google account.

▶ **NOTE**
Why should you ever bother to sign out of your Google account? Shouldn't you simply stay logged in forever? Not necessarily. The main reason to log out is to protect your privacy. While you're logged in, anyone using your computer can make full use of your account. This means they can read all your email in **Gmail**, send mail from **Gmail**, see your search history, and so on.

Now look at the links just above the search box. These links lead to several of Google's main services and tools. These links might change over time, but at the time this book was written, they linked to Google **Image Search** (**Images**); **Google Groups** (**Groups**); **Google News** (**News**); **Froogle** (**Froogle**); **Google Local**, which used to be called Google Maps (**Local**); and **Google Desktop** (**Desktop**). There's also a **more** link, which is covered in some more detail. In addition to these links, to the right of the search box are links to **Advanced Search** (for doing an advanced search), **Preferences** (which enables you to change your Google preferences), and **Language Tools** (which enables you to search through pages written in specific languages, and also includes language-translation tools).

Google prides itself on its barebones interface, so it's unlikely that you'll see many more links than what you see here on the front page. But this minimalist interface leads to a conundrum: As you'll see in this book, there are many more Google tools and services than there are links on Google's front page. In fact, this book doesn't cover all the tools and services that Google has because there are too many. So how do you find out about a tool or service, or even discover which ones exist?

That's where the **more** link comes in. Click it, and you'll see the **More, more, more** page with the current, comprehensive list of all Google's tools and services. So to get to any of these available features, head to the **More, more, more** page. For a description of the main tools and services here, see this book's Appendix.

A few links of note are on the page. The **web search features** link is a great place to go if you want to use Google's many specialized searches, such as for package tracking, stock quotes, music, and more. And the **Labs** link is the place to go if you want to see what new features Google is cooking up in its labs. New Google tools and services start here. Some experiments don't see the light of day, while others go on to fame and glory.

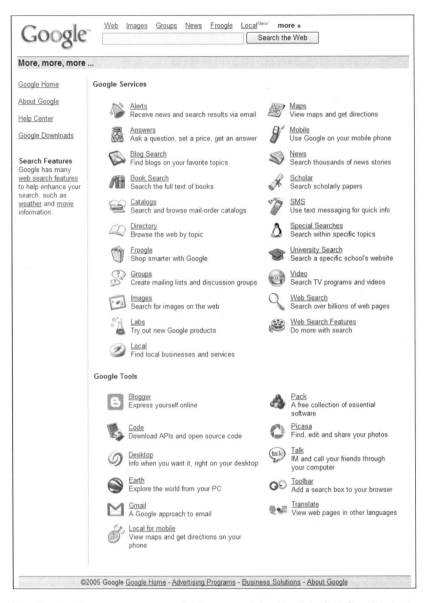

*The Google **More, more, more** page always contains the list of all Google's tools and services.*

2

Searching with Google

IN THIS CHAPTER:

Most of this book tells you how to use Google's specialized tools and to do special searches. But before you do any of that, you need to learn how to do basic Google searches. The fanciest tool in the world won't help you if you can't craft an intelligent search to find what you want—and fast.

In this chapter, you'll start with learning how to do a basic Google search, and then quickly go on to doing more advanced searches, using special search operators, and getting advice about strategies for doing smarter searching.

---

1 | **Perform a Basic Google Search**

→ **SEE ALSO**
_____

2 About Interpreting Google Results

3 Browse Through Search Results

4 Refine Your Search

Here's where it all begins—doing a basic Google search. Master this simple task, and you'll go a long way towards mastering Google.

1

1 Go to Google

To do anything, you need to head to the mother ship—www.google.com. Google works well with any browser, so it doesn't matter which one you use.

2 Set Your Preferences

If you're going to be a Google regular (and if you're reading this book, it means you are), you should set your preferences for how you want Google to perform searches. Click the **Preferences** link to the right of the main Google search box, and the **Google Preferences** page appears.

▶ **NOTE**

If you've disabled cookies in your browser, the Google preferences you set won't work. You need to enable cookies in your browser to use this feature of Google. Most likely, cookies are already enabled, but if not, here's how to do it: In Internet Explorer, choose **Tools, Internet Options** from the menu bar, click the **Privacy** tab, and make sure the slide is set to **Medium High** or a lower privacy setting. In Firefox, choose **Tools, Options** from the menu bar, click the **Privacy** tab, check the box next to **Allow sites to set cookies**, and click **OK**.

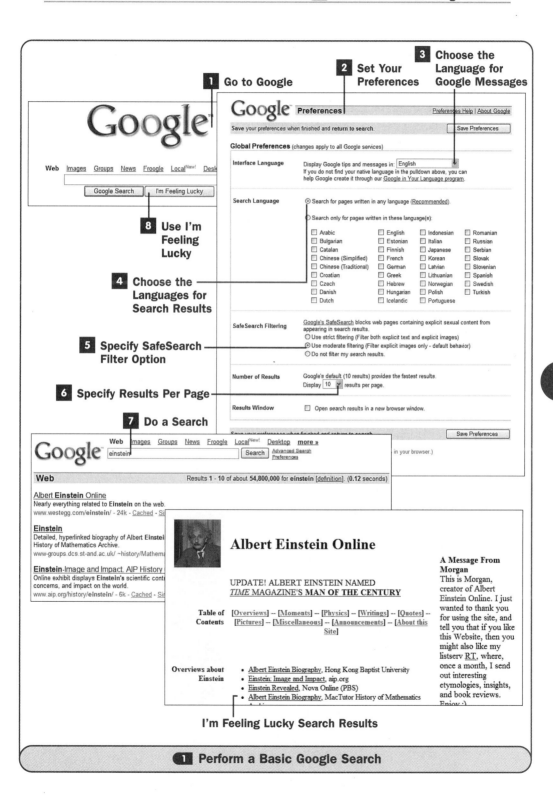

1 Go to Google

2 Set Your Preferences

3 Choose the Language for Google Messages

Google™

Web Images Groups News Froogle Local^{New!} Desk

Google Search   I'm Feeling Lucky

Google™ Preferences   Preferences Help | About Google

Save your preferences when finished and return to search.   Save Preferences

Global Preferences (changes apply to all Google services)

Interface Language   Display Google tips and messages in: English
                      If you do not find your native language in the pulldown above, you can
                      help Google create it through our Google in Your Language program.

Search Language   ⦿ Search for pages written in any language (Recommended).

                      ◯ Search only for pages written in these language(s):

☐ Arabic   ☐ English   ☐ Indonesian   ☐ Romanian
☐ Bulgarian   ☐ Estonian   ☐ Italian   ☐ Russian
☐ Catalan   ☐ Finnish   ☐ Japanese   ☐ Serbian
☐ Chinese (Simplified) ☐ French   ☐ Korean   ☐ Slovak
☐ Chinese (Traditional) ☐ German   ☐ Latvian   ☐ Slovenian
☐ Croatian   ☐ Greek   ☐ Lithuanian   ☐ Spanish
☐ Czech   ☐ Hebrew   ☐ Norwegian   ☐ Swedish
☐ Danish   ☐ Hungarian   ☐ Polish   ☐ Turkish
☐ Dutch   ☐ Icelandic   ☐ Portuguese

SafeSearch Filtering   Google's SafeSearch blocks web pages containing explicit sexual content from
                       appearing in search results.
                       ◯ Use strict filtering (Filter both explicit text and explicit images)
                       ⦿ Use moderate filtering (Filter explicit images only - default behavior)
                       ◯ Do not filter my search results.

Number of Results   Google's default (10 results) provides the fastest results.
                       Display 10 ▾ results per page.

Results Window   ☐ Open search results in a new browser window.

Save your preferences when finished and return to search.   Save Preferences

8 Use I'm Feeling Lucky

4 Choose the Languages for Search Results

5 Specify SafeSearch Filter Option

6 Specify Results Per Page

7 Do a Search

Google™   Web Images Groups News Froogle Local^{New!} Desktop more »
           einstein   Search Advanced Search   in your browser.)
                                               Preferences

Web   Results 1 - 10 of about 54,800,000 for einstein [definition]. (0.12 seconds)

Albert **Einstein** Online
Nearly everything related to **Einstein** on the web.
www.westegg.com/**einstein**/ - 24k - Cached - Si

Einstein
Detailed, hyperlinked biography of Albert **Einstei**
History of Mathematics Archive.
www-groups.dcs.st-and.ac.uk/ ~history/Mathema

Einstein-Image and Impact. AIP History
Online exhibit displays **Einstein's** scientific cont
concerns, and impact on the world.
www.aip.org/history/**einstein**/ - 6k - Cached - Si

Albert Einstein Online

UPDATE! ALBERT EINSTEIN NAMED
TIME MAGAZINE'S **MAN OF THE CENTURY**

Table of   [Overviews] -- [Moments] -- [Physics] -- [Writings] -- [Quotes] --
Contents   [Pictures] -- [Miscellaneous] -- [Announcements] -- [About this
                                 Site]

Overviews about   • Albert Einstein Biography, Hong Kong Baptist University
Einstein   • Einstein: Image and Impact, aip.org
                   • Einstein Revealed, Nova Online (PBS)
                   • Albert Einstein Biography, MacTutor History of Mathematics

A Message From Morgan
This is Morgan, creator of Albert Einstein Online. I just wanted to thank you for using the site, and tell you that if you like this Website, then you might also like my listserv RT, where, once a month, I send out interesting etymologies, insights, and book reviews. Enjoy :)

I'm Feeling Lucky Search Results

3 Choose the Language for Google Messages

From the **Interface Language** drop-down box, choose the language in which you want Google to display tips and messages from Google. (The language you choose affects messages such as the notice at the top of the page that tells you how many results you have and how long it took to get those results.) The choice you make here won't affect the language of the search results; it only affects the messages you get from Google.

4 Choose the Languages for Search Results

In the **Search Language** section, choose the languages whose pages you want to search. If you want to search all pages, regardless of the language in which they are written, choose the **Search for pages written in any language (Recommended)** option. You can limit your search to pages in only certain languages by choosing the **Search only for pages written in these language(s)** option and then enabling the check boxes next to those languages to which you want your search limited.

5 Specify SafeSearch Filter Option

In the **SafeSearch Filtering** section, choose what level of *SafeSearch* to use. SafeSearch blocks web pages that contain explicit sexual content. You can choose one of the following levels:

- **Strict filtering** filters explicit text and explicit images.

- **Moderate filtering** filters only explicit images (this is Google's default).

- **No filtering** does not filter search results.

▶ KEY TERM

SafeSearch—A Google feature that blocks any search results that contain explicit sexual content. You can choose from two levels of SafeSearch, or choose not to use it at all.

6 Specify Results Per Page

From the **Number of Results** drop-down box, choose how many search results to display per page. If you display 10 results at a time (the default), your search results are returned the quickest. But if you use a high resolution on your monitor, showing only 10 results per page means wasted screen space, and it takes longer to move from page to page. Experiment to find the best number of results per page based on how you use Google.

Finally, decide whether you want the search results returned in the same window in which you do a search or in a new window. Check the box next to **Open search results in a new browser window** if you want the results to open in a new window. Opening your search results in a new window leaves your search page intact, but requires you to juggle windows; opening your search results in the same window requires less juggling, but means that you have to keep clicking the **Back** button to get to your search results after you visit a page.

After you've made all your choices on the **Preferences** window, click the **Save Preferences** button. You are sent back to Google's main page.

7 Do a Search

To do a search, simply type your *search term* or terms into the search box and press **Enter** or click the **Search** button.

A page of search results is delivered to you. Browse through the results, and click the title of the web page you want to visit. (For more details about search results, see **2** About Interpreting Google Results. For more about browsing through search results, see **3** Browse Through Search Results.)

▶ KEY TERM

Search term—The string of characters you type into the search box for which you want Google to search the Internet.

8 Use I'm Feeling Lucky

Google does a very good job of taking search results and determining the most relevant pages. If you find yourself trusting Google's search results, click the **I'm Feeling Lucky** button after you type in your search term. Instead of showing you a page of search results, you are sent directly to the page Google thinks is most relevant to your search terms.

If the page Google's **I'm Feeling Lucky** feature opened for you isn't what you had hoped for, or if you want to see other results for your search term, return to the main Google search screen by clicking your browser's **Back** button. The Google search box retains the search term you typed; click the **Search** button to launch a traditional search.

2   About Interpreting Google Results

✔ BEFORE YOU BEGIN	→ SEE ALSO
1 Perform a Basic Google Search	**3** Browse Through Search Results

A Google search results page is a masterpiece of packing a great deal of information into a compact amount of space. But at first glance, it can be difficult to understand all that information and what it all means. Taking a moment or two to examine a typical page helps you get more out of Google.

On the typical search results page shown here, a search was done for **john lennon**. At the very top of the page is the total number of results Google found, the number of results on the current page, and the amount of time it took to do the search.

Just beneath that information are links for **News results**. These links all lead to recent news stories about the search term, *john lennon*. In the example, there are two recent news stories, one from *The Sunday Herald* and one from the BBC News. Click any link to go to the news story, or click the main link heading, **News results for john lennon**, to go to a full **Google News** page of search results. (For more information about using **Google News**, see **26** **Get the News with Google News**.

On the right side of the page is a list of sponsored links. These links have all been paid for, and are essentially advertising. But don't ignore them because of that; they often contain services, information, or items for which you're looking. In some instances, a sponsored link appears at the very top of the search results, if an advertiser has paid enough money for that positioning.

Directly below the News results are the heart of the page—the Google search results. Each result contains a great deal of information:

- The title of the page, which is also the link to the page.

- A short description of the page, just underneath the title.

- The actual *URL* of the page, underneath the description.

▶ KEY TERM

URL (uniform resource locator)—A web address that uniquely identifies a web page, such as **http://www.google.com**.

Title of Page

News Results   **Results on This Page**

Search Term   **Total Number of Results**

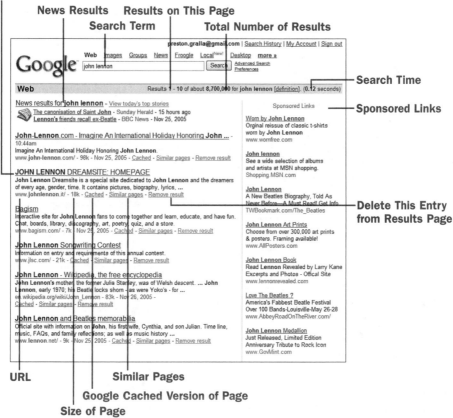

Search Time

Sponsored Links

Delete This Entry from Results Page

URL   **Similar Pages**

Google Cached Version of Page

Size of Page

A typical Google search results page.

- The size of the page, in kilobytes, to the right of the URL.

- The date the page was last updated, to the right of the URL. (This information is not always available and included.)

- A link to a *cached* version of the page, to the right of the date. The cached version of the page is a version of the page stored on Google's servers. This link can be useful if the page itself is not currently available, or if it has been moved or changed. In these circumstances, you can click the **Cached** link to see the version of the page that Google indexed.

▶ KEY TERM

Cached—A copy of something, such as a web page, that is stored locally or on a server. If the page is changed, the cached version is the old version of the page.

- A **Similar pages** link that displays a list of pages similar to the one listed; this link is located to the right of the **Cached** link. For example, if you did a search on **John Lennon**, and you came to a page that was from a biographical website with his biography, a page "similar" to that one would be the page of another biographical website.

- A **Remove result** link you can click if the result is off-target and you no longer want to see it on the results page.

---

3 **Browse Through Search Results**

✔ BEFORE YOU BEGIN	→ SEE ALSO
2 About Interpreting Google Results	**1** Perform a Basic Google Search

---

After you've typed your search term into the Google search box and received your search results, it's time to get to the good stuff—going through the actual results, the links to web pages that hopefully discuss the topic in which you're interested, as you'll learn how to do in this task.

1 Scroll Through the Results

Use the scrollbar on the right side of the page to scroll through the results. Read the description of each page as you scroll.

2 Visit a Page

When you find a page whose title or description interests you, click its link. You are sent to the actual page on the Web.

▶ NOTE

When you do a search on Google, it ignores certain common words, as well as digits and single letters. These are all called *stop words*. Stop words include *the*, *be*, *from*, and *about*, among others.

▶ KEY TERM

Stop word—A common word that Google ignores when it does a search, such as *the*, *be*, or *from*.

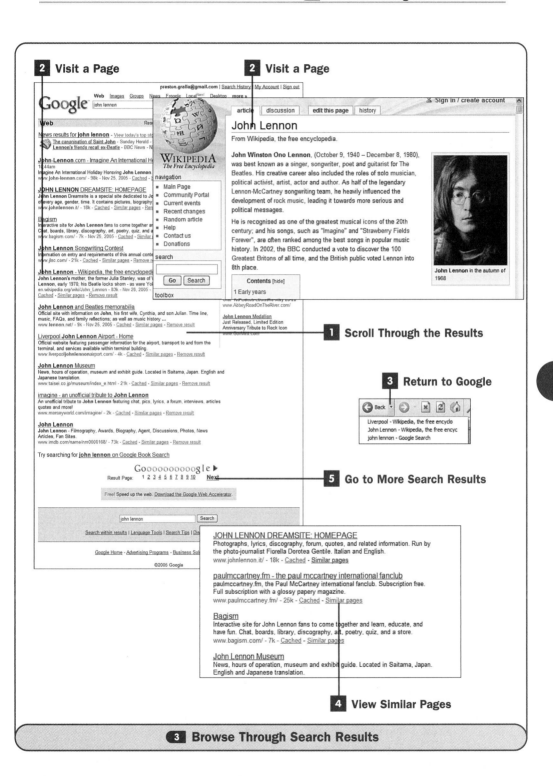

2 **Visit a Page**

2 **Visit a Page**

1 **Scroll Through the Results**

3 **Return to Google**

5 **Go to More Search Results**

4 **View Similar Pages**

❸ Return to Google

When you're done viewing a web page, click your browser's **Back** button as many times as you need to get back to your Google results page. As a shortcut, you can click the down arrow next to the **Back** button to see the most recent pages you've visited. Select the **Google Search** page to return to your results.

If you elected to open the search results in a new window, you must juggle the windows (that is, switch back to the results window, whether or not you close the viewing window).

❹ View Similar Pages

A good way to zero in on search results is to find a page that is relevant to your search, and then find pages most similar to that page. So when you find a page with useful information, click the **Similar pages** link next to it; you should get a list of pages that will help narrow down your search. In the example, I clicked the **Similar pages** link next to the **JOHN LENNON DREAMSITE: HOMEPAGE** search result and was shown links to several more pages that related to my search term.

❺ Go to More Search Results

At the bottom of the search results page is the navigation area for your search results. Click **Next** to get to the next page of results. Click **Back** to get to the previous page. You can also jump ahead several pages in the results (or go to a specific results page you might remember) by clicking a page number. If you've looked through many pages of search results, you can return to the first page of the results by clicking **1**.

---

❹ Refine Your Search

✔ BEFORE YOU BEGIN	→ SEE ALSO
❶ Perform a Basic Google Search	❺ Perform an Advanced Google Search
	❻ About Google Search Operators
	❼ About Power Searching Strategies

For many purposes, a straightforward search as shown in the previous task finds you the information for which you're looking. But there are also many occasions in which a simple search isn't good enough. In that case, you need to refine your search, as you learn to do in this task.

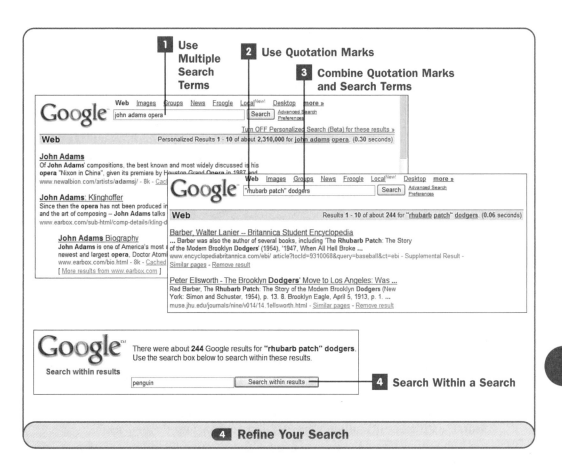

4 Refine Your Search

1 Use Multiple Search Terms

The single best way to narrow your results so you find exactly what you want is to use multiple search terms. For example, if you're looking for information about the contemporary classical music composer John Adams, using **John Adams** as your search terms does not work very well—you mainly get pages relating to the U.S. president John Adams. If you instead type **John Adams Opera**, you get the results you want.

2 Use Quotation Marks

When you use multiple search terms, Google does not look at them as a phrase. Instead, it thinks you are looking for pages that contain each of the search terms individually. If you typed the terms **Rhubarb Patch**, Google would return pages that contained the word *rhubarb* as well as pages that contained the word *patch*. You would get far more results than you wanted. If you type "**rhubarb patch**" in quotation marks, you would instead get only those pages that contained the phrase *rhubarb patch*.

3 Combine Quotation Marks and Search Terms

Suppose that you were looking for a book written in the early 1950s about the Brooklyn Dodgers, titled *The Rhubarb Patch*. The best way to find web pages about this book would be to combine the phrase "**Rhubarb Patch**" and the term **Dodgers**. (Google ignores capitalization, so it doesn't matter if you use uppercase characters or lowercase characters in your searches.)

▶ **NOTE**

It's a good idea to use multiple search terms to narrow your search, but if you use too many terms, Google ignores them. Google only pays attention to the first 32 words of a query, and ignores the rest.

4 Search Within a Search

Often the best way to narrow your search is to search within the results you've received from a previous search. To do that, start by performing a basic search. At the bottom of the search results page, beneath the results navigation area and the search text box located there, click the **Search within results** link. A new, blank search form appears. Type your additional search term or terms the way you normally would in Google and click the **Search within results** button or press **Enter**. Google uses the new search terms to narrow your search by searching only through the first set of search results.

5 Perform an Advanced Google Search	
✔ **BEFORE YOU BEGIN**	→ **SEE ALSO**
1 Perform a Basic Google Search	**6** About Google Search Operators
	7 About Power Searching Strategies

If you're doing a search that returns too many results and you want to zoom in on your search results as quickly as possible, the best way to do it is with an advanced search, as you'll learn to do in this task. An advanced search provides many more controls over what results are returned. For example, you can limit the search results to a specific language (instead of changing the options in the **Preferences** dialog box, as explained in **1** **Perform a Basic Google Search**, which affects *all* searches, you can limit just the *current* search to a specific language), specify words you do *not* want returned in the search results, and so on.

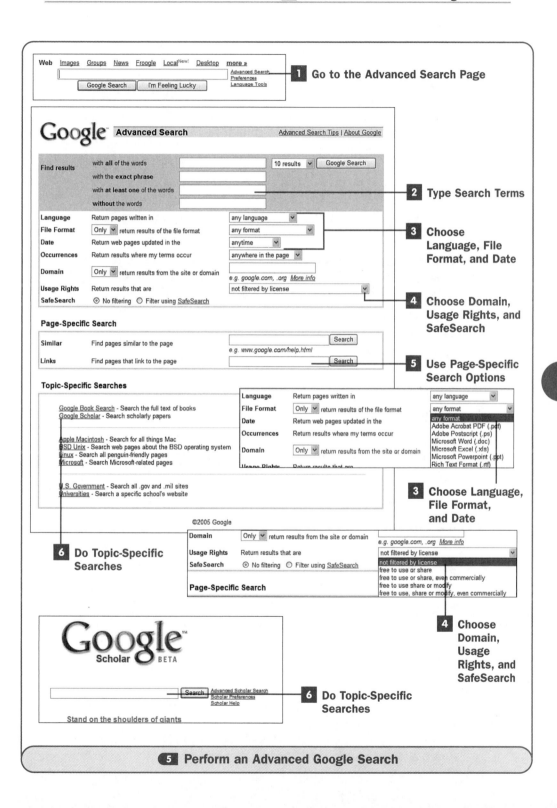

Web   Images   Groups   News   Froogle   Local^New!   Desktop   more »
Advanced Search
Preferences
Language Tools
Google Search   I'm Feeling Lucky

1 Go to the Advanced Search Page

Google Advanced Search   Advanced Search Tips | About Google

Find results
with **all** of the words   10 results ∨   Google Search
with the **exact phrase**
with **at least one** of the words
without the words

2 Type Search Terms

Language   Return pages written in   any language ∨
File Format Only ∨ return results of the file format   any format ∨
Date   Return web pages updated in the   anytime ∨
Occurrences Return results where my terms occur   anywhere in the page ∨
Domain   Only ∨ return results from the site or domain
            e.g. google.com, .org More info
Usage Rights Return results that are   not filtered by license ∨
SafeSearch   ⊙ No filtering ○ Filter using SafeSearch

3 Choose Language, File Format, and Date

4 Choose Domain, Usage Rights, and SafeSearch

Page-Specific Search

Similar   Find pages similar to the page   Search
          e.g. www.google.com/help.html
Links   Find pages that link to the page   Search

5 Use Page-Specific Search Options

Topic-Specific Searches

Google Book Search - Search the full text of books
Google Scholar - Search scholarly papers

Apple Macintosh - Search for all things Mac
BSD Unix - Search web pages about the BSD operating system
Linux - Search all penguin-friendly pages
Microsoft - Search Microsoft-related pages

U.S. Government - Search all .gov and .mil sites
Universities - Search a specific school's website

Language   Return pages written in   any language ∨
File Format Only ∨ return results of the file format   any format ∨
                                            any format
Date   Return web pages updated in the   Adobe Acrobat PDF (.pdf)
                                            Adobe Postscript (.ps)
Occurrences Return results where my terms occur   Microsoft Word (.doc)
                                            Microsoft Excel (.xls)
Domain   Only ∨ return results from the site or domain Microsoft Powerpoint (.ppt)
                                            Rich Text Format (.rtf)
Usage Rights Return results that are

3 Choose Language, File Format, and Date

©2005 Google

Domain   Only ∨ return results from the site or domain
            e.g. google.com, .org More info
Usage Rights Return results that are   not filtered by license ∨
                                            not filtered by license
SafeSearch   ⊙ No filtering ○ Filter using SafeSearch   free to use or share
                                            free to use or share, even commercially
Page-Specific Search   free to use share or modify
                                            free to use, share or modify, even commercially

6 Do Topic-Specific Searches

4 Choose Domain, Usage Rights, and SafeSearch

Google Scholar BETA

Search Advanced Scholar Search
        Scholar Preferences
        Scholar Help
Stand on the shoulders of giants

6 Do Topic-Specific Searches

5 Perform an Advanced Google Search

5

▌1▐ Go to the Advanced Search Page

From Google's main search page, click the **Advanced Search** link to the right of the main search text box at the top of the page. You are sent to the Google **Advanced Search** page.

▌2▐ Type Search Terms

The top part of the page, highlighted in blue, enables you to type search terms and to combine them in unique ways. Keep in mind that you can combine several of these options. For example, you can search for pages that have the exact phrase *rhubarb patch* but that *do not* have the word *Barber* on them. Here are your choices:

- The **with all of the words** option means that Google returns results in which pages contain *all* your search terms. If a page is missing just one of the terms, it won't be included in the search results.

- The **with the exact phrase** option means that Google returns results in which pages contain the exact phrase—it's the same as putting quotation marks around the words in your search phrase.

- The **with at least one of the words** option means that Google returns pages that contain *any* of your search terms. This is the default Google search method.

- The **without the words** option is meant to be used in combination with one of the previous search options as a way to narrow a search. When you use this option, Google excludes any pages that contain the search terms you type on this line.

▌3▐ Choose Language, File Format, and Date

The next set of options on the **Advanced Search** page allows you to narrow your search even further:

- The **Language** option enables you to narrow the results returned to pages that are primarily written in a single language. Click the drop-down box to make your choice of language. There are dozens of languages from which you can choose. The default search language is **any language**.

- The **File Format** option enables you to search for files, rather than web pages. So if you know that a particular piece of information is in a specific file format, use the **File Format** option to make it easier to find the file. You can search for files in half a dozen formats: Adobe Acrobat (**.pdf**), Adobe Postscript (**.ps**), Microsoft Word (**.doc**), Microsoft Excel (**.xls**),

Microsoft PowerPoint (**.ppt**), and Rich Text Format (**.rtf**). You can also tell Google to have your results *exclude* the selected file formats by choosing **Don't** from the drop-down list just to the right of **File Format**. (When you find a **.pdf** file, for example, Google gives you the option of viewing the content in HTML rather than as a **.pdf** file.)

- The **Date** option enables you to specify web pages that have been updated in a specific time period: in the past three months, the past six months, or the past year. You can also leave this option set to the Google default of **anytime**. Make your choice from the drop-down list.

4 Choose Domain, Usage Rights, and SafeSearch

The next set of choices on the **Advanced Search** page allow you to narrow your search in these ways:

- The **Domain** option enables you to search through only a specific domain or domains, such as **www.cnn.com**. To search multiple domains, separate the URLs by commas. You can also *exclude* domains from your search by selecting **Don't** from the drop-down box to the right of **Domain**. (A domain is a main location such as **www.weather.com** or **www.cmp.com**.)

- The **Usage Rights** option enables you to search through pages or material that is bound—or not bound—by specific usage rights (that is, by the way in which the information can be used). The default is **not filtered by license**, which means that Google searches for any material. From the drop-down list, you can make a wide range of choices, from **free to use or share**, up to **free to use, share or modify, even commercially**.

▶ NOTE

The **Usage Rights** section of the **Advanced Search** page is primarily of use to those searching for software, not for material on web pages.

- The SafeSearch option enables you to filter searches so they do not contain sexually explicit or inappropriate material.

5 Use Page-Specific Search Options

The **Page-Specific Search** section of the **Advanced Search** page enables you to do two types of searches:

- **Similar** enables you to find pages similar to a page you've already found. For example, let's say you've found a page about the

Hindenburg disaster, you want to find other pages about the disaster, and you've found that the site www.otr.com/hindenburg.html gave you a great deal of information about the topic. Type that page's URL here and click the related **Search** button to get similar pages. This option functions the same as if you clicked the **Similar pages** link on a search results page.

- **Links** enables you to find pages that link to a specific page. For example, you could type the URL **www.otr.com/hindenburg.html** and click the related **Search** button to see all the pages that link to the specified URL. This is a very useful tool if you run a website and you notice a sudden surge in traffic; you can find out where that traffic came from by typing the URL for your home page in the **Links** box.

6 Do Topic-Specific Searches

The final section of the **Advanced Search** page enables you to search through topic-specific pages (such as pages related to Microsoft or Apple Macintosh) or through scholarly pages. When you click any of the topic-specific searches, you are sent to a new Google page (Google determines which page has the most relevant information). Type your search term on that page, and you'll do a topic-specific search.

6

6 About Google Search Operators

✔ BEFORE YOU BEGIN	→ SEE ALSO
1 Perform a Basic Google Search	**7** About Power Searching Strategies
4 Refine Your Search	
5 Perform an Advanced Google Search	

Google enables you to search using *search operators*, special words and symbols that make it easy to get search results that match as closely as possible the information for which you're looking. You can combine search operators with search terms to form a query, like this:

zeppelin -"Led Zeppelin"

The minus sign in this search string means *not*, so this search would bring back pages that had the word *zeppelin* on them but *did not have* the term *Led Zeppelin* on them.

▶ KEY TERM

Search operator—Special words or symbols you can use in concert with search terms to make it easier for you to narrow your search.

Table 2.1 contains the common operators you can use with Google (you do not have to use all capital letters when you type the operators).

TABLE 2.1 Common Google Search Operators

Operator	Description
AND	You don't need to use this operator because Google adds it by default to searches in which you use multiple terms. It returns results that contain all the terms in the search. So a search for **cow collagen** (with the implied operator **AND**—**cow AND collagen**) returns only those pages in which both **cow** *and* **collagen** appear.
OR	When you use this operator, Google returns pages on which *any* of the words are found. So a search for **cow OR collagen** returns pages in which the word **cow** appears and pages on which the word **collagen** appears. An **OR** search returns many more results than an **AND** search.
–	The minus sign is called the *exclusion operator*; it returns pages on which the specified search term *does not* appear. You can combine it with other operators and terms to exclude certain words from the search results. The search for **cow –collagen** returns pages on which the word **cow** appears but only if that same page does *not* include the word **collagen**. The – operator must go next to the word (or the phrase within quotes) that you want to exclude; there can be no spaces between them, like this: **cow –"skim milk"**.
+	The plus sign is called the *inclusion operator* and serves an interesting purpose—it tells Google to use stop words in a search that it normally ignores. If you wanted to make sure that Google included the word *to* in a search (Google typically ignores this word when searching), put it in the search as **+to**. As with the inclusion operator, the plus sign must go next to the word (or next to the quotes surrounding a search phrase) you want to include; there can be no spaces between them.
*	The asterisk is called a *wildcard*. For those who are familiar with searches on a computer, Google uses the asterisk in a search similarly to a computer wildcard search. The asterisk must be used in a quoted phrase, like this: **"I * New York"**. When you use this character, Google returns pages that have any words in place of the * on them. A search for **"I * New York"** would return pages with **I Love New York**, **I Hate New York,** and so on.
~	The tilde is called the *fuzzy operator* or *synonym operator*. When you use this operator, Google searches for pages that contain the specified term as well as synonyms for the term. For example, a search for ~**generous** would return pages on which the word **generous** appears, as well those pages that contain synonyms of *generous*, such as *munificent* and *charitable*.

6

▶ **NOTE**

Google does not recognize the **NOT** operator; instead, use the − operator.

---

7   About Power Searching Strategies

✔ **BEFORE YOU BEGIN**

1 Perform a Basic Google Search
5 Perform an Advanced Google Search
6 About Google Search Operators

Knowing how to do a search, how to do an advanced search, and how to use search operators goes a long way toward effective Google searching. But even knowing all that won't go *all* the way.

You need to combine all that technical information you acquired in the first tasks in this chapter with power searching strategies—techniques for crafting searches that give you results as close to possible to that for which you're searching.

Everyone has his own strategies for better searching, and so it's always a good idea to ask others for their ideas. But here are a few hints that should help you with your Google searches:

- **Be specific**—The Web is an enormous place, containing literally billions of pages. Almost any search you do brings back far too much information. So make sure your search is as specific as possible. If you're looking for a history of the making of the album *Blonde on Blonde* by Bob Dylan, don't just search for "**Blonde on Blonde**". Try **history "Blonde on Blonde"** and you'll get better results.

- **Be brief**—More is not always better when it comes to searching. Be as precise as possible with the terms you search for, and you'll get the best possible results. A short, precise search is much more effective than a rambling, imprecise one. So the search term **history of castrati** is better than **history of castrati who were special boy child singers starting in 1600**.

- **Vary the order of search terms**—When you do a search, Google looks not only at the terms themselves, but at the order in which you type them. Google applies more weight to the first terms than it does to later terms in the search string. So use more important terms first. However, it's also worth trying to do a search that uses the same search terms, but with the order varied; rearranging your terms sometimes returns exactly the results you want.

3

Finding Pictures with Google Images

IN THIS CHAPTER:

Google isn't limited to finding web pages and text—it's also great for finding pictures. Literally millions of photographs and other images are on the Web, available free. And **Google Images** is the best way to find them.

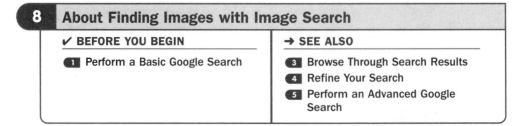

Finding pictures with Google **Image Search** is much like finding anything on Google. As you can see in the nearby figure, the search interface is the same bare-bones search you've come to know and love for basic Google.

You perform a basic search for images in the same way you do a basic search on Google. Type your search terms (including any advanced search operators), and Google does its searching magic, combing through hundreds of millions of images to find one that matches that for which you're looking.

8

Google **Image Search** *features the same bare-bones search interface as does normal Google.*

But some significant differences exist between using Google **Image Search** and using Google, and they have to do with the nature of images themselves.

In a normal Google search, Google looks through text it has indexed from hundreds of millions of web pages. Using a complicated series of rules, it decides which pages best match your search terms.

With images, though, things are different. An image is not made up of text; it contains no words. As smart a company as Google is, its search engine cannot examine a picture and know what it's a picture *of*. To Google, a picture of a zeppelin is no different than a painting by the Renaissance artist Caravaggio or a photograph of Hawaii. Basically, to Google, all three of these images are just bunches of bits.

So how can Google know what those pictures are if it can't decipher them? By using detective work that even Sherlock Holmes would envy. For a start, it looks at the image's filename. If the filename is **Caravaggio.jpg**, for example, there's a good chance that the image contained in the file is either a portrait of Caravaggio or a painting by Caravaggio.

Google also looks at the text near the image on a web page as well as at the text on the entire web page. Very frequently, web pages include a caption directly above, beneath, or next to an image. Google can associate that caption information with the image. In addition, other text on the web page itself provides more information about the image, and Google extracts that information as well. As an example, look at the nearby figure. The page is a biography of the painter Caravaggio and includes images of his paintings, with the names of the images and more information next to each painting.

So keep in mind when you're doing your Google **Image Search** that you're actually searching for information Google can find about each image. As you'll see in **11 Perform an Advanced Image Search**, this knowledge can help you better narrow your search.

8

WebMuseum, Paris

Caravaggio, Michelangelo Merisi da

Caravaggio (1573-1610). Probably the most revolutionary artist of his time, the Italian painter Caravaggio abandoned the rules that had guided a century of artists before him. They had idealized the human and religious experience.

He was born Michelangelo Merisi on Sept. 28, 1573, in Caravaggio, Italy. As an adult he would become known by the name of his birthplace. Orphaned at age 11, he was apprenticed to the painter Simone Peterzano of Milan for four years. At some time between 1588 and 1592, Caravaggio went to Rome and worked as an assistant to painters of lesser skill. About 1595 he began to sell his paintings through a dealer. The dealer brought Caravaggio to the attention of Cardinal Francesco del Monte.

Through the cardinal, Caravaggio was commissioned, at age 24, to paint for the church of San Luigi dei Francesi. In its Contarelli Chapel Caravaggio's realistic naturalism first fully appeared in three scenes he created of the life of St. Matthew. The works caused public outcry, however, because of their realistic and dramatic nature.

 _The Calling of Saint Matthew_

 The Inspiration of Saint Matthew
1602; Oil on canvas, 9' 8 1/2" x 6' 2 1/2"; Contarelli Chapel, Church of San Luigi dei Francesi, Rome

Despite violent criticism, his reputation increased and Caravaggio began to be envied. He had many encounters with the law during his stay in Rome. He was imprisoned for several assaults and for killing an opponent after a disputed score in a game of court tennis. Caravaggio fled the city and kept moving between hiding places. He reached Naples, probably early in 1607, and painted there for a time, awaiting a pardon by the pope. Here there was a in his painting style. The dark and urgent nature of his paintings at this time must have reflected Caravaggio's desperate state of mind.

Early in 1608 Caravaggio went to Malta and was received as a celebrated artist. Fearful of pursuit, he continued to flee for two more years, but his paintings of this time were among the greatest of his career. After receiving a pardon from the pope, he was wrongfully arrested and imprisoned for two days. A boat that was to take him to Rome left without him, taking his belongings. Misfortune, exhaustion, and illness overtook him as he helplessly watched the boat depart. He collapsed on the beach and died a few days later on July 18, 1610.

 David and Goliath
undated; Oil on canvas; Prado, Madrid

 Medusa
after 1590; Oil on canvas mounted on wood; Uffizi

Google can extract information from this page to help it index every image on the page.

8

---

9 | **Browse Through Image Search Results**

✔ BEFORE YOU BEGIN	→ SEE ALSO
8 About Finding Images with Image Search	**2** About Interpreting Google Results
	3 Browse Through Search Results

When you do a search on Google **Image Search**, the search results are not the same as they are when you do a normal Google search. This task shows you how to browse through the results.

1 Go to Google Image Search

Get to the Google **Image Search** by going to http://images.google.com or by starting at the Google home page (www.google.com) and clicking the **Images** link just above the search box.

2 Type Your Search Terms

Google **Image Search** works like the normal Google search site, so type your search term or terms and press **Enter** or click **Search Images**.

3 Browse the Results

The search results page looks different from the normal Google results. You see thumbnails of pictures that match your search. Beneath each picture is information about the image, including the filename; the resolution of the image in pixels; the size of the image in kilobytes; and the site on which the image is found.

4 Sort Images by Size

After you've done your search, you can choose to show only those images of a certain size—small, medium, or large. From the **Images Showing** drop-down list box, select **Large Images**, **Medium Images**, or **Small Images** to specify which size images to display. Note that the image *size* in this context refers not to the size of the image in kilobytes, but to its resolution size.

▶ **NOTE**

Sometimes, at the top of your **Google Image** search results page, you see a news photograph. That photograph is delivered from the **Google News** service. News is time-sensitive, so you might see a different photo or no photo at all the next time you do the same search.

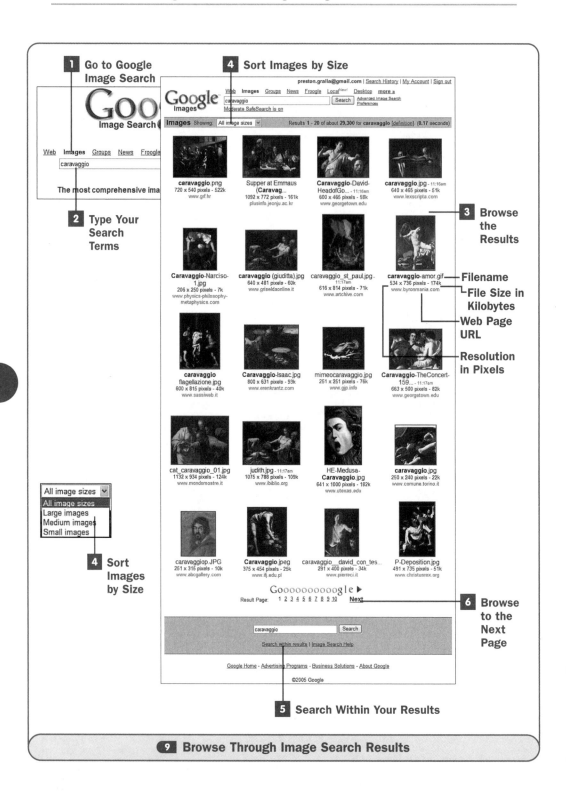

1 Go to Google Image Search

2 Type Your Search Terms

4 Sort Images by Size

3 Browse the Results

Filename
File Size in Kilobytes
Web Page URL
Resolution in Pixels

6 Browse to the Next Page

5 Search Within Your Results

9 Browse Through Image Search Results

5 Search Within Your Results

If you get too many search results, you can fine-tune your search by searching within your results. Scroll to the bottom of the results screen, and click the **Search within results** link located underneath the search box. A new page appears. Type your new search term (don't retype your original term), and you search within the original results.

6 Browse to the Next Page

As you can with any Google search results page, you can browse to the next page of results by clicking the **Next** button, located in the navigation area at the very bottom of the results page. Go to a specific page of results by clicking the page number you want to view (click the **1** to return to the first page of results), or click the **Back** button to go backward through multiple pages of results.

10	**Use the Image Viewer Interface**	
✔ **BEFORE YOU BEGIN**		→ **SEE ALSO**
9 Browse Through Image Search Results		**13** Use an Image As Your Desktop Wallpaper

10

When you do a normal Google search and then click a search result, you're sent to a web page. That's not how Google **Image Search** works. Instead, you're sent to an image viewer that gives you more information about the image and takes some actions on the image, as this task shows.

1 Click a Search Result

When you see an image that you want more information about or that you want to use, click the image thumbnail on the search results page.

2 Get Information About the Image

At the top of the page that appears, you find information about the image. You see a thumbnail of the image, the size of the image in pixels and kilobytes, and the URL of the web page on which the image is found. There also might be copyright information about the image. (For more information about images and copyright, see **12** About Images and Copyright Law.

Image Viewer

1 Click a Search Result

2 Get Information About the Image

4 See the Full-Size Image

4 See the Full-Size Image

3 View the Image on Its Original Page

5 Save the Image to Disk

10 Use the Image Viewer Interface

10

3 View the Image on Its Original Page

The bottom half of the page shows the image on the page on which it was found by Google. If you want more information about the image, it's a good idea to read through the page.

4 See the Full-Size Image

Click the **See full-size image** link located at the top of the image page to launch the image in its original size in a browser window.

▶ **NOTE**

If you no longer want to use the Google image viewer and the Google **Image Search**, you can go to the page that has the image on it. To do that, click the **Remove Frame** link at the top of the page. You can still click the browser's **Back** button to return to the Google results page.

5 Save the Image to Disk

To save the image to your computer's hard disk, right-click the image on its source web page or in the full-size browser window. From the context menu that appears, select **Save Picture As**. Then select the folder to which you want to save the picture and click **Save** to save it.

---

11   **Perform an Advanced Image Search**

✔ BEFORE YOU BEGIN	→ SEE ALSO
8 About Finding Images with Image Search	**5** Perform an Advanced Google Search

---

Because Google indexes hundreds of millions of images, your search results might return hundreds or thousands of images, many of which do not match that for which you're looking. What to do? Use Google's **Advanced Image Search** feature that enables you to fine-tune your searches. The **Advanced Image Search** includes features specific to images, such as file size.

1 Go to Advanced Image Search

Starting on the main page of the Google **Image Search**, click the **Advanced Image Search** link, located on the right side of the page, just to the right of the **Search Images** button.

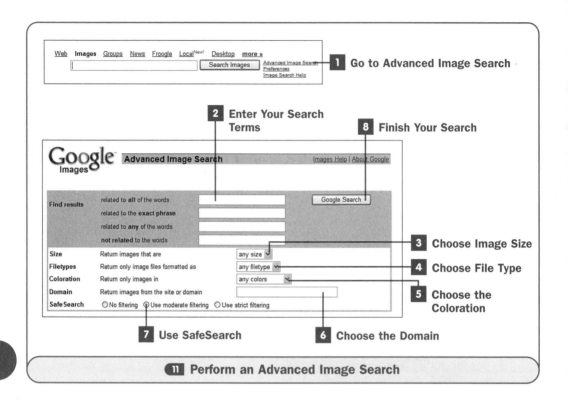

2 Enter Your Search Terms

The top part of the **Advanced Image Search** page enables you to enter search terms and phrases. It works exactly the same way as does Google's normal **Advanced Search**, so see **5** **Perform an Advanced Google Search** for details.

3 Choose Image Size

You can narrow your search by specifying a file size. *File size* refers to image resolution rather than to the size in kilobytes. Choose **small**, **medium**, or **large**, or **any size** if you want to search for images of any size.

4 Choose File Type

Google **Image Search** indexes images that it finds in three formats: **.gif**, **.jpg**, and **.png**. Most images on the web are in **.gif** or **.jpg** format; the **.png** format is much rarer. Choose the type of file you want to search for from the **Filetypes** drop-down list.

Why would you search for a **.gif** rather than a **.jpg**, and vice versa? Although any image can be saved in either format, each format has its strengths and weaknesses, which you should take into account when searching:

- **.gif** files are primarily used for simple graphics and illustrations that have 256 or fewer colors. The **.gif** format is best for logos, banners, web page buttons, and similarly simple graphics. Files in **.gif** format tend to be small and download quickly.

- **.jpg** files are use for photographs and complex graphics and illustrations that use more than 256 colors.

- **.png** files are a relatively new, high-quality format. Compared to **.gif** and **.jpg** files, relatively few **.png** files are on the Web.

If you're searching for photographs or complex graphics, search for a **.jpg** file; if you're looking for a logo, line illustration, or simple graphic, the **.gif** format is a better choice. It's rare that you would want to search only for **.png** files because there are relatively few of them online compared to files in **.jpg** and **.gif** format.

5 Choose the Coloration

Google can limit its search for images by color. Although you cannot search for images that are predominately red or mostly yellow, you *can* limit your search to black-and-white images, grayscale, or full-color images. From the **Coloration** drop-down box, choose **any colors**, **black and white**, **grayscale**, or **full color**. The **any colors** option returns black-and-white, grayscale, and full-color pictures. The **full color** option does not return black-and-white or grayscale pictures.

▶ **TIP**

You can also search for images using your cell phone. Go to www.google.com/xhtml, select **Images**, and then do a search. For more details about using Google on your cell phone, see ③① **About Searching Google with Your Cell Phone.**

6 Choose the Domain

If there is a specific website or domain to which you want to limit your search for images, type its URL in the **Domain** text box. For example, you could search an entire domain, such as www.prestonspictures.com, or an area inside that domain, such as www.prestonspictures.com/Caravaggio.

7 Use SafeSearch

The Web is full of inappropriate graphics, and although Google **Image Search** does not index pornographic sites, inappropriate pictures still might show up inadvertently on some searches. Use the SafeSearch feature, located at the bottom of the **Advanced Image Search** page, to filter out inappropriate pictures. You can choose **No filtering**, **Use moderate filtering**, or **Use strict filtering**.

8 Finish Your Search

After you've filled out the **Advanced Image Search** form, click the **Google Search** button or press **Enter** to finish your advanced search. Google returns image results in the standard way. See **9** **Browse Through Image Search Results** for more information.

---

12 About Images and Copyright Law

✔ BEFORE YOU BEGIN	→ SEE ALSO
8 About Finding Images with Image Search	**10** Use the Image Viewer Interface

The use of copyrighted material online has become one of the most contentious issues in all of cyberspace, particularly when it comes to music, movies, and books. The truth is that a great deal of material you can find online is actually owned by a copyright holder, and using it without the copyright holder's permission violates the laws.

The issues are not quite so contentious when it comes to the use of images online, but you still need to adhere to copyright laws when you use images. Many images you find using the Google **Image Search** might be copyrighted, so you cannot use them for certain purposes.

As a general rule in the United States, you can use a copyrighted image for an educational, research, or not-for-profit purpose. If you or your child are using an image for a school research project, for example, that should be fair game. If you're using a copyrighted image as wallpaper for your computer, as described in **13** **Use an Image As Your Desktop Wallpaper**, you should be fine as well. But if you're using a copyrighted image for a for-profit purpose, that breaks the law.

Sometimes, a copyrighted image on the Web carries a copyright notice, but more often than not, it doesn't. An image can still be copyrighted, even if it does not carry that notice. So be careful how you make use of images you find online.

▶ **TIP**

For more information about U.S. copyright law, go to the Library of Congress website dealing with copyright issues at www.loc.gov/copyright. For information about international copyright laws, go to the International Federation of Reproduction Rights Organizations at www.ifrro.org.

---

13 **Use an Image As Your Desktop Wallpaper**	
✔ **BEFORE YOU BEGIN**	→ **SEE ALSO**
8 About Finding Images with Image Search	**10** Use the Image Viewer Interface
9 Browse Through Image Search Results	
11 Perform an Advanced Image Search	

What can you do with images you find online? One great thing you can do is use an image as your background *wallpaper* in Windows. It's really quite easy to do, as you'll see in this task.

▶ **KEY TERM**

Wallpaper—The background image on your PC's desktop.

1 Find Your Screen Resolution

Finding the right picture for your background wallpaper isn't as easy as you might think. One of the key factors you should look for when searching for images to use for wallpaper is that the image be the same general dimensions and size as your computer screen. If the image is much smaller than your screen's dimensions, the image looks extremely distorted.

Computer monitors are wider than they are tall and have a ratio of 4:3 (width compared to height). Common screen resolutions are 800×600 pixels, 1024×768 pixels, and so on.

If you don't know the resolution for your screen, right-click a blank area of the desktop, choose **Properties** from the context menu that appears, and then click the **Settings** tab. Look for the **Screen resolution** section; it tells you your current resolution.

13

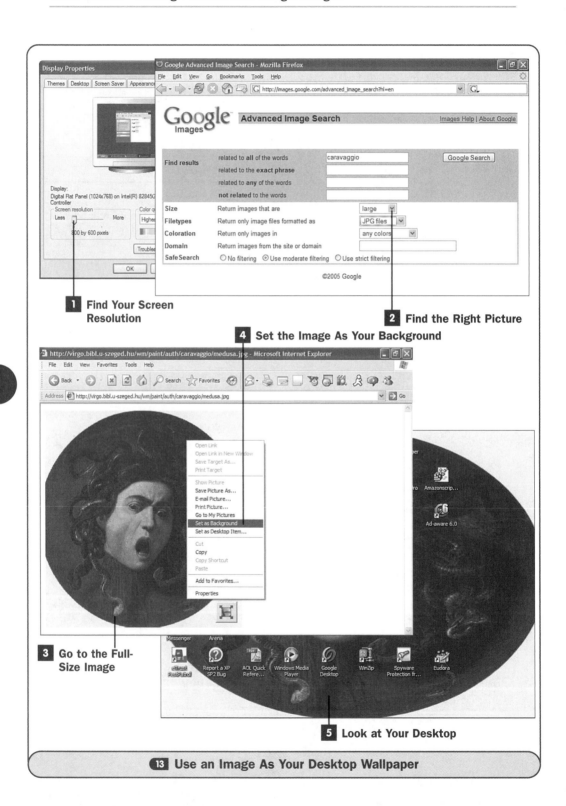

1 Find Your Screen Resolution

2 Find the Right Picture

4 Set the Image As Your Background

3 Go to the Full-Size Image

5 Look at Your Desktop

13 Use an Image As Your Desktop Wallpaper

2 Find the Right Picture

After you know your screen resolution, you need to find a picture of that approximate size. Use the **Advanced Image Search**, as outlined in **11** **Perform an Advanced Image Search**. If you have a screen resolution of 800×600 or more, specify the **large** option in the **Size** drop-down list. Unless you want a line drawing or a simple graphic, you can limit your search to photographs and more complex graphics by selecting **.jpg** from the **Filetypes** drop-down list. Press **Enter** or click **Google Search** to perform the search using your search terms and options.

After you do a search, look at the file sizes of the images on the results page. Try to find one that best matches your screen resolution. Don't worry if it's not exact, but do try to find one as close as possible to your screen's size and dimensions.

3 Go to the Full-Size Image

When you find the right image, view it at full size, as outlined in **9** **Browse Through Image Search Results**.

4 Set the Image As Your Background

When you are viewing the image at full size, right-click it and select **Set as Background** from the context menu. This command makes the image appear as your Windows wallpaper. (The image is stored in the **Windows\Web\Wallpaper** folder.)

5 Look at Your Desktop

Minimize or close the web browser window to go to the Windows desktop. The image appears as your wallpaper.

▶ **TIP**

These instructions show you how to set an image as your wallpaper when you use Internet Explorer. The name of the command you choose might vary if you're using a different browser. For example, in Firefox, you right-click the image and choose **Set As Wallpaper** from the context menu.

13

4

Searching Discussion Boards with Google Groups

IN THIS CHAPTER:

The Internet is all about communication. So it should be no surprise that one of its earliest uses was public discussion boards, which allow people to have conversations about any topic you can imagine—and many topics you probably can't imagine.

The mother of all discussion boards is called Usenet, which is a vast collection of thousands of discussions organized by topic. Each of these discussions is called a *newsgroup*. These newsgroups continue to be popular today. But they have one drawback—they're not particularly easy to use. In fact, they can be downright intimidating. You need a special piece of software to read and respond to them, called a newsgroup reader. And even with that software, newsgroups are not that easy to use.

▶ **KEY TERM**

Newsgroup—An Internet-based discussion board. Thousands of newsgroups are available, and you can read them using **Google Groups**.

Enter **Google Groups**. **Google Groups** give you an easy way to read any newsgroup straight from the Web or even through email. And in addition to newsgroups, Google has added discussion groups of its own. Anyone can set up her own **Google Group** for private or public discussions of any topic she wants.

So if you want to participate in the discussions on any topic you've ever been interested in, read this chapter—and get prepared to yak.

▶ **NOTE**

Google calls many of its services beta, which typically means that a service is in a test phase. But Google uses that term very liberally, and labels services as being in beta even after they've been around for a year or more.

14 **Browse Through Google Groups**	
✔ **BEFORE YOU BEGIN**	→ **SEE ALSO**
③ Browse Through Search Results	⑮ Search Through Google Groups

The most basic way to find a discussion group in which you're interested is to browse through those that are available. **Google Groups** are organized in directory fashion, and browsing to find the one you want is quite easy. But as you'll see, after you find a group you want to participate in, the interface you use to read the postings for the group can be a bit confusing. The following steps help you out so you'll be able to do it in a snap.

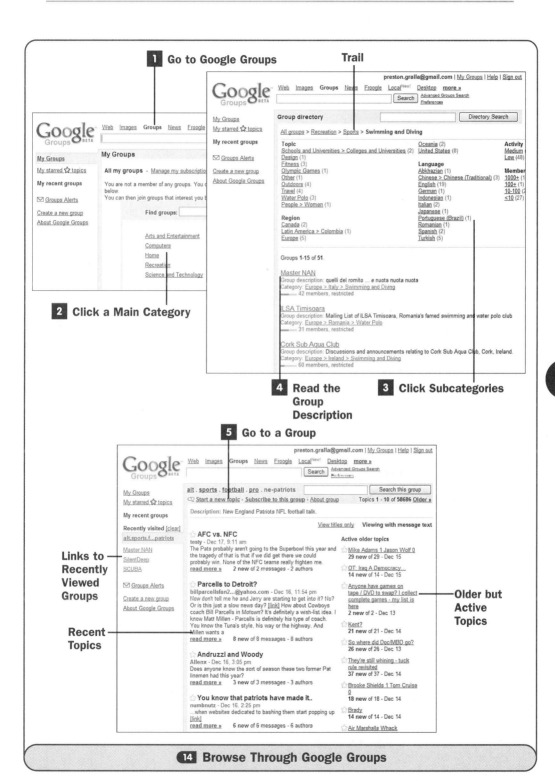

1 Go to Google Groups

Trail

2 Click a Main Category

4 Read the Group Description

3 Click Subcategories

5 Go to a Group

Links to Recently Viewed Groups

Recent Topics

Older but Active Topics

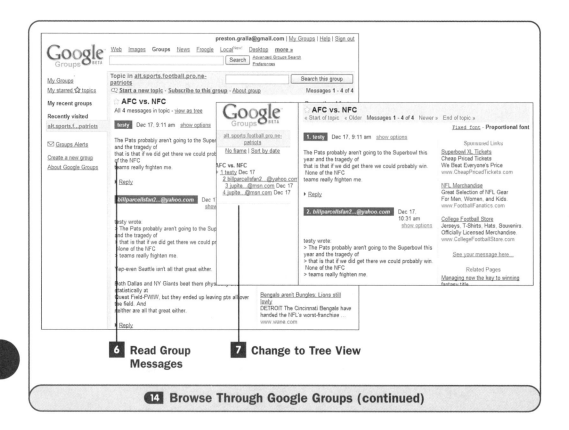

6 **Read Group Messages**   **7** **Change to Tree View**

14 Browse Through Google Groups (continued)

1 Go to Google Groups

Get to the main **Google Groups** site by entering the following URL in your browser's address bar: **http://groups.google.com**. (Alternatively, click the **Groups** link at the top of any Google page.) Before going to the **Google Groups** site, sign into your Google account because doing so enables you to customize how the **Google Groups** page looks.

2 Click a Main Category

The main **Google Groups** page lists top-level categories, such as **Arts and Entertainment**, **Computers**, **Home**, **Recreation**, and so on. Click the category in which you're interested.

▶ TIP

If you're familiar with Usenet, you know that Usenet newsgroups are organized in top-level categories such as **alt** (for alternative), **rec** (for recreation), and so on. If you'd like to browse by the traditional Usenet categorization scheme, click the **Browse all of Usenet** link on the main page of **Google Groups**.

3 Click Subcategories

At the top of the category results page, Google lists all the appropriate sub-categories. Each category has subcategories, and those subcategories might have sub-subcategories beneath them. Next to each subcategory you see the number of groups within that category. Keep clicking until you find the group you want. Note that as you click deeper into subcategories, you are able to see the trail you've taken near the top of the page, such as **All groups > Recreation > Sports > Swimming and Diving**. You can click on any part of the trail to move up to a higher level in the trail. The listings at the top of the category results page are also organized by topic, language, region, activity, and members. Follow those links to help you more quickly find the group you want.

4 Read the Group Description

As you browse through categories and subcategories, look for the discussion groups listed underneath the subcategory listings. For each group, you see a name, a description, and the number of members in the group. Read through this information to determine whether this might be a group that interests you. If a group name has the word **restricted** next to it, that means someone has set up the group and restricted it to only members he invites to the group.

5 Go to a Group

To go to a group, click its name. On the group page that appears, you see a list of the titles of the most recent topics, along with the first several lines of each topic, how many responses are in each topic, and how many authors are participating in each topic. Down the right side of the page you find older topics that are still active—in other words, people are still posting messages to them.

On the left side of the page are links to any groups you've recently visited. To clear out the list of recently visited groups, click the **Clear** link. Note that this action clears your **Recently visited** groups, but not the groups underneath **My recent groups**. The **My recent groups** list contains groups to which you subscribe; The **Recently visited** list contains groups you've recently visited but to which you have not subscribed. You might want to clear the **Recently visited** list if it becomes too long and unwieldy.

14

6 Read Group Messages

Click the **read more** link underneath a topic, and you are able to read the messages posted in that topic. Messages are organized in chronological order—the first message is listed first, the second message listed second, and so on. That means that the newest messages are at the bottom of the list. There is a limit of 10 posts per page; to get to the next 10 posts, click the **Newer >>** link at the bottom of the page.

At the top of each post you see the name of the person who wrote the post—the name is in colored, reverse text. To learn how to respond to a message, see **17 Participate in Google Group Discussions**.

7 Change to Tree View

If you prefer, you can view the group in tree view. In a tree view, on the left side of the page, you see a list of all the messages in the topic and can navigate to any by clicking on it. The tree view also shows you which messages are in response to other messages by indenting them. To change to the tree view, scroll to the post at the top of the message thread and click the **view as tree** link located just underneath the thread title. When you click the link, all threads are displayed in the tree view. To leave the tree view, click the **No frame** link in the left pane of the tree view.

14

▶ NOTE

Google Groups has a somewhat confusing and inconsistent interface. Depending on what page you're on, you might see a variety of options on the upper-right portion of the page. For example, on some pages, you can change the font by clicking either **fixed font** or **proportional font**. And you might also see a **view titles only** and **viewing with message text** link there as well. Keep in mind that Google has been experimenting with the display on **Google Groups**, so don't be surprised if what you see today changes tomorrow.

Note that some groups require that you first apply for membership before you can read them. For these membership groups, you see a **Join this group** link. Click the link and sign in to Google if you haven't done so already. After you sign in, a new page appears. Select how you want to read messages from the group (as email messages, on the Web, and so on), type the name you want to appear when you participate, and then click **Apply to this group**. The group owner will review your request and either allow or disallow you from participating in the group.

---

15 | Search Through Google Groups

✔ BEFORE YOU BEGIN	→ SEE ALSO
1 Perform a Basic Google Search **5** Perform an Advanced Google Search **14** Browse Through Google Groups	**17** Participate in Google Group Discussions

One of the best reasons for using **Google Groups** to access Usenet discussions is that you can use all of Google's searching power to find the discussion and messages you want. Here's how to do it.

1 Search for a Message

The search box at the top of any **Google Groups** screen enables you to search for individual messages and groups. Type your search term or terms just as you would normally in Google. You'll find the groups, message, or messages that match your search terms.

2 Browse Messages

The search results display groups or individual messages that match your search term or terms. For each message, you'll see the subject line; the first several lines of the message; the time, date, and author of the message; and the group in which the message appeared. Click any message to read it.

3 Search for a Group

You might be interested in finding a group that matches your interest, not just an individual message. To search for a group, go to the main **Google Groups** page by clicking the **Google Groups** logo on any page, type your search term or terms in the **Find groups** box, and click the **Group lookup** button.

4 Browse Groups

The search results display all the groups that match your search term or terms. For each group, you see the group name, description, category, and type—whether it's a public group in which anyone can participate or a private group in which only members can participate.

To visit the group, click the group name. If you prefer to read only matching message within that group, click the **Show matching messages from this group** link next to the group's name.

15

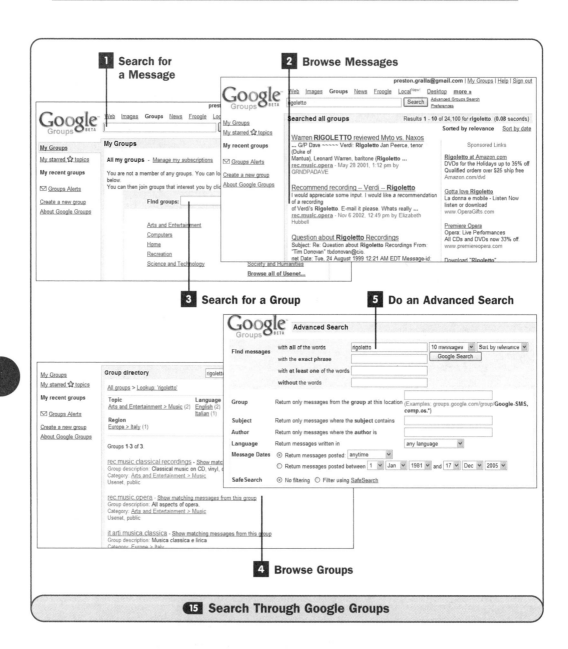

1 Search for a Message

2 Browse Messages

3 Search for a Group

5 Do an Advanced Search

4 Browse Groups

15 Search Through Google Groups

5 Do an Advanced Search

Google Groups' advanced search enables you to easily narrow your search. Click the **Advanced Group Search** link next to the search box at the top of any **Google Groups** page to do an advanced search.

The **Find messages** section works like most Google advanced search pages, and it enables you to enter specific search terms and how to use them. For more details, see **5** **Perform an Advanced Google Search**.

The rest of the page enables you to search by group name, subject, author of the message, date, and by language. You can also specify whether to use SafeSearch, which filters out objectionable language and content.

▶ **TIP**

It's a good idea to use the SafeSearch filter when doing an advanced search. Usenet is filled with a great deal of pornographic and objectionable content, and the SafeSearch feature filters that out.

---

16 | **About Tracking Your Favorite Topics**

✔ **BEFORE YOU BEGIN**

14 Browse Through Google Groups
15 Search Through Google Groups

16

The terminology of **Google Groups** can be confusing at times, so before tackling how to track your favorite topics, here's a quick rundown about what you need to know:

- A *group* is a Usenet discussion group about a subject, such as rec.music.classical, which is a discussion group about classical music.

- A *topic* is a single discussion thread inside a group, such as Stravinsky's Rites of Spring inside rec.music.classical.

- A *message* is a single posting inside a topic.

As you participate in more groups, you'll find more topics that interest you—you might find several dozen topics. It can be maddeningly difficult to keep track of them all. But Google gives you a simple way to keep track of your favorite topics. You can star those topics you want to follow, and they show up when you click the **My starred topics** link on any **Google Group** page.

▶ **TIP**

To keep track of starred topics, you have to be signed in to your Google account. For information about how to create a Google account, see Chapter 1, "Start Here."

Every topic title has a blue outline of a star next to it. To star a topic you want to refer to again, simply click the blue-outline star next to the topic name. When you do that, the star fills in with yellow. When you want to see all your starred topics, click the **My starred topics** link on the left side of any **Google Groups** page, and they show up, as you can see in the nearby figure.

Viewing your starred topics.

17

17 Participate in Google Group Discussions

✔ **BEFORE YOU BEGIN**

14 Browse Through Google Groups
15 Search Through Google Groups

Google Groups are useful for more than just reading—you'll want to participate in them as well. As you'll see in this task, it's as easy to participate in groups as it is to read them.

1 Sign into Your Google Account

Before you can post messages to a group, you must have a Google account. So before participating, sign up for an account, and sign in. For details, see Chapter 1, "Start Here."

2 Read Messages

Browse groups and topics, and read the messages that interest you. Find a message to which you want to reply.

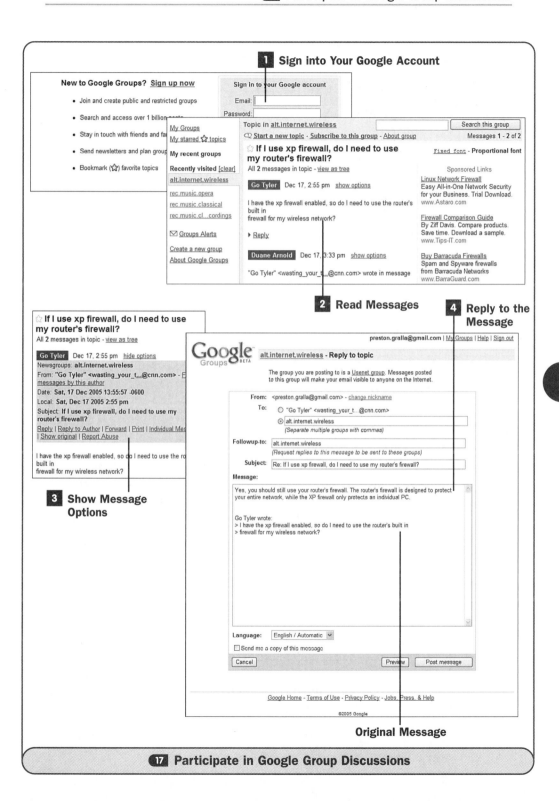

1 Sign into Your Google Account

New to Google Groups? Sign up now

- Join and create public and restricted groups
- Search and access over 1 billion posts
- Stay in touch with friends and family
- Send newsletters and plan group events
- Bookmark (☆) favorite topics

Sign in to your Google account

Email: [   ]
Password:

My Groups
My starred ☆ topics

My recent groups

Recently visited [clear]
alt.internet.wireless

rec.music.opera
rec.music.classical
rec.music.cl...cordings

✉ Groups Alerts

Create a new group
About Google Groups

Topic in alt.internet.wireless   [   ] [Search this group]

📢 Start a new topic - Subscribe to this group - About group   Messages 1 - 2 of 2

☆ **If I use xp firewall, do I need to use my router's firewall?**   Fixed font - Proportional font

All 2 messages in topic - view as tree   Sponsored Links

[Go Tyler] Dec 17, 2:55 pm show options

I have the xp firewall enabled, so do I need to use the router's built in
firewall for my wireless network?

▶ Reply

[Duane Arnold] Dec 17, 3:33 pm show options

"Go Tyler" <wasting_your_t...@cnn.com> wrote in message

Linux Network Firewall
Easy All-in-One Network Security
for your Business. Trial Download.
www.Astaro.com

Firewall Comparison Guide
By Ziff Davis. Compare products.
Save time. Download a sample.
www.Tips-IT.com

Buy Barracuda Firewalls
Spam and Spyware firewalls
from Barracuda Networks
www.BarraGuard.com

2 Read Messages

4 Reply to the Message

☆ **If I use xp firewall, do I need to use my router's firewall?**

All 2 messages in topic - view as tree

[Go Tyler] Dec 17, 2:55 pm hide options
Newsgroups: alt.internet.wireless
From: "Go Tyler" <wasting_your_t...@cnn.com> - F
messages by this author
Date: Sat, 17 Dec 2005 13:55:57 -0600
Local: Sat, Dec 17 2005 2:55 pm
Subject: If I use xp firewall, do I need to use my
router's firewall?
Reply | Reply to Author | Forward | Print | Individual Mes
| Show original | Report Abuse

I have the xp firewall enabled, so do I need to use the ro
built in
firewall for my wireless network?

3 Show Message Options

preston.gralla@gmail.com | My Groups | Help | Sign out

Google Groups BETA   alt.internet.wireless - Reply to topic

The group you are posting to is a Usenet group. Messages posted
to this group will make your email visible to anyone on the Internet.

From: <preston.gralla@gmail.com> - change nickname
To: ○ "Go Tyler" <wasting_your_t...@cnn.com>
        ⊙ alt.internet.wireless   [   ]
        (Separate multiple groups with commas)
Followup-to: alt.internet.wireless
        (Request replies to this message to be sent to these groups)
Subject: Re: If I use xp firewall, do I need to use my router's firewall?

Message:

Yes, you should still use your router's firewall. The router's firewall is designed to protect
your entire network, while the XP firewall only protects an individual PC.

Go Tyler wrote:
> I have the xp firewall enabled, so do I need to use the router's built in
> firewall for my wireless network?

Language: [English / Automatic ▾]
☐ Send me a copy of this message
[Cancel]   [Preview] [Post message]

Google Home - Terms of Use - Privacy Policy - Jobs, Press, & Help

©2005 Google

Original Message

17

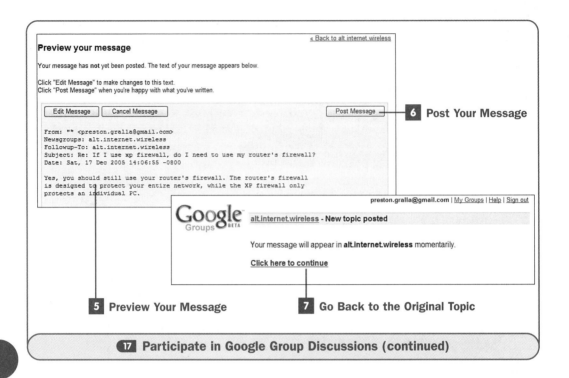

5 Preview Your Message   **7** Go Back to the Original Topic

17 Participate in Google Group Discussions (continued)

17

3 Show Message Options

You have a number of options for participating in groups, so when you find a message to which you want to reply, click the **show options** link next to the name of the person who posted the message. Several lines of message option links appear. To hide the list of message options again, click the **hide options** link. The message options available are

- **Reply**—Reply to the entire group. If you don't see a **Reply** link, look at the top of the topic page, where you will undoubtedly see the **You cannot post messages because only members can post, and you are not currently a member** message. You must become a member of this group before you can post to it, as explained in **14 Browse Through Google Groups**.

- **Reply to Author**—Reply only to the author of the message. When you click this link, you can send an email to the author *and* you make a post to the group, but that post can be read only by the author of the original message.

- **Forward**—Forward the message to someone else in an email message.

- **Print**—Print the message.

- **Individual Message**—Display only the message you are reading and reply to it.

- **Show original**—Show the *header* information along with the message in a separate window. The header information includes technical information about the ISP, where the message originated, the route it traveled across the Internet, the newsgroup reader used to create the program, and similar information.

▶ KEY TERM

Header—Information about a newsgroup message or email message that includes information such as the ISP, where the message originated, the servers the message traversed, and more.

- **Report Abuse**—Bring up a form that enables you to send a message to Google if you believe the post is spam or the post contains illegal content, such as copyrighted material. (For information about what is suitable and what isn't for posting, see the terms of service for **Google Groups** at http://groups.google.com/googlegroups/terms_of_service.html.

4 Reply to the Message

Click the **Reply** link to reply to the entire group, or click **Reply to Author** to reply only to the author. A form appears into which you type your response. If you want to receive a copy of the message, check the box next to **Send me a copy of this message** near the bottom of the form.

5 Preview Your Message

It's a good idea to preview your message before posting it. Click the **Preview** button at the bottom of the form, and you are able to see a preview of the message you're about to post. Read it, and if you want to make changes, click the **Edit Message** button near the top of the **Preview your message** page. To cancel the message (that is, to delete it without posting it to the group), click the **Cancel Message** button.

6 Post Your Message

To post your message, click the **Post Message** button on either the **Preview your message** page or at the bottom of the original message reply form.

17

7 Go Back to the Original Topic

After you properly post your message, you receive a confirmation that your message has been posted. Click the **Click here to continue** link to go back to the topic you were reading. Your message appears in the topic after several moments.

---

18   Subscribe to Google Groups

✔ BEFORE YOU BEGIN	→ SEE ALSO
14 Browse Through Google Groups **15** Search Through Google Groups	**16** About Tracking Your Favorite Topics

---

With the many thousands of groups you can read and participate in, you'll no doubt find a number of them that you would like to check regularly. To do that, you can subscribe to them. When you subscribe to a group, it shows up as a permanent link whenever you visit **Google Groups**, so the group is easy to revisit whenever you want.

▶ **NOTE**

A *topic* is a discussion within a group that enables you to hone in on a specific discussion in a specific group. When you subscribe, you subscribe to the entire group, not to a specific discussion within the group. When you subscribe to a group, the group shows up on the left side of the page, underneath the **My recent groups** heading. To unsubscribe from a group, click the **My Groups** link; on the page that appears, click **Manage my subscriptions**. From the new page that appears, choose **Unsubscribe** from the drop-down list next to the name of the group from which you want to unsubscribe. Then click **Save group settings**.

1 Search or Browse for Groups

As detailed in **14** Browse Through Google Groups and **15** Search Through Google Groups, find a group in which you're interested.

2 Show Suggested Groups

After you use **Google Groups** for a while, Google learns what kind of interests you have. Based on that, it suggests groups you might be interested in viewing. Click the **Show suggested groups** link on the **Google Groups** page to view these groups.

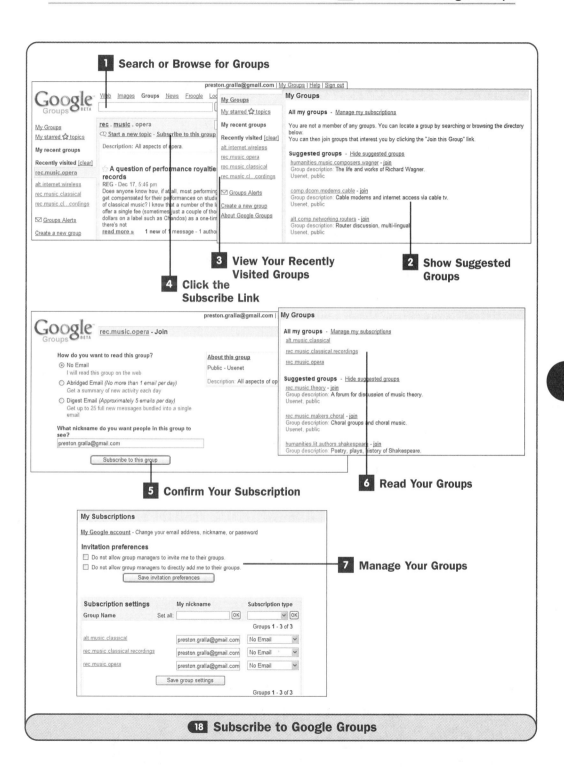

1 Search or Browse for Groups

3 View Your Recently Visited Groups

2 Show Suggested Groups

4 Click the Subscribe Link

5 Confirm Your Subscription

6 Read Your Groups

7 Manage Your Groups

18

3 View Your Recently Visited Groups

On the left side of the **Google Groups** page, you see a list of all the groups you've recently visited. Click any of these links to view that group.

4 Click the Subscribe Link

When you visit a group, you see a **Subscribe to this group** link at the top of the page. Click it to subscribe to it. When you do that, the group shows up on the left side of the **Google Groups** page, underneath **My recent groups**. To quickly jump to your favorite groups, click the group name in the list.

5 Confirm Your Subscription

The next page asks how you want to read messages from the group to which you want to subscribe. You have these options:

- **No Email**—When you choose this option, you have to go to **Google Groups** on the Web to read the group messages.

- **Abridged Email**—When you choose this option, you receive a summary of all new messages in an email message sent once a day to the email account you specified when you created your Google account. To read the complete messages, you have to visit **Google Groups** on the Web.

- **Digest Email**—When you choose this option, you get the complete messages from the group every day, bundled into separate emails of up to 25 messages per email. The digest is sent to the email address you specified when you created your Google account.

Choose the way you want to read the messages from this group and click the **Subscribe to this group** button. Set your nickname as well. Your nickname is the name that people see when you post messages.

6 Read Your Groups

From now on, the groups you've subscribed to are listed whenever you visit **Google Groups**. They are in the main part of the page, under the heading **My Groups**.

7 Manage Your Groups

You can change your subscription settings by clicking the **Manage my subscriptions** link on your **My Groups** page. The **My Subscriptions** page enables you to change your subscription choices—for example, you can unsubscribe, or you can change the way you read your subscriptions. For

18

each group to which you have subscribed, make a choice from the **Subscription type** drop-down list.

You can also change the name that people see when you write messages. To give yourself a nickname, type it in the **My nickname** box and click **OK**.

▶ **TIP**

People who set up and manage their own Google groups can send you invitations to join their groups or can add you directly to their groups. If you don't want to receive invitations or be added to groups by group managers, check the appropriate boxes beneath **Invitation preferences** at the top of the page.

When you're done making changes to your group subscriptions, click the **Save group settings** button to return to your **My Groups** page.

---

19 | **Create Google Groups Alerts**

✔ **BEFORE YOU BEGIN**

16 About Tracking Your Favorite Topics
17 Participate in Google Group Discussions

→ **SEE ALSO**

18 Subscribe to Google Groups

19

A topic that interests you might appear in almost any Google group. For example, if you're interested in cloning, messages about it might appear in many dozens of groups, not just one devoted to cloning. **Groups Alerts** send you email messages when a topic you're interested in is mentioned in any group, anywhere. When you get an alert email message that there is a new topic, click the link in the email message to go straight to that topic.

1 **Click Groups Alerts**

On the left side of any **Google Groups** page, click the **Groups Alerts** link. This action brings you to the **Create a Google Alert** page.

2 **Type Your Search Terms**

In the **Search terms** box, type the term or terms about which you want to create an alert. If you type multiple terms, you'll get an alert only when *all* the terms are mentioned in the same post.

1 Click Groups Alerts

5 Choose Your Email Type

2 Type Your Search Terms

3 Choose the Alert Type

6 Create the Alert

4 Choose the Alert Frequency

7 Check Your Email

List of Active Alert Terms

8 Edit Your Alerts

19 Create Google Groups Alerts

▶ **TIP**

Be careful not to use a very common word for your alert. If you do, you'll be inundated with alert email messages. So, for example, if you were interested in reading about the New England Patriots football team, make sure to use the term **New England Patriots**. If you use only the term **Patriots**, you'd get notification every time the word **Patriots** was used.

3 Choose the Alert Type

You can create alerts not only for **Google Groups**, but also for when the term or term appears on a web page or in a news article. Choose the alert type from the **Type** drop-down list. Again, make sure that the term is not a common one, or you'll be inundated with results.

4 Choose the Alert Frequency

From the **How often** drop-down list, choose how often you want your alert results to be sent to you in email messages—once a day, when it happens, or once a week.

5 Choose Your Email Type

You can have alerts sent to you as text email or as HTML email. (Text mail is mail with just plain text; HTML mail includes pictures and formatting.) Make your choice by clicking the link at the top of the page. Now Google will send the alerts to the email address you used when you registered with Google.

6 Create the Alert

When you've made your choices concerning this alert, click the **Create Alert** button. Your alert is created. You see a list of your alerts at the bottom of the page, underneath **Your Google Alerts**.

7 Check Your Email

When your alert terms appear in a message in any Google group (or on a web page or in a news article, depending on the option you selected in step 3), you receive an email message according to the schedule you've set. The email contains links you can click to bring you to the relevant messages.

8 Edit Your Alerts

To edit your alerts, click the **edit** link next to the alert in the **Your Google Alerts** area and make your edits by changing your search term, how often you want to be notified, and the type of alert you want to receive. To delete the alert, click the **delete** link instead.

19

20 Create Your Own Google Group

✔ **BEFORE YOU BEGIN**

14 Browse Through Google Groups

15 Search Through Google Groups

One of **Google Groups'** most useful features is that it enables you to create your own groups, which you can make private or public. (A private group is one in which only people who have been invited are allowed to join.) And particularly useful is that you can create groups in which people participate using email in addition to postings on the Web. To post messages, people send a message to an email address. That message is then sent to everyone in the group, who can then read it and respond to it.

1 Click Create a New Group

Click the **Create a new group** link on any **Google Groups** page. You go to the **Create a group** page. You can create a group for any reason you want—for example, to converse with other like-minded people about a topic or to communicate with friends and family.

2 Fill in the Name, Address, and Description

In the **Group name** box at the top of the page, type your group's name, for example, **Godzilla Lovers**. In the **Group email address** text box, type the email address that is the group email address. An **@googlegroups.com** is added to the email address you type, so don't include the domain name when you type the address. The email address has the **googlegroups.com** domain name. This email address is the email address to which people will send mail if they want to participate in the group using email rather than the Web. So, for example, they could send an email message to **godzillalovers@googlegroups.com**, and the message would go to every member of the group.

▶ **TIP**

The email address you give determines the exact URL of your group on the Web. All groups start with http://groups.google.com/group/. Appended to that is the email address (sans domain name) of your group. For example, if I specify an email address of **preston**, the URL of my group will be http://groups.google.com/group/preston. People can also send emails to participate in the group's discussions by addressing them to **preston@googlegroups.com**.

In the **Group description** text box, type a description for your group. There is a maximum of 300 characters. As you type, you see how many characters you have remaining.

If your group is going to have content that is adult-only, check the box next to **This group may contain content which is only suitable for adults.**

3 Set the Access Level

You can choose from three access levels. Click the appropriate radio button to specify the kind of group you want to create:

- **Public**—The messages and *archives* for this group are open to anyone. Anyone is allowed to join the group. If someone wants to post messages, he must join the group.

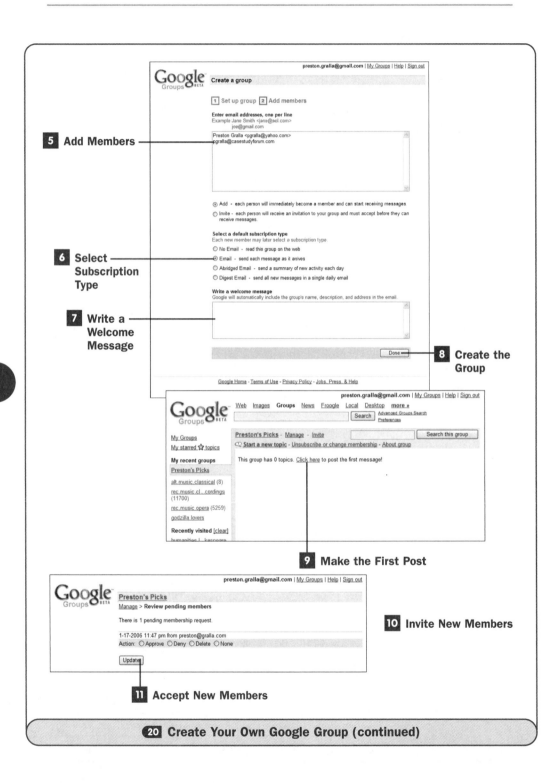

20

5 Add Members

6 Select Subscription Type

7 Write a Welcome Message

8 Create the Group

9 Make the First Post

10 Invite New Members

11 Accept New Members

20 Create Your Own Google Group (continued)

▶ **KEY TERM**

Archive—A list of messages in a group that are more than 30 days old.

▶ **NOTE**

You do not have to do anything special to search or read through archives. But you cannot reply to a message that is more than 30 days old—that's why those messages are termed archives.

- **Announcement-only**—Anyone can read the messages in this type of group, and anyone can join the group. But only those who have been given moderator rights can post messages.

- **Restricted**—Membership to this private group is available by invitation only. The group, its messages, and its archives don't appear in the **Google Groups** directory and can't be found using searches. The owner of the group sends you an email if she wants you to join. And if someone tells you the name and email address of the owner, you can send an email to the owner, asking to join the group. After you're a member of a restricted group, you can post and reply to all messages.

▪4 Create Your Group

When you've made your choices, click **Create my group**.

▪5 Add Members

From the page that appears, enter the email addresses of people you want to be members of your group. Enter one email address per line. If you want to have people's names as well as email addresses, enter them like this:

Preston Gralla preston.gralla@gmail.com

After listing all the people you want to be members of your group, select the **Add** option if you want to add these people automatically to your group; select the **Invite** option if you want to first send an invitation, which they must accept before they can participate in the group.

▪6 Select Subscription Type

At the bottom of the page, select the default type of subscription you want to assign to the people who join your group. (They can change the type of subscription afterwards, if they want.) Your choices are

- **No Email**—Members can participate in the group only over the Web, not using email.

20

- **Email**—Members can participate using the Web and email. As soon as a member posts a message, an email message is sent to all the members in the group.

- **Abridged Email**—Members can participate in the group using the Web and email. Members receive a summary of activity on the group every day, but have to go to the Web to read the full messages.

- **Digest Email**—Members can participate in the group using the Web and email. Once a day, a single digest is sent as an email message; the digest has all the day's messages in it.

7 Write a Welcome Message

When your welcoming email message is sent to the members you listed in step 5, the group's name, description, and address is included in the email. If you also want to include a welcome message, enter your text in the box at the bottom of the page.

8 Create the Group

After you've made all your choices, click **Done**. Your group is created. Members can participate in the group, according to the rules you've established.

20

9 Make the First Post

Now that you've created your group, you can create the first post. Go to your group. There are no topics or messages posted yet. Click the **Click here** link, and you are brought to a page that enables you to create a message. Fill out the subject and the body text boxes, and click **Post message** to create the first post.

10 Invite New Members

After you've created your group and invited your initial list of members, you can still add new members to your group. When you're in your group, click the **Manage** link to get to the group's management page. Click the **Invite or Add members** button to invite a new member. You see the same screen you did in step 5. Follow the directions in step 5 to add the new members.

11 Accept New Members

When you receive emails from people accepting your invitation to join your group (or if someone sends you an email asking to join your group), you must approve those people individually before they can join the group and post messages. On the page where you manage your group, look in the **Tasks** area in the upper-right corner of the page. You see a notification that you need to review a member who wants to join. The message reads **1 new membership to review** (or more than one, if there is more than one message waiting for you). Click the link. A page appears that allows you to approve or deny the request. You can also take no action by selecting **None**, or delete the request by selecting **Delete**. If you select **None**, the request still shows up in your **Tasks** area so you can review it at a later time. If you select **Delete**, the request is deleted, but no notification is sent to the requester. Use this option if you don't want someone to join your group, and don't want to have *any* communication with them, even an automated email. When you've made your membership-approval choice, click **Update** to update the membership roster for your group.

When you approve a member, that person can immediately start posting. An email is sent to the new member, telling her that she has been approved—or that she has not been approved, if you selected the **Deny** option.

20

5

Specialized Google Searching

IN THIS CHAPTER:

Want to get health information or the run-down on your new doctor? Like to find out how to fix your broken computer? Want to find the latest news, get travel information, or translate pages from French or German into English? You can do all that and more with Google specialized searches, as you'll see in this chapter.

---

21 Find People with Google

✔ BEFORE YOU BEGIN	→ SEE ALSO
1 Perform a Basic Google Search	**7** About Power Searching Strategies
5 Perform an Advanced Google Search	**27** Search Through Blogs with Google
6 About Google Search Operators	

Have you ever been Googled? Whether you know it or not, you most likely have. When you Google someone, you search with Google to find out information about that person.

You can use Google to find substantial amounts of information about people, and you can use it to find long-lost friends as well. Want to get in touch with your old boyfriend or girlfriend from high school? Turn to Google. Need to find out about someone you plan to hire or about your kid's school principal? Google is the place to turn. In this task, you'll learn how to find information about anyone with Google.

21

1 Create a Search Checklist

Before you begin searching, you should create a list of everything you know about the person, such as the following:

- Full name, including the middle name
- Maiden name
- Place of birth
- Current residence or last known address
- Place of work
- Names of parents, siblings, children, and relatives
- Current and past employers
- Interests and hobbies
- Awards and recognitions
- High school and university attended

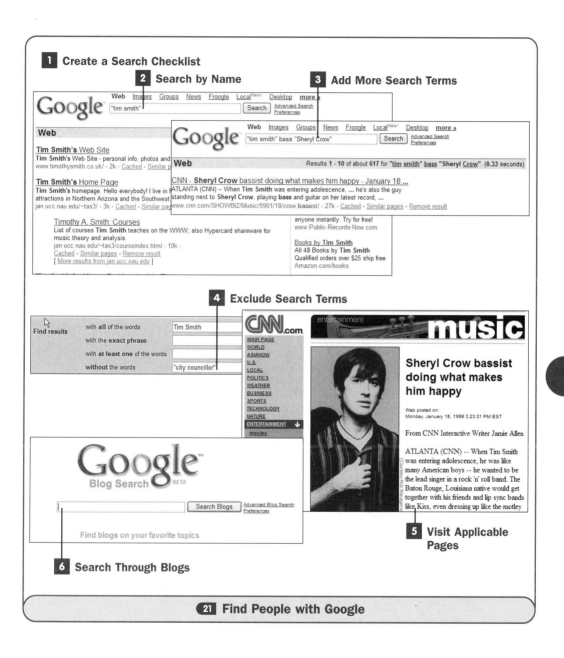

1. **Create a Search Checklist**
2. **Search by Name**
3. **Add More Search Terms**
4. **Exclude Search Terms**
5. **Visit Applicable Pages**
6. **Search Through Blogs**

21 Find People with Google

▶ **NOTE**

Make sure you check the spelling of the person's name, place of work, residence—everything you know about the person. If you spell the name wrong, it's unlikely you'll find the person.

2 Search by Name

The first step is the most obvious—search for the person's name by typing it into the Google search box. Make sure that you put quotations marks around the name before you press **Enter**, like this: "**Tim Smith**". If you don't use quotation marks, you might find odd results, such as towns or cities, land-marks, and so on.

3 Add More Search Terms

The odds are that your first search won't come up with information about the person for whom you're looking, unless you're searching for someone with a unique name. Instead, it will most likely come up with thousands of results, most of which are not useful. So now begin to add search terms, one by one. Use the search checklist you created in step 1. For example, try adding the person's last known address, university, personal interests, and so on. Make sure to use quotation marks when applicable, around the name of a univer-sity, for example. (When you're searching for an exact phrase, use quotation marks.)

4 Exclude Search Terms

21

If you're searching for someone who happens to have the same name as a person relatively well known or who has many Google results, you're going to run into trouble. It will be very hard to find the object of your search, and information about him might be buried several hundred or more results deep. To get around the problem, use the **Advanced Search** feature to exclude many of the search results of the more well-known person. (You can also use search operators to exclude search terms. For details, see **6 About Google Search Operators**.

Get to the **Advanced Search** page by clicking **Advanced Search** next to the Google search box. (For more information about **Advanced Search**, see **5 Perform an Advanced Google Search**.) Then in the **without the words** box, type any words that describe the well-known person—for example, "**city councilor**" or **musician**. Make sure that the **with all of the words** box includes the person's name and any other search terms you've added. When you're done, click **Search**.

5 Visit Applicable Pages

Using multiple search terms should bring you relevant results. Visit them, one by one. What you find on one page might also give you ideas for more search terms to use to fine-tune your search; use those terms for subsequent searches.

6 **Search Through Blogs**

A surprising number of people have their own blogs these days, so don't be surprised if who you're looking for has one. If he does, a blog is the best way to find someone or find information about that person because blogs are often very personal.

To search through blogs, go to the Google Blog Search at http://blogsearch. google.com. For more details, see **27** **Search Through Blogs with Google**.

---

22 **Find Health Information with Google**

✔ BEFORE YOU BEGIN	→ SEE ALSO
1 Perform a Basic Google Search	**7** About Power Searching Strategies
5 Perform an Advanced Google Search	
6 About Google Search Operators	

Searching for health information is one of the most common activities on the Internet. In fact, a study for the Pew Internet & American Life Project found that more than 80% of Internet users have searched the Internet for health-related information. More likely than not, a high percentage of those people used Google to find their results. This task shows you how to find health information using Google.

1 **Formulate a Search**

You search for health information on Google as you do for any other information; there is no health-specific Google website. When searching for health-related information, be as specific as possible about the condition for which you're looking. An exceptional amount of health information is on the Internet, and if you don't narrow your search, you'll soon become overwhelmed.

2 **Examine Search Results Carefully**

You should be very skeptical about health information you find online. There are plenty of scammers and crackpots out there, and you don't want to be victimized. So no matter what results are returned, check whether the source is a reputable one. Is it from a large, well-known website such as www.webmd.com or from a site associated with a major medical association, university, hospital, or medical school? If so, the information you read there should be trustworthy. But if the search result links to a site that's not from a known, reputable source, be very, very leery of what you find there.

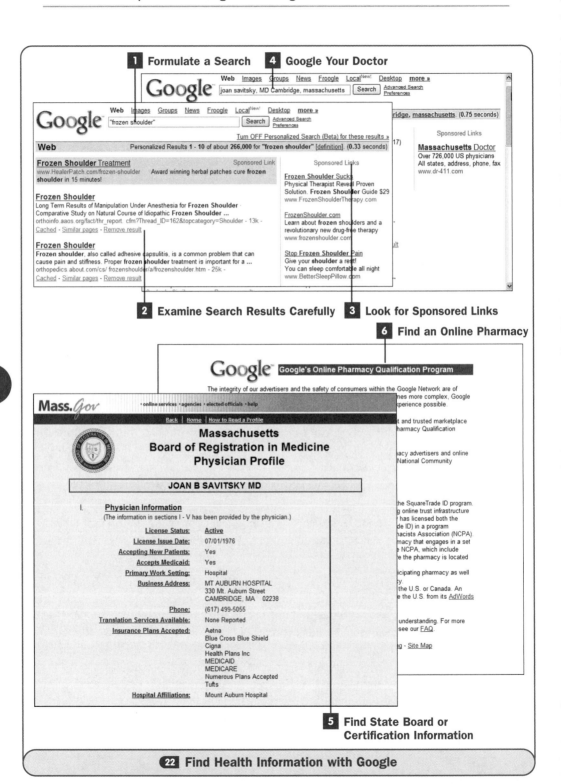

1 Formulate a Search   **4** Google Your Doctor

2 Examine Search Results Carefully   **3** Look for Sponsored Links

6 Find an Online Pharmacy

5 Find State Board or Certification Information

22 Find Health Information with Google

▶ TIPS

Just because someone includes the honorific "Dr." in front of his name does not mean that he is a medical doctor. Anyone who has received a doctorate (in English literature or chemical engineering, for example) can use "Dr." in front of his name.

Similarly, if someone calls himself a medical practitioner, that does not mean he is a doctor. So if you see someone referred to as Dr. Joe Smith, medical practitioner, the odds are he is not a medical doctor qualified to dispense medical advice.

3 Look for Sponsored Links

Often, the **Sponsored Links** area on the right side of the Google page has sites relevant to the information you're looking for, so make sure to check out those links as well as your search results. However, keep in mind that to show up as a sponsored link, all a company has to do is pay Google—Google does not check the medical qualifications of companies who buy ads.

4 Google Your Doctor

Google can help you find information about your existing doctor or a doctor you're considering using. Search using your doctor's name, affiliation, address, and any other identifying information.

You'll most likely find a wide variety of search results. Look at the doctor's or practice's website, and look for affiliations, education, internship, board certifications, and similar information. Follow up each of those facts—for example, if the doctor claims a specialty from a board or group, search for that board or group, and then do a search on the site you find to determine whether the doctor in fact has been certified for that specialty by that board or group.

5 Find State Board or Certification Information

Doctors are certified by a state board. Increasingly, the websites for these state boards include a great deal of information about every doctor in the state, including data about the physician's specialties, education, employment background, and other basic information. And the state boards often provide information about any disciplinary action taken, or malpractice claims filed, against the doctor. Search for your state's name, along with terms such as **"doctor certification"** to find the site. You might also be able to check with your state's department of consumer affairs to determine the name of the site.

22

6 Find an Online Pharmacy

Many pharmacies sell prescription medications online, and you can find them by searching for the name of the drug you've been prescribed or that you're investigating. But you need to be careful about buying from an online pharmacy: Make sure it's reputable, will deliver the medications, and that the product you will actually receive is a valid medication.

Don't trust search results when looking for an online pharmacy. The sponsored links are more trustworthy because of Google's Online Pharmacy Qualification Program. In order for a site to be allowed to buy ads and show up in the **Sponsored Links** list for pharmacy searches, the site must be qualified by the program, which uses the SquareTrade ID program. SquareTrade verifies that the pharmacy and its pharmacist have been properly licensed and that they adhere to the industry practices of the National Community Pharmacists Association (NCPA). Be aware, though, that this applies only to the ads—not to the general search results.

▶ WEB RESOURCE

www.google.com/adwords/pharmacy_qualification.html
This site offers details about Google's Online Pharmacy Qualification Program.

23

23 Get Technical Support with Google	
✔ BEFORE YOU BEGIN	→ SEE ALSO
1 Perform a Basic Google Search **5** Perform an Advanced Google Search **6** About Google Search Operators **15** Search Through Google Groups	**7** About Power Searching Strategies

Thanks to Google, gone are the days of waiting on hold for 30 minutes on a technical support line, only to be "helped" by someone whose grasp of English is as poor as her ability to solve technical problems. And gone are the days of paying $25 for a single technical support phone call.

Instead, you can turn to Google, which can help solve many problems quickly—in particular, those questions having to do with computer problems—without having to resort to technical support, as you'll see in this task.

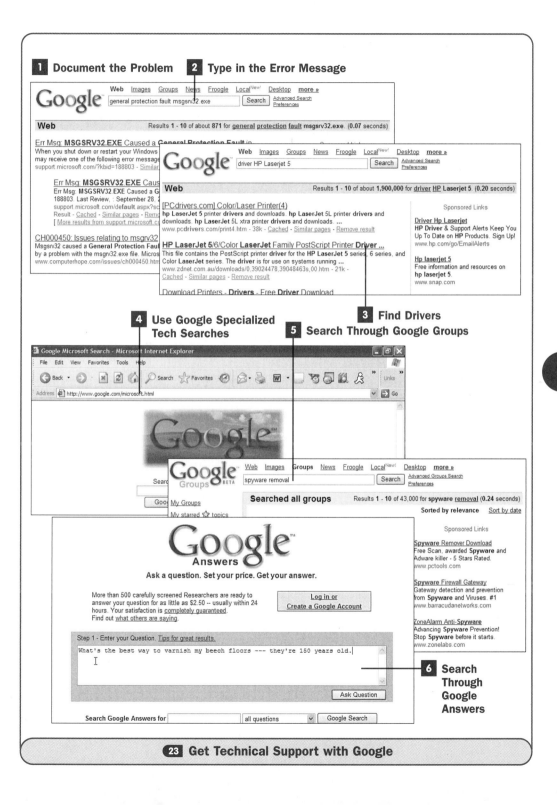

1 Document the Problem

Computer problems often have very specific causes and solutions, and unless you very precisely detail your problem, it's unlikely you'll find a solution to it. So first write down everything you know about the problem, including the software version or hardware make and manufacturer, and any error messages you might have received as part of the problem.

2 Type in the Error Message

The odds are that someone else has gotten the error message you've received, for example, General protection fault msgsrv32.exe. Type the error message into the Google search box exactly as it appeared on the computer screen—you'll be surprised at how often you'll find a match for it.

Click several of the results you find and follow the directions for fixing the problem.

3 Find Drivers

A common cause of many computer problems is out-of-date *drivers*, pieces of software that hardware needs to function. For example, printers, scanners, and digital cameras require specific drivers to function properly with your computer.

▶ KEY TERM

Driver—Software that hardware (such as printers, scanners, and digital cameras) need in order to work with your computer.

Updating the driver for the piece of hardware you're having difficulty with is often the simplest way to fix a wide variety of hardware problems. Google does an excellent job of helping you find those drivers. Copy down the manufacturer and model number of your hardware. Then type it in the search box and add the term *driver* as well, like this: **driver HP LaserJet 5**.

Among the search results, you find pages that have links to download the driver. It's a good idea to first try downloading the driver from the official website of the manufacturer because that site is most likely to have the latest drivers.

23

▶ **NOTE**

If you're going to download a driver from a manufacturer's website, you might think that it's easier to go to the website and try to find the driver using the manufacturer's own search. It's worth a try, but you'd be surprised at how difficult some manufacturers make it to find drivers on their sites. Google is really your better bet in locating driver files to download.

4 Use Google Specialized Tech Searches

Google recognizes that many people search for technical information, and so it has created four specialized search sites for technical problems. These search sites search only through other sites that specialize in that particular kind of technical information. Because of that, they return the best and most accurate results. The four sites Google supports are listed here:

- **Microsoft**

  www.google.com/microsoft

  This site searches for anything related to Microsoft products.

- **Apple**

  www.google.com/mac

  This site searches for anything related to Apple products.

- **Linux**

  www.google.com/linux

  This site searches for anything to do with Linux.

- **BSD**

  www.google.com/bsd

  This site searches for anything to do with Berkeley Software Distribution (BSD), a version of the Unix operating system.

5 Search Through Google Groups

Very often, the best answers come directly from people who have had the exact same technical support problem you're having. The best place to find technical support discussions, in which people share their problems and solutions, is in **Google Groups** at http://groups.google.com. **Google Groups** are actually Internet newsgroups, which are world-wide discussion groups spanning many topics. For help searching through **Google Groups**, go to **15 Search Through Google Groups**. Use search terms that describe your problem.

23

6 Search Through Google Answers

Google has a for-pay site called **Google Answers** in which you type a question and pay to receive an answer for it. Head to **Google Answers** at http://answers.google.com/answers. You type in your question, specify the price range you're willing to pay, and you receive an answer. You can follow up with the answerer. If you're not satisfied with the answer, you can get your money refunded. You pay for the service using a credit card, and usually get answers within 24 hours in an email message. Some answers cost as little as $2.50. If you need a refund, go to http://answers.google.com/answers/createaccount?qe_destination=%2Fanswers%2Frefundrequest.

---

24 About Getting Travel Information with Google

✔ BEFORE YOU BEGIN	→ SEE ALSO
1 Perform a Basic Google Search	**7** About Power Searching Strategies
5 Perform an Advanced Google Search	**43** Find Local Information with Google Local
6 About Google Search Operators	

24

Google is great at many things—but when it comes to travel information, it's not always a spectacular success. It has some exceptionally strong points as well as some weak ones, so the key is in knowing when to use it to get travel information and when to stay away.

If you're looking to find flight information, ticket prices, package deals, and cut-rate hotel bargains, there are better places to go. Sites such as www.expedia.com, www.orbitz.com, www.smartertravel.com, www.travelocity.com, www.hotwire.com, www.priceline.com, and www.bookingbuddy.com are better than Google for ferreting out this kind of pricing information.

That's not to say that you shouldn't use Google for researching *any* of your travel plans. Google does a great job of finding off-the-beaten-path information, for example. Let's say you're looking to rent a house on the big island of Hawaii. Travel sites tend not to have this kind of information; they're better at finding hotel rates and package deals. So doing a simple search such as **house rentals big island Hawaii** leads you to plenty of resources.

And, of course, you can use Google to research any place you're planning to visit or considering visiting using the normal Google search tools.

Where Google really shines for travel information is with **Google Local**, formerly known as Google Maps. The site does far more than merely enable you to find maps and driving directions. It also helps you find any kind of local sightseeing information, restaurants, information, and resources. If you're looking for Cuban restaurants in Cambridge, Massachusetts, or museums and art galleries in Orem, Utah, **Google Local** is the best place to go. For details, see **43** **Find Local Information with Google Local**.

*Looking to find Cuban restaurants in and around Cambridge, Massachusetts? **Google Local** (formerly known as Google Maps) is the place to go.*

25

25 | About Google's Search-by-Number Feature

✔ BEFORE YOU BEGIN

1 Perform a Basic Google Search
5 Perform an Advanced Google Search
6 About Google Search Operators

Our lives are filled with numbers—ZIP Codes, area codes, UPCs (universal product codes), Federal Express tracking numbers, and more. One of Google's least-known capabilities is its capability to ferret out information based on numbers you type into it—in most instances, you don't even need to tell Google what kind of number it is. Google can figure it out for itself.

For example, let's say you're considering buying a used car. You'd like to find out whatever you can about the car before you buy it. Look through the front of the windshield and find the vehicle's 17-character Vehicle Information Number (VIN). (The VIN number might also be in the owner's manual.) Type the VIN number into Google as you see it, without hyphens or spaces (for example, **1g2pm37rxfp271693**), and you'll find a link to a page on the CARFAX service, which gives you the basic information about the car, including its year, make, model, body style, engine type, and the country in which it was manufactured. If you want a complete history of the car from CARFAX, you can pay $19.99 for a more complete report, including a record of accidents (major or otherwise), the number of owners, and so on.

You can type many other numbers into Google to find information. Here's a list:

- Type a product's UPC code and you are sent to the UPC Database, which gives you manufacturer information about products.

- Type a Federal Express tracking number, and you are given a link to a FedEx page that supplies tracking information. Google does not work with United States Postal Service (USPS) or United Parcel Service (UPS) tracking numbers.

- Type a U.S. Postal Service tracking number, and you are sent to a page that links you to the U.S. postal website with tracking information. You can do this only for packages you can also track through the U.S. Postal Service website, which means you can Google only those letters or packages you've sent using a means that allows tracking. So, for example, if you simply have a USPS number from having shipped a package, but haven't paid for a service that offers tracking, such as registered mail or certified mail, the Google search won't work.

- Type the flight number of an airplane, including the name of the airline, such as **Delta 1098**, and you get a top-of-the-page result that reads **Track status of Delta Air Lines flight 1098 on Travelocity - Expedia - fboweb.com**. Click any of the links to track the status of a flight.

- Type the tail number of an airplane, and you see the full registration form for the plane.

- Type **Patent** and then a patent number, within quotation marks, like this: **"patent 5123123"**. You can get patent information about any United States patent.

26   Get the News with Google News

✔ BEFORE YOU BEGIN	→ SEE ALSO
47 Add News and Information to Google Personalized Home	**84** About Google Reader and RSS Feeds

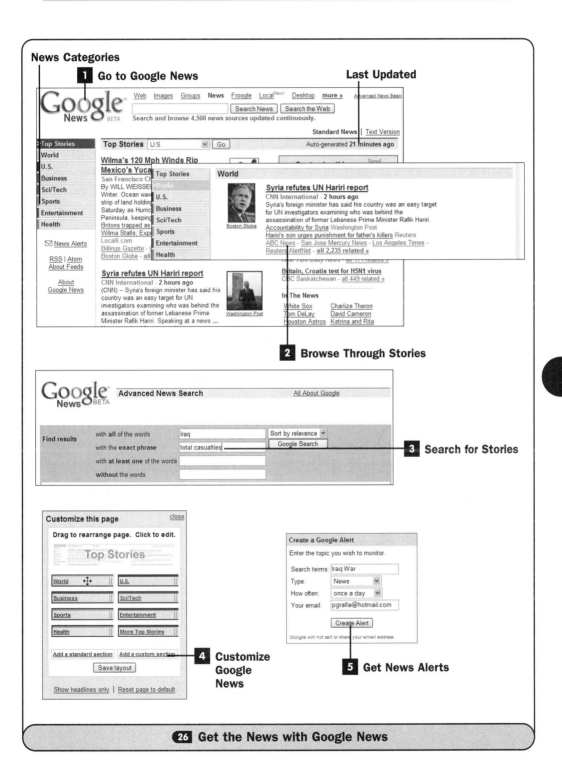

The circulation of daily newspapers has been shrinking at an alarming rate, and with good reason—more and more people are using the Internet to get their news.

No doubt, **Google News** has contributed to the number of people who read news online. It collates news reports from reputable sources all over the world—everything from major daily newspapers such as the *Washington Post* and the *New York Times*, to international news sources such as the BBC News and international news agencies such as Reuters, to TV news sites such as CNN and ABC news, to local newspapers not only in the United States, but in many other countries as well. It's the single best place online to get your news—and possibly the single best place anywhere.

The news is constantly updated on the **Google News** site, so you always get the latest news. You can also customize the site to deliver the exact news you want when you want it. This task shows you how to get the most out of it. Make sure to log in to your Google account if you want to get the most out of using **Google News**.

1 Go to Google News

When you type **http://news.google.com** in your browser's address bar, you go to the **Google News** site. Alternatively, click the **News** link at the top of the main Google page. There you see the top news stories, when the page was last updated with news, and news in many categories.

2 Browse Through Stories

The main stories on the page have synopses underneath them, and if there are multiple reports about the same event, you are shown links for each separate report. Choose which source to read by clicking the desired link.

Scroll down the page to see the top stories in various categories, such as **World, U.S. Sci/Tech, Business**, and so on.

The left side of the **Google News** page lists the top news categories. Click any category and you go to a new page with a listing of the top stories in that category.

► **NOTE**

If you want to read stories of the most interest to places in the world other than the United States—in that country's native language—choose the country from the drop-down box next to **Top Stories** at the top of the display area and click **Go**.

26

3 Search for Stories

You can search for news stories on **Google News**. Type your search term or terms into the search box at the top of the page and click **Search News**. If you instead want to do a normal Google search, click **Search the Web**.

For best results, do an advanced news search by clicking the **Advanced News Search** link. You are able to target your search by searching only through specific news sources, only through articles from news sources in specific countries or states, by the date the article was published, and even where your search terms appear (for example, in the headline, body, URL, or anywhere in the article).

4 Customize Google News

If you'd like to change the order of the categories on the **Google News** page, you can customize the way the page appears when you open it. Click the **Customize this page** link; a box appears with small boxes inside it representing each of the news categories. Hover your mouse over a category you want to move, and a four-sided arrow appears. Drag the category to where you want it to appear on the page and release the mouse to drop the category in its new location. Click **Save layout** when you're done.

You can also change how many items appear in each category. Click the category link, and from the **Customize this page** box that appears, choose the number of stories you want to appear on the page from the **Stories** drop-down list. You can also have the section display news from a different part of the world by choosing the country from the **Edition** drop-down list. If you don't want this news category to appear on the page, delete it by checking the box next to **Delete section**. Click **Save changes** when you're done, or click **Cancel** to cancel your changes.

In addition, you can add an entirely new, customized section that displays news about only a specific topic. After you've clicked **Customize this page**, click the **Add a custom section** link. Type a word or words that describes the customized news in which you're interested, select how many items you want displayed, and then click **Add section**. The new section now appears on your page.

5 Get News Alerts

One of the most powerful features of **Google News** is its capability to deliver news to your email inbox so you don't actually have to visit **Google News** to get the news. All you have to do is log into your email service.

26

To create a news alert that generates an email message to you, click the **News Alerts** link. From the **Create a Google Alert** page that appears, type the term or terms that describe the news you want to track, select the type of articles you're interested in from the **Type** drop-down list (you can choose from **News**, **Web**, **News & Web**, and **Groups**), select how often you want the news delivered (choose from **once a day**, **when it occurs**, or **weekly**), type your email address, and click **Create Alert**. From now on, you get links to the kind of news you described, on the schedule you've chosen, delivered to your inbox.

▶ NOTE

In Google terminology for news alerts, *Web* refers to any pages on the Web that mention your search term, not news stories.

You can create multiple alerts in this way. To manage your alerts and edit them, sign into your Google account, and go to www.google.com/alerts/manage.

27

27 Search Through Blogs with Google

✔ BEFORE YOU BEGIN	→ SEE ALSO
1 Perform a Basic Google Search	**7** About Power Searching Strategies
5 Perform an Advanced Google Search	**15** Search Through Google Groups
6 About Google Search Operators	
84 About Google Reader and RSS Feeds	

Several years ago, **blogs**, also sometimes called weblogs, took the world by storm. Blogs are, in essence, online journals or columns that are often personal or political in nature, typically written by a single person.

▶ KEY TERM

Blog—An online journal or column, typically written by one person, that is often personal or political in nature.

Hardly thought of several years ago, blogs have not just gone mainstream—they have become enormously influential as well. They were instrumental in forcing Trent Lott to resign as Senate Majority Leader after he praised Senator Strom Thurmond's 1948 run for president on a segregationist platform, for example, and took center stage during the 2004 presidential campaign. Today, blogs are written by well-known journalists, celebrities, your neighbor down the street, and everyone in between. (For details on how to build your own blog using Google's **Blogger** service, see **77** **Create a Blogger Account**. To find out how to subscribe to blogs, see **84** **About Google Reader and RSS Feeds**.)

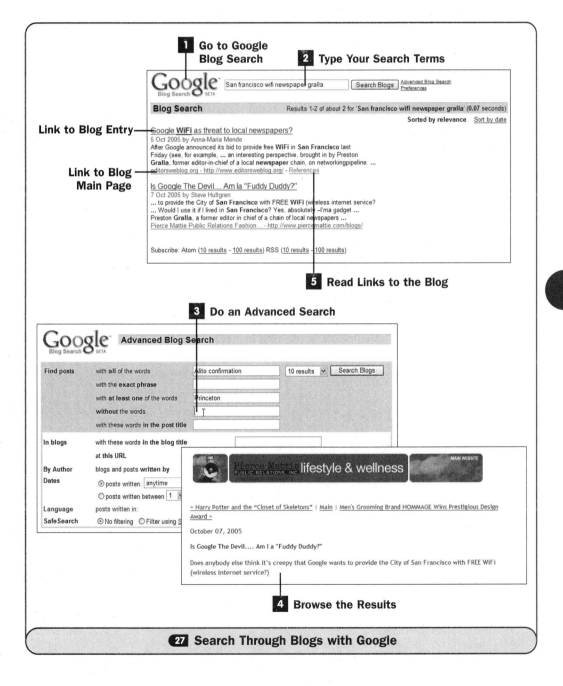

An enormous amount of talk, information, and frankly, hot air, is in what's called the blogosphere, a term that has come to mean the world of blogs. How do you find exactly what you want in it all? Head to Google's **Blog Search**. It searches only through blogs and makes it easy to read blog entries.

1 Go to Google Blog Search

The normal Google search doesn't do blog-specific search, so you have to go to Google **Blog Search** at http://blogsearch.google.com if you want to search only through blogs.

2 Type Your Search Terms

The Google **Blog Search** works like other Google searches. To search for a term or terms, type them into the search box and click **Search Blogs**. If you're looking for a specific blog or person, type the name of the blog or person.

3 Do an Advanced Search

Google **Blog Search** also has advanced tools for searching through blogs. To get to them, click **Advanced Blog Search**. In addition to the usual search features, you are able to search for terms only in the blog title, to search for blogs only by specific authors, to search for blogs written on or between specific dates, and to search for blogs written in specific languages.

4 Browse the Results

Search results are returned in the familiar Google fashion. You see the title of the specific blog entry, and just beneath that is the date and author of the entry. There is a synopsis of the blog as well. Underneath that is the name of the blog (for example, editorsweblog.org), and the overall blog's URL.

Click the result's title to visit the blog entry; click the link at the bottom of the result's entry to visit the blog's main page.

5 Read Links to the Blog

Next to some blog entries is a link titled **References**. Click it to see a list of blogs that have linked to the original blog entry.

27

28 Search Books with Google Book Search

✔ BEFORE YOU BEGIN	→ SEE ALSO
1 Perform a Basic Google Search	**7** About Power Searching Strategies
5 Perform an Advanced Google Search	
6 About Google Search Operators	

Google doesn't confine itself to enabling you to find information on the Web—it has expanded into the book world as well. The **Google Book Search** service enables you to search for information in many books. It does this by scanning books, making them available online, letting you search through the contents of books, and showing you results. You won't be able to see the entire book, but you can see snippets from the book.

▶ NOTE

The **Google Book Search** project is a very controversial one. Google scans copyrighted and out-of-copyright books, which makes those books available online, without permission of the copyright holders. Google argues that it shows only snippets of the books, and that therefore, it can legally scan the books under "fair use" guidelines. A number of authors and publishers disagree, and both the Author's Guild and the Association of American Publishers sued Google, claiming copyright infringement. As this book went to press, the case had not yet been heard.

Every day, more books become available online. Google's ultimate plan is to make literally millions of books available online by scanning books from Harvard, Stanford, the University of Michigan, Oxford University, and the New York Public Library.

When you search in **Google Book Search**, the results you see vary somewhat according to the type of book from which the results come. If it's a book whose copyright has run out, you might be able to see the entire book. If the book is still copyrighted, you see only a snippet from the book. Depending on whether the copyright owner has made an agreement with Google, you might also be able to click a link to buy the book.

1 Go to Google Book Search

Get to the **Google Book Search** main page by going to http://books.google.com.

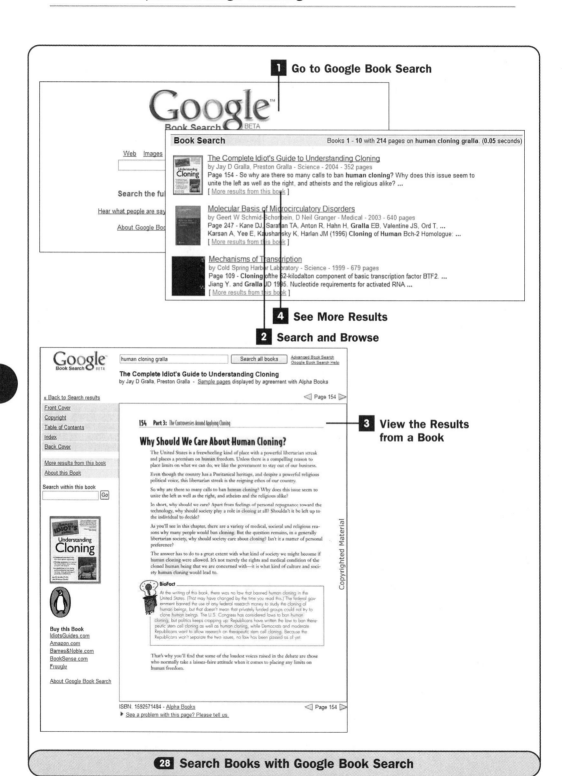

1 Go to Google Book Search

Google™
Book Search BETA

Web   Images

Search the ful

Hear what people are say

About Google Boo

Book Search   Books 1 - 10 with 214 pages on human cloning gralla. (0.05 seconds)

The Complete Idiot's Guide to Understanding Cloning
by Jay D Gralla, Preston Gralla - Science - 2004 - 352 pages
Page 154 - So why are there so many calls to ban **human cloning**? Why does this issue seem to
unite the left as well as the right, and atheists and the religious alike? ...
[More results from this book]

Molecular Basis of Microcirculatory Disorders
by Geert W Schmid-Schonbein, D Neil Granger - Medical - 2003 - 640 pages
Page 247 - Kane DJ, Sarafian TA, Anton R, Hahn H, **Gralla** EB, Valentine JS, Ord T, ...
Karsan A, Yee E, Kaushansky K, Harlan JM (1996) **Cloning** of Human Bch-2 Homologue: ...
[More results from this book]

Mechanisms of Transcription
by Cold Spring Harbor Laboratory - Science - 1999 - 679 pages
Page 109 - **Cloning** of the 62-kilodalton component of basic transcription factor BTF2. ...
Jiang Y. and **Gralla** JD 1995. Nucleotide requirements for activated RNA ...
[More results from this book]

4 See More Results

2 Search and Browse

Google™
Book Search BETA

human cloning gralla   Search all books   Advanced Book Search
                                                Google Book Search Help

The Complete Idiot's Guide to Understanding Cloning
by Jay D Gralla, Preston Gralla - Sample pages displayed by agreement with Alpha Books

« Back to Search results   ◁ Page 154 ▷

Front Cover
Copyright
Table of Contents
Index
Back Cover

More results from this book
About this Book

Search within this book

[   ] [Go]

3 View the Results
from a Book

154   Part 3: The Controversies Around Applying Cloning

Why Should We Care About Human Cloning?

The United States is a freewheeling kind of place with a powerful libertarian streak
and places a premium on human freedom. Unless there is a compelling reason to
place limits on what we can do, we like the government to stay out of our business.

Even though the country has a Puritanical heritage, and despite a powerful religious
political voice, this libertarian streak is the reigning ethos of our country.

So why are there so many calls to ban human cloning? Why does this issue seem to
unite the left as well as the right, and atheists and the religious alike?

In short, why should we care? Apart from feelings of personal repugnance toward the
technology, why should society play a role in cloning at all? Shouldn't it be left up to
the individual to decide?

As you'll see in this chapter, there are a variety of medical, societal and religious reasons why many people would ban cloning. But the question remains, in a generally
libertarian society, why should society care about cloning? Isn't it a matter of personal
preference?

The answer has to do to a great extent with what kind of society we might become if
human cloning were allowed. It's not merely the rights and medical condition of the
cloned human being that we are concerned with—it is what kind of culture and society human cloning would lead to.

BioFact
At the writing of this book, there was no law that banned human cloning in the
United States. (That may have changed by the time you read this.) The federal government banned the use of any federal research money to study the cloning of
human beings, but that doesn't mean that privately funded groups could not try to
clone human beings. The U.S. Congress has considered laws to ban human
cloning, but politics keeps cropping up: Republicans have written the law to ban therapeutic stem cell cloning as well as human cloning, while Democrats and moderate
Republicans want to allow research on therapeutic stem cell cloning. Because the
Republicans won't separate the two issues, no law has been passed as of yet.

That's why you'll find that some of the loudest voices raised in the debate are those
who normally take a laissez-faire attitude when it comes to placing any limits on
human freedom.

Buy this Book
IdiotsGuides.com
Amazon.com
Barnes&Noble.com
BookSense.com
Froogle

About Google Book Search

ISBN: 1592571484 - Alpha Books
▶ See a problem with this page? Please tell us.   ◁ Page 154 ▷

Copyrighted Material

28

28 Search Books with Google Book Search

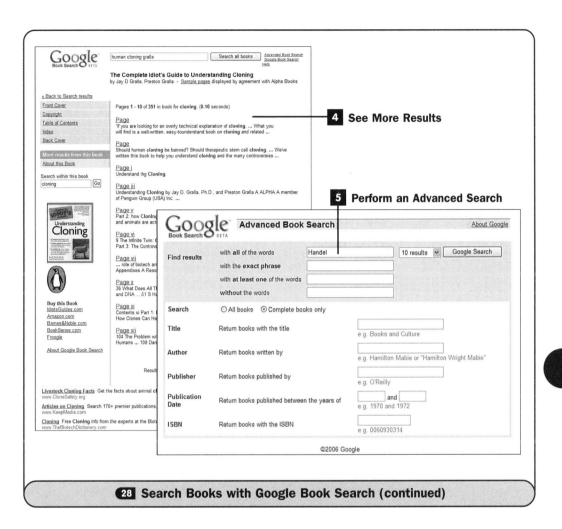

4 See More Results

5 Perform an Advanced Search

28 Search Books with Google Book Search (continued)

2 Search and Browse

Type a search term in the same way you type any other search term in Google. The results you see, though, look different. You see a list of books, including the covers, and information about each book, including its authors, total number of pages, and a brief list of the first several search results found in the book.

3 View the Results from a Book

Click the link to any book to see results from the book. You see the original page, with your search term or terms highlighted. In many instances, you are able to see the previous or next page by clicking the arrows at the top or bottom of the screen.

In many cases, you won't be able to copy and paste the information you find in the book because pages are often displayed as graphics rather than text. You can, however, print out the page using your browser's **Print** command.

For many books, you are able to click links to buy the book from a variety of sources. You might also find links to the book's table of contents, index, back cover, and similar information. The exact information of this type displayed for the book varies according to the information Google has been able to gather about the book, and whether Google has an agreement with the copyright holder.

▶ **NOTE**

Although you can search and browse without logging in, you must be signed in to your Google account to see the *results* from the book search. If you're not signed in, you come to a page that enables you to sign in.

4 See More Results

If other results for your search are within the book, you see a **More results from this book** link on the results page. Click it to see additional results. You can browse them and view them as you can any other search result.

5 Perform an Advanced Search

When you're searching for information from books, you can narrow your search using **Google Book Search's Advanced Print Search** feature. From the main **Google Book Search** page, click **Advanced Book Search**. You are able to search by title, author, publisher, and ISBN number (a number that uniquely identifies a book), and by using the usual Google **Advanced Search** features.

---

29 Find Online Bargains with Froogle

✔ BEFORE YOU BEGIN	→ SEE ALSO
1 Perform a Basic Google Search	7 About Power Searching Strategies
5 Perform an Advanced Google Search	
6 About Google Search Operators	

2 Search and Browse

1 Go to Froogle

Product Ads

Price Range

3 Fine-tune Your Search

2 Search and Browse

Best Buy Designation

Compare Prices

Product Reviews

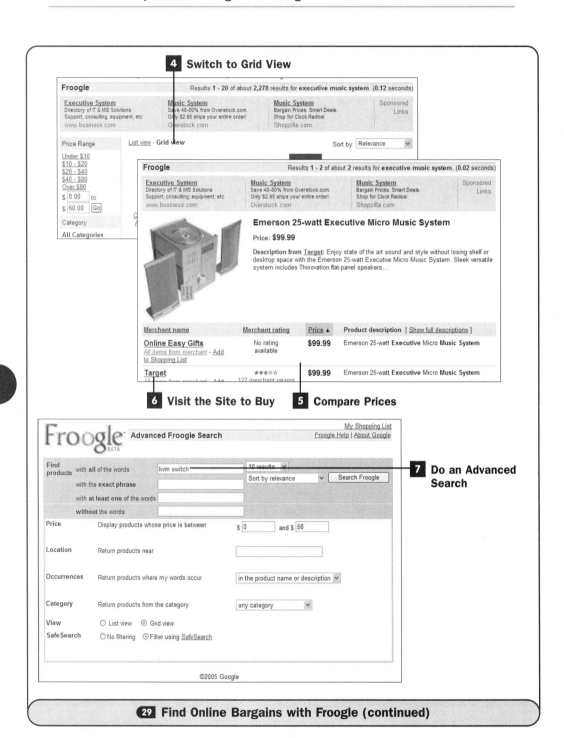

4 **Switch to Grid View**

6 **Visit the Site to Buy**   **5** **Compare Prices**

7 **Do an Advanced Search**

29 **Find Online Bargains with Froogle (continued)**

29

Online shopping accounts for billions of dollars a year in sales, and with good reason. You can buy almost any product imaginable online—and get bargains, to boot.

Froogle, Google's shopping site, is a great place to find those bargains. You are able to find great deals, as well as find reviews about what you plan to buy. **Froogle** searches through multiple shopping sites and finds the lowest prices for products. **Froogle** also enables you to comparison shop among those sites.

1 Go to Froogle

Get to the main Froogle page by heading to www.froogle.com or http://froogle.google.com. Alternatively, click the **Froogle** link at the top of the main Google page.

2 Search and Browse

Type your search term or terms as you would normally in Google. You come to a page with results that match your search query. At the top of the page are ads from stores that have the products for which you're searching. The main part of the page is taken up by results for products that match your query. The page lists descriptions of each of the products, as well as price information. If Froogle finds multiple sites that sell the same product, it shows you the price range for them.

3 Fine-tune Your Search

You can fine-tune your search by specifying a price range for the product. On the left side of the results page, click the price range in which you're interested, or type a price range in the text boxes and click **Go**. The results page now shows products only in that price range.

▶ **TIP**

When you're browsing or searching, look for **Best Buy** search results. When you find one and click it, you'll find reviews of the product from one or more shopping sites— including PriceGrabber.com, ResellerRatings.com, Shopping.com, and Shopzilla.com. In addition to the **Best Buy** designation, look at the end of each product's description on the results page to see whether there are product reviews.

4 Switch to Grid View

If you prefer to see listings in a grid rather than in a list, click the **Grid View** link at the top of the results page. When you do that, you see more search results per page, but you can't see the details for each item.

5 Compare Prices

When you find a product in which you're interested, click it, or click the **Compare Prices** button. You come to a page that has a more complete description of the item and a larger picture of the item (if it's available). The page also has listings of every site Froogle found that stocks the item and from which you can order. The results are sorted by price, with the lowest price first.

The page not only enables you to compare prices, it enables you to compare the sites that sell the item as well. Look in the **Merchant Rating** column in the results list. If the merchant's site has been reviewed by customers, you see a star rating for the site, as well as the total number of reviews. Click the link to read the actual reviews. Note that the reviews are not about the product, but about the store or merchant itself, as well as reports about the consumers' experiences with the site—reporting, for example, whether the site shipped the items on time, whether they returned items if they were defective, and so on.

6 Visit the Site to Buy

To buy the item, click the link on the left side of the page for the merchant from which you want to buy the product. You are sent to that merchant's site, specifically to a page that has the site's description of the product you're interested in buying. At this point, you've left Froogle, and so you buy from the site itself, not from Froogle. Froogle has nothing to do with the transaction at this point.

7 Do an Advanced Search

If the searching and browsing doesn't help you find the item you want to buy, try doing an advanced Froogle search. From the main page of Froogle, click **Advanced Froogle Search**. In addition to the normal Google searching, you are able to search by price and product category, and specify whether you want the results to be displayed in a normal listing or in a grid.

---

30 | About Translating Web Pages with Google

✔ BEFORE YOU BEGIN	→ SEE ALSO
1 Perform a Basic Google Search	**7** About Power Searching Strategies
5 Perform an Advanced Google Search	
6 About Google Search Operators	

The World Wide Web, as the name implies, is a worldwide phenomenon—you'll find web pages in many languages. What if you find a page written in Korean, Japanese, German, or another language, but you don't speak that language?

Google has translation tools that enable you to read the information you find. You can automatically translate entire pages—or just sections of a page—from other languages to English, and from English to other languages.

You can translate information from other languages into English in several ways. If you do a search and find pages in Italian, French, Spanish, German, or Portuguese, you see a **Translate this page** link next to the search results, as you can see in the nearby figure.

Le site du projet de réaménagement du quartier des **halles** - [Translate this page]
Le site du projet de réaménagement du quartier des **halles**.
www.projetleshalles.com/ - 4k - Cached - Similar pages - Remove result

Les Halles de Schaerbeek - [Translate this page]
Centre culturel européen situé au coeur de Bruxelles, **les Halles** accueillent **les** manifestations artistiques **les** plus diverses : concerts (rock, hip-hop,.
www.halles.be/ - 12k - Oct 29, 2005 - Cached - Similar pages - Remove result

If you find a page with Google in Italian, French, Spanish, German, or Portuguese, click the Translate this page link and you get an English translation of the page.

30

The translated page includes all the original graphics, but the text is in English. At the top of the translated page is a **View Original Web Page** link so you can immediately jump to the original page itself.

What if you come across a page in language other than Italian, French, Spanish, German, or Portuguese? Depending on the language, you might still be able to have Google translate it for you. Go to www.google.com/language_tools and look toward the bottom of the page. In the **Translate a web page** section, enter the URL (including the **http://**) of the page you want to translate, and from the drop-down list, choose the language from which you want to translate to English. As of this writing, the languages you can translate from are

- German
- French
- Italian
- Portuguese
- Spanish
- Japanese
- Korean
- Chinese

New languages may be added as well. After you type the URL and choose the language, click **Translate** to be sent to a web page that has the translation.

Google can translate a word or phrase—or an entire web page if you give it the URL of the page.

You can also translate English pages into these same languages, and translate from one language to another—for example, from German to Spanish. Just make your choices from the drop-down lists.

▶ TIP

The **Language Tools** page has other language tools in addition to translations. You can use it to search for pages written in specific languages or that are hosted in specific countries. To do it, use the drop-down boxes in **Search Specific Languages or Countries** at the top of the page.

You can also translate sections of pages, not entire pages. To do that, start at www.google.com/language_tools and copy and paste the text you want to translate into the **Translate text** box. Then make your language choice and click **Translate** to go to a page that shows the translated text.

Be aware that the translations are done by computer, not by human beings. Nuances are lost, and meanings might be distorted, sometimes significantly so. For example, here's what you get if you use Google to translate the first sentence from Lincoln's Gettysburg Address into French, and then translate that French version back into English:

> Four points and there are seven years our fathers brought on this continent, a new nation, conceived in freedom, and devoted to the proposal that all the men equal are created.

---

31 About Searching Google with Your Cell Phone

✔ BEFORE YOU BEGIN

1 Perform a Basic Google Search
5 Perform an Advanced Google Search
6 About Google Search Operators

→ SEE ALSO

7 About Power Searching Strategies

Google isn't just available from your computer—it's now available anywhere you are if you carry a cell phone. Google offers services specifically targeted at those who use cell phones.

You can search through Google from your cell phone in two ways. You can use your phone's built-in web browser to search Google, or you can use the text messaging Short Message Service (SMS) to do it.

You don't need to do much special to search Google using your cell phone's web browser; it's surprisingly simple to do. Just follow these steps:

1. Launch your cell phone's browser.

2. In the URL field, type **www.google.com**. If you get an error message, instead type **www.google.com/xhtm**.

3. You see the familiar Google interface, shrunk to fit for your cell phone's display area. Type your search term or terms.

4. Select the kind of search you want to do. You can search the Web, search for images, do a search to find local information and maps, or search the Mobile Web. The Mobile Web is made up of web pages that have been specifically designed to work with cell phones.

5. After you've typed your search terms and chosen the kind of search you want to do, press **Enter**. A search page with 10 search results appears. The page looks like a normal Google results page.

6. Scroll through the results and choose the page you want. You can also scroll to the bottom of the page and click **Next** to see 10 more results.

Searching Google using SMS is simple as well:

1. Enter your search term or terms as a text message on your phone. (Follow the phone's instructions for doing this.)

2. Send the message to the U.S. shortcode **46645**. (On most phones, that's **GOOGL**.)

3. Usually within a minute you get a text message or messages with your results.

▶ **TIP**

If you want to get help searching Google using SMS, send the word *help* as a text message to the U.S. shortcode **46645**.

---

32   **Search Through TV Shows with Google Video**

✔ BEFORE YOU BEGIN	→ SEE ALSO
1 Perform a Basic Google Search	**7** About Power Searching Strategies
5 Perform an Advanced Google Search	
6 About Google Search Operators	

32

Google doesn't confine you to the world of the Web—with **Google Video**, you can search through and then view TV shows, including news, entertainment, and more, for free. You can search through not only national networks (such as ABC, CBS, NBC, and CNN), but also local programming, programming from around the world, and videos that individuals upload to the service.

When you type a search term, **Google Video** searches through closed-caption transcripts of TV shows and videos, and then displays a list of show results that contain the term in the transcripts. Click the show result for more details, including the date and time it was broadcast. In some instances, you are able to see only stills of the show and a transcript. In other instances, you view the video when you click it.

1 **Go to Google Video**

Find **Google Video** at http://video.google.com. You'll see the familiar Google search box. In addition, you'll see several videos that you can click on and play. The highlighted videos are often created by individuals, rather than news videos, TV shows, or other commercial videos.

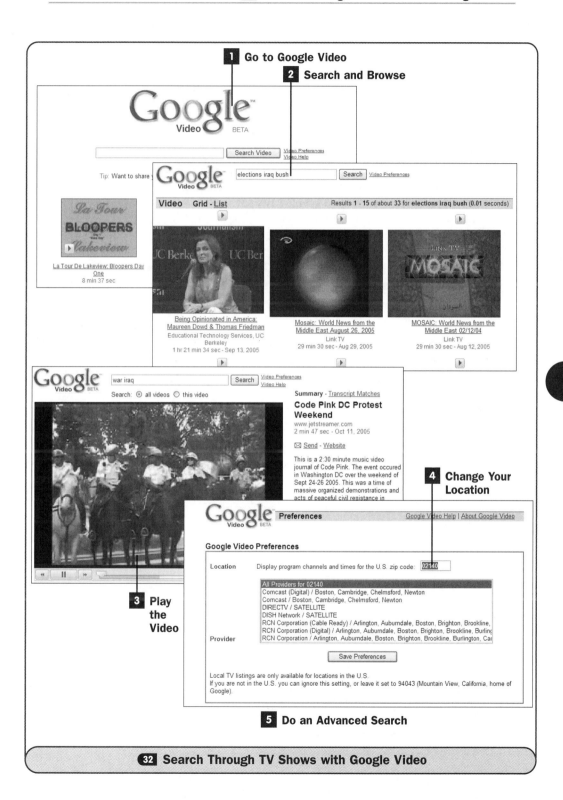

1 Go to Google Video

2 Search and Browse

4 Change Your Location

3 Play the Video

5 Do an Advanced Search

32

2 **Search and Browse**

Search for videos in the same way you search for anything else on Google—type your search term(s) and press **Enter** or click **Search**.

► **TIP**

Have a worthwhile video you want to share with the world? You can upload it and make it available through **Google Video**. For instructions on how to do it, go to https://upload.video.google.com. You have to include metadata about the video (*metadata* includes keywords that describe the content of the image or video). If you have a transcript through which you want people to be able to search, you can upload that as well.

A page appears with still images from videos that match your search. Beneath each images is a description of the video, including the source, length, and sometimes a brief description.

You can switch between two views of your search results—a **Grid** view (in which the videos are laid out in a grid, several videos across) or a **List** view (in which they are listed one above the other). The **List** view has transcript excepts with each video, but the **Grid** view doesn't. To switch between the views, click either the **Grid** or **List** link.

32

3 **Play the Video**

Click the video or the link beneath it to play the video. You are brought to a page in which the video plays. At the bottom of the video are controls that enable you to fast forward, rewind, pause, and play the video, as well as increase or decrease the volume.

► **NOTE**

If you want to play the video full screen on your PC, click the small, rectangular button just to the left of the down arrow at the bottom of the screen. The video plays full screen. Click the button again to return to normal viewing mode.

If you'd prefer that the video instead play directly on the search results page, click the arrow above the video, and the video plays right on the page itself. In some instances, you have to go to the page to see the whole thing.

4 **Change Your Location**

The news and videos you find are localized—you are able to view results from local TV stations. But the only way that localization can work is if you set your preferences to your local area. Click the **Video Preferences** link next to the search box, and in the page that appears, enter your ZIP Code in the

Location box and press **Enter**. A list of TV outlets for that ZIP Code appears in the **Provider** box. If you want to always search through all outlets, choose the **All Providers for** option in the **Provider** box. If you want to search through only specific outlets, select them. When you're done making your selection, click **Save Preferences**.

5 Do an Advanced Search

There is no advanced search page for **Google Video**, but you can fine-tune your search by using the proper search syntax. You can, for example, search only through a particular network, by typing **channel:**, the channel you want to search, and then your search term, like this:

Channel:CNN Iraq

▶ WEB RESOURCE
http://video.google.com/video_about.html#channels
This site provides a list of channels you can search on **Google Video**.

You can also search through only a specific show, by typing **title:** in front of your search, the title of the show, and then your search term, like this:

Title:Nightline Iraq

33

---

33 | **About Other Google Specialized Searches**

✔ BEFORE YOU BEGIN	→ SEE ALSO
1 Perform a Basic Google Search	**7** About Power Searching Strategies
5 Perform an Advanced Google Search	**8** About Finding Images with Image Search
6 About Google Search Operators	**15** Search Through Google Groups
	27 Search Through Blogs with Google

You can do far more specialized searches with Google than can possibly be covered in this chapter, and probably even in an entire book. And more specialized search opportunities become available all the time. Following is a brief list of other areas of Google you can use for specialized searches:

- **Google Answers**

  http://answers.google.com/answers

  This is the ultimate specialized search site. Pose a question, and you get an answer, although for a fee. It works quite simply: Type your question, and it is sent out via email to researchers who have been screened by Google. You then get a list of researchers and the prices they'll charge to answer your question. Click one, and you can get the answer and pay for it.

- **Google Zeitgeist**

  www.google.com/zeitgeist

  Zeitgeist is a German word that means the general cultural and intellectual climate of the moment. How to measure the current zeitgeist? Google has come up with a clever solution—look at what search terms are the most popular on Google. Head to this site, and that's exactly what you see. It changes weekly.

- **Google Catalogs**

  http://catalogs.google.com

  Are you a big fan of catalog shopping—businesses such as L.L.Bean, Williams-Sonoma, Crutchfield, and more? Head to this site, and you can search through multiple catalogs or browse individual catalogs.

- **Google University Search**

  www.google.com/options/universities.html

  If you're looking to search through university websites, here's the place to go. Look on the list for a university, click the link, and then do a search on that university's site for whatever you're interested in.

33

▶ **TIP**

Want to test-drive Google's newest features? Head to the **Google Labs** site at http://labs.google.com. That's where Google introduces and tests new features and products. Not all of them make the cut, so you might find features there that are eventually killed. But most new features start off in the labs first.

If that's not enough for you, Google has put together a page that enables you to do many kinds of specialized searches—everything from searching for books to searching dictionaries, finding movie reviews, and more. Go to www.google.com/help/features.html and click the kind of search you want to do. You are sent to a search box. Use that box as you would normally use Google, and it does your specialized search for you.

▶ **NOTE**

Alternatively, click the **More** link above the search box on the main Google screen to see the **More, more, more** page with a similar list of search options—including a link to **Google Labs**. The www.google.com/help/features.html page is more comprehensive than the **more, more, more** page, and better still is that you can do searches right from the features page—in many cases, there's no need to click to another site.

If you're the trusting sort, you can do an **I'm Feeling Lucky** search from Google's main page. Type your search terms and click the **I'm Feeling Lucky** button; Google sends you straight to the most relevant page it finds—the search result that would normally be at the top of a search results page.

PART II

Unleash the Power of Google's Special Tools

IN THIS PART:

6

Searching Your Computer with Google Desktop

IN THIS CHAPTER:

If Google is good for searching the Web, why not use it to search your PC? After all, the information on your hard disk is probably just about as hard to find as information on the Web.

Why not indeed? In fact, you *can* do it, using **Google Desktop**, available for a free download at http://desktop.google.com.

After you install **Google Desktop**, it indexes the files on your computer. Although you can immediately start using it to search through your PC, it's better to wait until it finishes its indexing. If you search while it's still indexing, you only find results for those files that **Google Desktop** has already indexed.

How long **Google Desktop** takes to finish indexing varies according to how many files you have on your hard disk, the speed of your processor, and whether you use your PC while it's indexing. In most instances, indexing your hard disk for the first time can take several hours. After the initial index is created, indexing happens automatically as you use your computer.

After you install **Google Desktop** and it indexes your computer's hard disk, you are able to search through your computer's hard disk using the same Google technology you use to search the Web. The program has many extras as well, including its **Sidebar** that delivers news, email, and information straight to your desktop.

34

---

34 Search Your PC with Google Desktop

✔ BEFORE YOU BEGIN	→ SEE ALSO
1 Perform a Basic Google Search	**5** Perform an Advanced Google Search
	6 About Google Search Operators
	7 About Power Searching Strategies
	35 Browse Search Results

After you've installed **Google Desktop**, you can start using it to search your PC. You don't have to wait until all the indexing is done; you can search even while it's indexing. If you do that, of course, you can only find content that has already been indexed. So it's best to wait...but if you can't wait, you can get started right away.

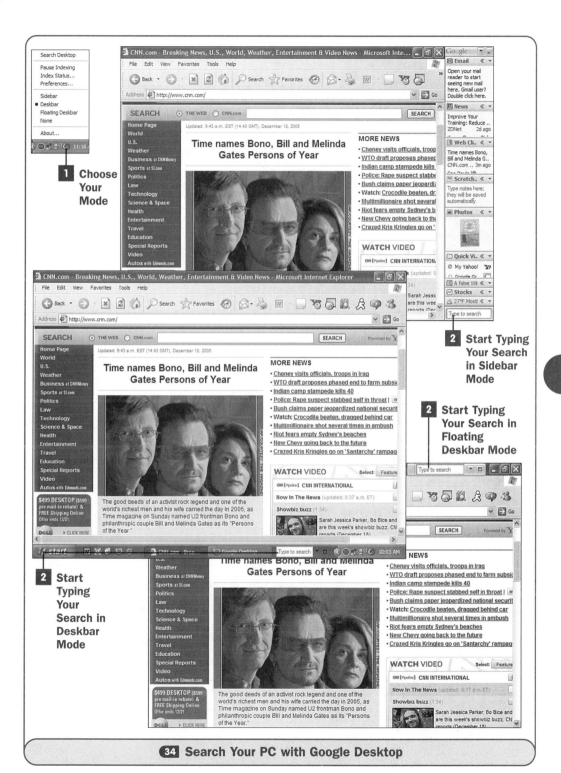

1 Choose Your Mode

2 Start Typing Your Search in Sidebar Mode

2 Start Typing Your Search in Floating Deskbar Mode

2 Start Typing Your Search in Deskbar Mode

34

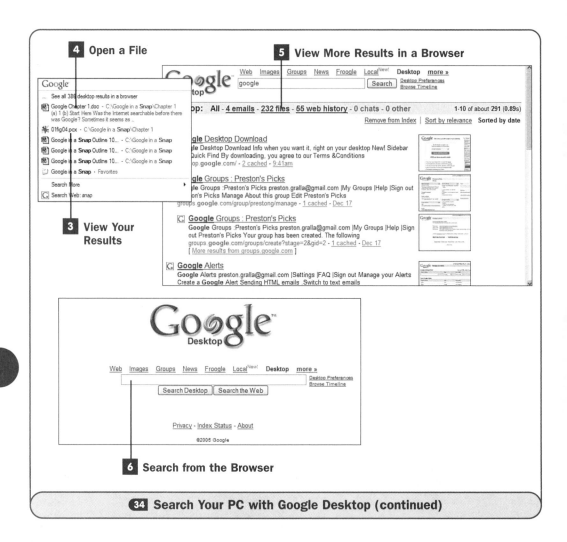

4 Open a File

5 View More Results in a Browser

3 View Your
   Results

6 Search from the Browser

34 Search Your PC with Google Desktop (continued)

1 Choose Your Mode

Google Desktop can run in one of three modes—**Sidebar**, **Deskbar**, or **Floating Deskbar**. In the **Sidebar** mode, **Google Desktop** runs down the side of the screen; in the **Deskbar** mode, it appears as a search box in your taskbar at the bottom of the Windows desktop; and in the **Floating Deskbar** mode, **Google Desktop** appears as a floating search box you can place anywhere on your desktop. To change between the modes, right-click the **Google Desktop** icon in the taskbar and choose your mode. (You can also change between them by setting your preferences, as described in **39 Set Indexing and Desktop Preferences**.)

2 Start Typing Your Search

No matter which mode you use, you type your search into the Google search box on your desktop—the search box is in the taskbar in **Deskbar** mode, at the bottom of the sidebar in **Sidebar** mode, or floating somewhere on your desktop in **Floating Deskbar** mode. Type your search term just as you would normally with Google.

3 View Your Results

As you type your search term, **Google Desktop** displays matching results in a pop-up list. As you continue typing, Google narrows down the results. For example, if you were searching for **prince**, as you typed **pr**, **Google Desktop** would display all files it found with the letters **pr** in them, such as **predict**, **president**, and so on. When you type **pri**, it would display all the files that contain words with those letters in it, and so on.

▶ **NOTE**

Click **Search More** in the list of results that **Google Desktop** displays if you want to search for your term on the Internet using Google. You have a choice of searching **Froogle**, **Google News**, **Google Images**, and other Google services.

34

4 Open a File

If you find what you want in the pop-up list and want to open the file, highlight the entire entry with your mouse and press **Enter**. The file opens in the application that created it. For example, if you select a Word file, Microsoft Word loads and opens the highlighted file.

5 View More Results in a Browser

Often, **Google Desktop** finds more results than can be displayed in the pop-up list. In those instances, at the top of the list you see the note **See all xxx desktop results in a browser**, in which **xxx** is the number of results **Google Desktop** found on your computer. Highlight the entire phrase and press **Enter**. Your default browser launches, showing you all the results of your search of the computer. Click the link next to the file you want to open. (For more information about browsing search results, see **35** **Browse Search Results**.

6 Search from the Browser

If you prefer, you can do a desktop search from your web browser, using the familiar Google interface. Double-click the **Google Desktop** icon, which is always found in the corner of the taskbar, and your browser launches. The page that loads is similar to the Google home page, except that it's labeled **Google Desktop**. Type your search term into the text box and click **Search Desktop**. **Google Desktop** searches your PC and returns the results in your browser window. If you instead want to search the Web, click the **Search the Web** button.

35	**Browse Search Results**

✔ BEFORE YOU BEGIN	→ SEE ALSO
34 Search Your PC with Google Desktop	**37** Browse and Search with the Timeline

---

The search results you see displayed by **Google Desktop** differ from those you see on a normal Google page—for example, you see email messages and information specific to your PC rather than information from the Internet. Here's how to understand and use the search results returned by **Google Desktop**.

35

1 View All Results

When you do a search with **Google Desktop**, all of the matching results are initially displayed, no matter what those results are—emails, files, websites you've visited, and chats. Each search result includes a link; the first several lines of the file, website, email, or chat; and the date the file was last accessed. Browse until you find a file in which you're interested. Note that when **Google Desktop** finds web pages you've visited, it shows you a thumbnail of them.

2 Open a File

To open a file, click its link. It opens in the program that created it—for example, a web page you've visited opens in your browser, and a Word document opens in Word.

3 Open a Folder

For each file that **Google Desktop** finds, there is an **Open Folder** link next to it. Click this link, and Windows Explorer opens to the folder that contains the file. This is useful when you're trying to track down not just a file, but a group of related files you've stored in the same folder.

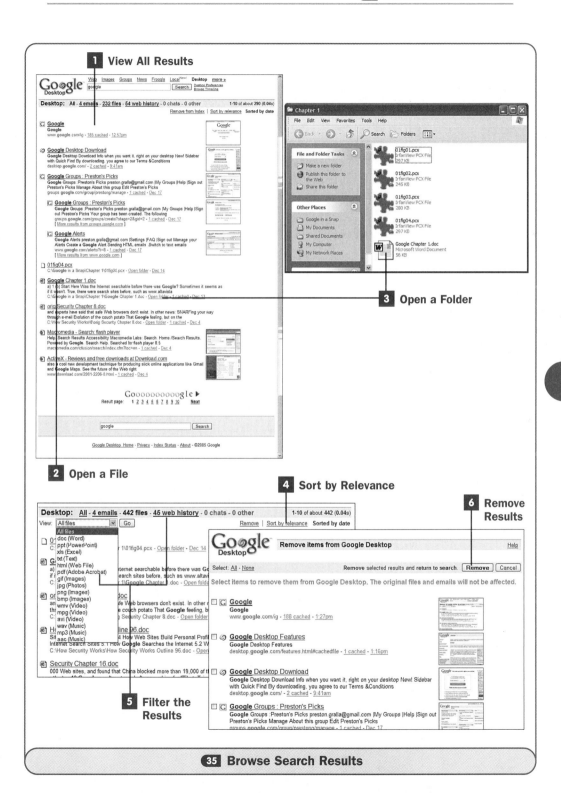

1 View All Results

2 Open a File

4 Sort by Relevance

6 Remove Results

3 Open a Folder

5 Filter the Results

▶ **TIP**

Google Desktop makes a copy of information in the files it finds and stores it in its cache—a special area used for **Google Desktop** storage. Next to each of your search results, you see **xx cached**, where **xx** is a number. Click that link to see a copy of the file from the cache. The results are displayed in your browser, not in the program that created the file, so it's a quick way to preview the information for which you're looking. Google typically keeps only one cached version of a file. But if you've visited a website multiple times, it keeps a copy of a snapshot of the site for each of the times you've visited.

4 Sort by Relevance

Google Desktop returns search results with the newest (most recently modified) on top and the oldest at the end of the results list. You can instead display the results so that the most relevant results appear on top, and less relevant results are displayed in descending order. To do it, click the **Sort by Relevance** link in the upper-right corner of the screen.

5 Filter the Results

Instead of seeing all results grouped together, you can filter them to only show emails, files, websites you've visited, or chats. To do this, click the appropriate link at the top of the search results.

When you're viewing files, you can further filter the search results to display only a particular file type; for example, only Word files or only **.jpg** files. After you've clicked the **Files** link at the top of the search results page, open the **View** drop-down list, choose the file type you want displayed, and click **Go**; only those file types are displayed in the results list.

6 Remove Results

If you would prefer that certain search results not show up in future searches, you can remove them from the **Google Desktop** index. Click the **Remove from Index** link in the upper-right corner of the search results page. A new page appears. Check the boxes next to the results you want to remove from the index and then click the **Remove** button. Note that when you do this, the files themselves remain on your PC, but they are removed from the **Google Desktop** index and won't show up on any future searches.

36 Use and Customize the Sidebar

✔ BEFORE YOU BEGIN	→ SEE ALSO
34 Search Your PC with Google Desktop	39 Set Indexing and Desktop Preferences

The **Sidebar** extends the usefulness of **Google Desktop** by giving you instant access to information from the Web and your email, all from a sidebar panel that appears on your desktop. It displays constantly changing information that you can access with a click.

1 Turn on the Sidebar

To turn on the **Sidebar**, right-click the **Google Desktop** icon in the system tray and choose the **Sidebar** option. The **Sidebar** panel appears on the right side of your PC's desktop.

2 Display Information from a Module

The **Sidebar** has separate modules that display many kinds of information:

- **Email** displays your most recently received emails, whether or not you've actually read the email messages.

- **News** displays news from a variety of websites. At first, the news you see is Google's choice, but you can add your own preferred news sites as explained in 39 **Set Indexing and Desktop Preferences**.

- **Web Clips** displays information from *RSS feeds*, which can be from blogs, news sites, or other sources of information.

▶ KEY TERM

Really Simple Syndication (RSS) feeds—A technology that allows websites to send a feed of information to subscribers. You can subscribe free to RSS feeds. A typical RSS feed includes a summary of information. To read more, you click a link to go to the site that originally published the information.

- **Scratch Pad** is a small note-taking module that enables you to jot down notes and ideas. You can save these notes as text files that are stored in the **Google Desktop** program folders.

- **Photos** displays photos from your PC, one after another, in a kind of slideshow. You can specify the folders and websites from which you want to pull the images for the slideshow.

- **Quick View** displays recent or frequently used files and web pages.

- **What's Hot** displays current trends on the Web. The content for this module is automatically generated by Google and is compiled from many sources.

- **Stocks** displays stock information for the stocks you choose.

- **Weather** displays weather information.

- **Maps** enables you to view maps of your choosing.

- **Todo** enables you to create a to-do list.

For each module, you see only one or two pieces of information. To see more, click the double-left arrow in the module's title bar. A larger pane slides out, displaying more information from the module. Click the information you're interested in, and you go to the web page that has the information, or a new pane slides out with more details.

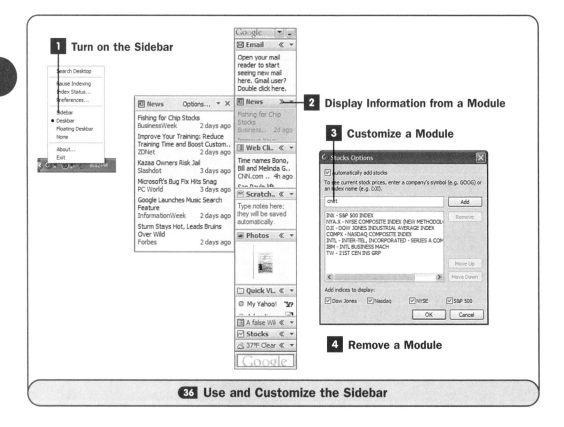

36

1 Turn on the Sidebar

2 Display Information from a Module

3 Customize a Module

4 Remove a Module

36 Use and Customize the Sidebar

3 Customize a Module

Many modules enable you to customize the information they display—for example, the **Stocks** module allows you to choose which stock information to display. To customize a module, click the down arrow in the module's title bar and choose **Options**. A dialog box of options for that module opens. Then fill out the form for customizing the module and click **OK**.

4 Remove a Module

Most likely, you won't want to use all the modules in the **Sidebar**, especially because as you remove some modules, you leave room for others. So, for example, if you remove several modules, you are able to see more information in each of the remaining modules without having to slide out its pane. To remove a module, click its down arrow and select **Remove**.

---

37 Browse and Search with the Timeline

✔ **BEFORE YOU BEGIN**

35 Browse Search Results

37

One of **Google Desktop**'s least-known features can at times be the most useful—its **Timeline**. The **Timeline** enables you to browse through all your computer activity by day and time of day. This can be useful for more than just finding information—for those who charge by the hour, such as consultants, the **Timeline** can help re-create the work you've done and help you determine how much time to invoice.

1 Double-click the Google Desktop Icon

To use the **Timeline**, you must be on the main browser page of **Google Desktop**. Double-click the **Desktop** icon in the system tray or on the Windows desktop to get there.

2 Click Browse Timeline

Click the **Browse Timeline** link, next to the search text box at the top of the main **Google Desktop** web page. When you do, you are sent to a page with the current day's **Timeline**. On the left side of the page you see a list of files and websites, along with the times they were visited (for files, the time shown is the time at which you started editing the file). Browse the search results the same way you do any search results returned on **Google Desktop**, as outlined in **35** **Browse Search Results**.

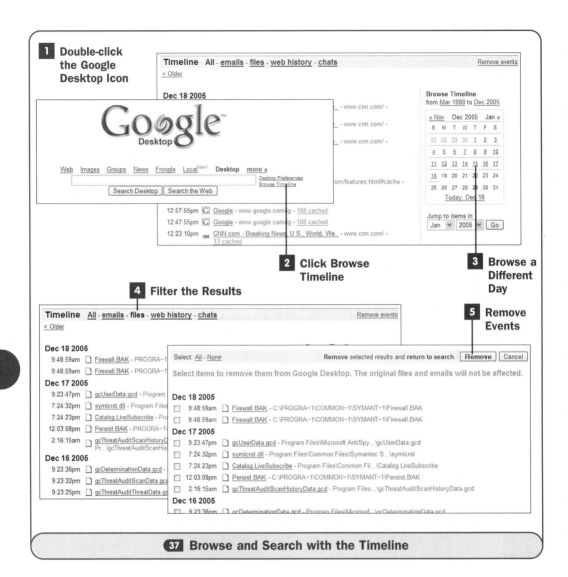

37 Browse and Search with the Timeline

3 Browse a Different Day

To browse the **Timeline** for another day, click the day you want to view on the calendar on the right side of the page. You can also jump to a day by choosing it from the drop-down boxes on the right side of the page.

4 Filter the Results

You can browse the **Timeline** only for email, files, your websites, or chats. Click the appropriate link at the top of the page to do so.

▶ **NOTE**

Google Desktop shows 20 events on a single screen; if you don't have many events for a single day, you might see more than one day's worth of events.

5 Remove Events

To remove an event (and in the **Timeline**, an "event" includes files you've opened, chats you've had, emails you've read, as well as websites you've visited), click the **Remove events** link in the upper-right corner of the **Timeline** page. From the page that appears, check the boxes next to the results you want removed, and then click the **Remove** button. Note that when you do this, the files themselves remain on your PC, but they are removed from the **Google Desktop** index and won't show up in the **Timeline** again.

▶ **TIP**

When you remove an event, you remove it from the **Google Desktop** index. That means you won't be able to find it when you do a **Google Desktop** search or when you browse the **Timeline**. You can't remove an event from the **Timeline** without also removing it from the index.

38 **Search Outlook with Google Desktop**

✔ **BEFORE YOU BEGIN**

34 Search Your PC with Google Desktop
35 Browse Search Results

38

Outlook users have an additional bonus when they use **Google Desktop**—it integrates directly into Outlook. This allows you to search your Outlook email using **Google Desktop**, without actually leaving Outlook.

1 Turn on the Google Desktop Toolbar

If you want to search your messages in Outlook using **Google Desktop**, you must turn on the special **Google Desktop** toolbar. From within Outlook, choose **View**, **Toolbars**, **Google Desktop Toolbar** so that there is a check mark next to that option. An input text box appears in the Outlook toolbar, next to an icon for the **Google Desktop**.

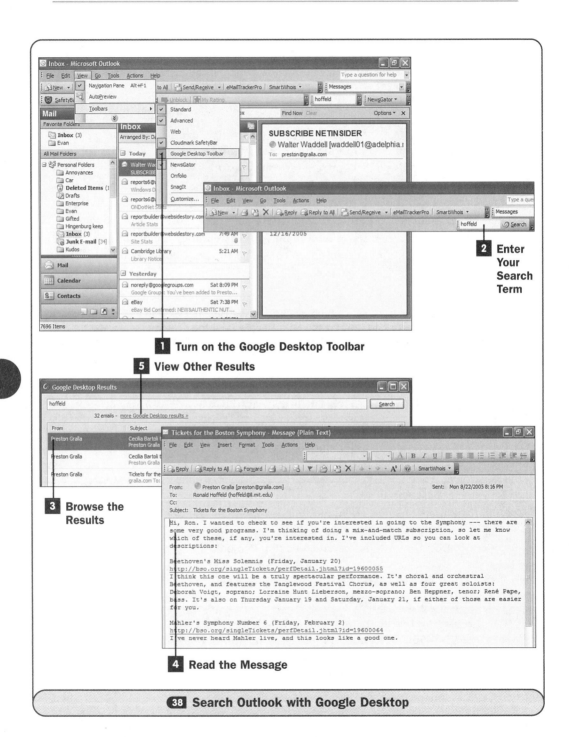

1 Turn on the Google Desktop Toolbar

5 View Other Results

38

3 Browse the Results

4 Read the Message

2 Enter Your Search Term

38 Search Outlook with Google Desktop

Enter Your Search Term

In the input text box in the Outlook toolbar, enter your search term or terms and press **Enter** or click the **Google Desktop Search** icon. Google searches all text in the email messages: text in the To, From, CC, and BCC lines; text in the Subject line; the text of the message itself; as well as the message's header information.

Browse the Results

A new window opens, listing the search results. For each email message that matches your search terms, you see who sent the message, the message subject, the date of the message, and the beginning of the message text.

Read the Message

To read any message, double-click it in the results page. The message opens in Outlook. You can now use the message as you would normally.

▶ NOTE

When you use Outlook integration to search with **Google Desktop**, you are only able to search through your email. The **Google Desktop** integrated into Outlook won't find contacts, appointments, or any other kind of Outlook information other than what's contained in your email messages. However, the standard **Google Desktop** normally finds that kind of Outlook information, so if you're looking for contacts or appointment details, search using **Google Desktop**, but not from within Outlook.

View Other Results

If you want to see other search results using the normal **Google Desktop** interface, click the **more Google Desktop results** link at the top of the results page. You go to the **Google Desktop** search results page, which returns information found in addition to Outlook's email.

39 Set Indexing and Desktop Preferences

✔ BEFORE YOU BEGIN	→ SEE ALSO
34 Search Your PC with Google Desktop	**36** Use and Customize the Sidebar

To get the most out of **Google Desktop**, you should customize it. There's plenty you can change, including which files to index and how many search results to show on a page. Here's how to do it.

1 Go to the Preferences Page

Right-click the **Google Desktop** icon in the system tray or on the Windows desktop and choose **Preferences** from the context menu. You go to the **Google Desktop Preferences** page in your browser.

2 Choose Indexing Options

The top part of the page enables you to select your indexing preferences. In the **Search Types** section, choose the kinds of items you want to index by putting a check mark in the box next to them.

For email, **Google Desktop** indexes **Gmail**, Outlook, Outlook Express, Netscape Mail, Thunderbird, and Mozilla Mail, but no other kinds of email. For documents, it indexes Word, Excel, PowerPoint, Acrobat, graphics, and audio files, among others.

Under the series of check boxes detailing the items you want to index, you find a check box option for whether to search password-protected Office documents, such as Word and Excel files. It's a good idea to leave this box disabled if you're worried about someone else using your computer. If you enable the check box next to **Password-protected Office documents**, Google indexes those documents and anyone who uses your PC is able to search through those files without using your password.

The **Secure pages (HTTPS) in web history** check box should also be left disabled if you're worried about privacy. If you enable the check box, Google indexes pages on which you've entered your credit card number and on which you do online banking. If you index these pages, other people who use your PC could get personal, financial information about you.

39

▶ NOTE

If you want to add to the power of **Google Desktop**, you can install plug-ins, which are small programs that give **Google Desktop** more features. For example, plug-ins can allow **Google Desktop** to search for extra file types, can have **Google Desktop** integrate with Outlook Express in the same way it integrates with Outlook, and more. To see them, in the **Plug-ins** section of the **Preferences** page, click the **Plug-ins Download page** link and install those plug-ins in which you're interested.

If you want **Google Desktop** to index your **Gmail** files, enable the check box next to **Index and search email in my Gmail account** and type your username and password for your **Gmail** account.

Google Desktop can search multiple hard disks. It can even search the hard disks and folders of computers on your home network if you've set up those disks and folders to be available over the network.

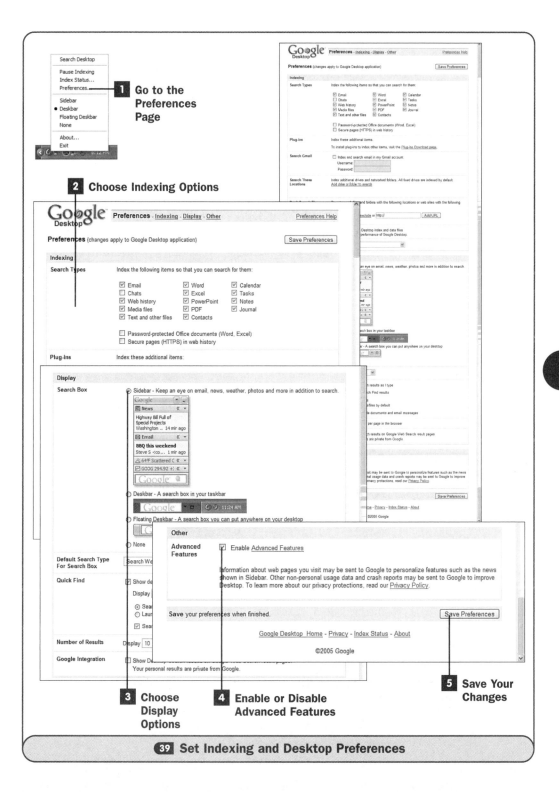

1 Go to the Preferences Page

2 Choose Indexing Options

3 Choose Display Options

4 Enable or Disable Advanced Features

5 Save Your Changes

39

When you install **Google Desktop**, it automatically indexes all the hard disks on your PC. If you have added extra hard disks (or folders or disks on other computers on your network) and want to index those, too, in the **Search These Locations** section, click the **Add drive or folder to search** link and choose the hard disks or networked drives or folders you want to index and search. When you add them, they show up underneath the **Add drive or folder to search** link. If you no longer want these locations to be indexed, click the **Delete** link next to the location you want to remove from the index.

You can also *exclude* folders, files, or websites from being indexed. To exclude a folder or a file, click the **Add file or folder to exclude** link and browse to select the file or folder you don't want to be indexed. To add a website to the excluded list, type its URL in the box, including the **http://** in front of it, and click **Add URL**. The list of excluded files, folders, and websites shows up underneath the **Add file or folder to exclude** link. If you no longer want these items to be excluded from the index, click the **Delete** link next to the item, and the item will be indexed.

After the initial index is created, **Google Desktop** updates the index with file information whenever your computer is idle. The index is updated with Outlook email information on the fly, whenever you send or receive email.

39

If you want the index encrypted so only you can use it, in the **Encrypt Index** section, enable the **Encrypt Google Desktop index and data files** check box. This option works only if you have Windows XP because it uses XP's Windows Encrypted File System. Note that if you use this feature, it slows down indexing and searching. Encrypting the index ensures that if someone hacks into your PC, they can't read your index. Only people with access to your encrypted files can read the index.

You can turn off indexing for any future files and events. To do it, in the **Enable Indexing** section, choose the **Disabled** option from the drop-down list. All files and events that have already occurred remain indexed and searchable, but none that you add after you disable indexing are included in the index. You can always turn the indexing feature back on if you want.

3 Choose Display Options

The next section of the **Preferences** page enables you to customize how **Google Desktop** should display information. The **Search Box** section allows you to display **Google Desktop** as the **Sidebar**, the **Deskbar**, the **Floating Desktop**, or not display it at all. Choose which option you want.

▶ **TIP**

You can also set your display by right-clicking the **Google Desktop** icon in the system tray and choosing the appropriate option from the context menu.

The **Default Search Type For Search Box** section enables you to set what kind of search should be done when you use the **Google Desktop** search box. Choose your option from the drop-down list. You can have **Google Desktop** search your desktop, search the Web, search **Google Images**, search **Google Groups**, search **Google News**, search **Froogle**, search **Google Local** (previously called Google Maps), and do an **I'm Feeling Lucky** search (in which **Google Desktop** automatically goes to the page with the top search result).

The **Quick Find** section comes next. If you want **Google Desktop** to display results as you type, enable the **Show desktop search results as I type** check box. From the drop-down list beneath it, select the number of these **Quick Find** results you want to appear, from 1 to 10. (The **Quick Find** option is not available if you choose **None** for the **Search Box** type.)

▶ **NOTE**

The number of results you choose to display for **Quick Find** affects only the results that appear in the **Quick Find** pop-up window as you type your search terms. It does not affect how the results appear on the normal **Google Desktop** results page.

The next set of preferences, **Search by default** or **Launch programs/files by default** enables you to launch programs using **Quick Find**. If you want to launch Microsoft Word, for example, you can type **wor** in the search box, select **Microsoft Word** from the results that appear, and Word launches.

If you want to be able to search for text inside documents and email, enable the **Search text inside documents and email messages** check box. If you don't check this box, you are only able to search for filenames and for text in the subject lines of email messages.

The **Number of Results** section enables you to set how many results to show on a page. Select the number from the drop-down list.

The final area of the **Display** section allows you to determine whether, when you do a normal Google search, you also see **Google Desktop** search results. If you enable the **Show Desktop Search results on Google Web Search result pages** check box, whenever you search on Google, you also see the results of a search on your hard disk. Note that these results are not sent back to Google; they are displayed only on your PC.

4 Enable or Disable Advanced Features

The last section of the page, **Advanced Features**, determines whether information about how you use **Google Desktop** should be sent to Google. When you enable the **Enable Advanced Features** check box, information about the web pages you visit are sent to Google. Google claims that this information helps the **Sidebar** better deliver customized results to you—for example, to deliver more relevant news. Google also claims that the information is not personally identifiable, and that it is used to help Google engineers understand how people use the **Google Desktop**, and so make better versions of the program.

5 Save Your Changes

When you're done, click **Save Preferences**. The new settings you specified take effect. **Google Desktop** updates the original index when your computer is idle; the changes you've specified here will take effect the next time **Google Desktop** updates the index.

40

40 About Advanced Desktop Searching	
✔ **BEFORE YOU BEGIN**	→ **SEE ALSO**
6 About Google Search Operators **7** About Power Searching Strategies	**34** Search Your PC with Google Desktop

---

Google Desktop enables you to use all the advanced searching tools that you normally use with Google, including search operators, as detailed in **6** **About Google Search Operators**. Using these search operators can help narrow your search results tremendously.

Some other Google advanced searching features can help as well. Probably the most useful is the **file type** filter. This comes in handy when you want to only find a file, and especially a file of a particular file type. For example, let's say that you want to find a Word file with the word *clone* in it. You could type this search string in the **Google Desktop** search box:

Clone filetype:doc

This search returns all Word files on your hard disk with the word *clone* in them. To do this kind of file type search, you need to know the extension of the file for which you are looking. Table 6.1 shows common file types that **Google Desktop** can search for, along with their extensions.

TABLE 6.1   Common File Extensions

File Type	Extension
Word	doc
Excel	xls
PowerPoint	ppt
Adobe Acrobat	pdf
Text files	txt

40

7

Getting Maps and Directions with Google Local

IN THIS CHAPTER:

The best place to go on the Internet for maps is **Google Local**, which is now officially known as **Google Local**, but most people still call it **Google Maps**.

Google Local does more than just display maps—it also gives step-by-step driving directions and enables you to find businesses and resources anywhere in the United States and in many places in the world. Want to find Japanese restaurants in South Bend, Indiana or zoos in London? **Google Local** is the place to go. It also includes close-up satellite maps. (Although it provides maps of the world, **Google Local** only includes local information on certain areas of the world; Google plans to expand its local coverage over time.)

---

41   **Map a Location**

✔ BEFORE YOU BEGIN	→ SEE ALSO
1 Perform a Basic Google Search	**42** Navigate Through Google Local
	69 Navigate Through Google Earth

41

The simplest and most basic thing you can do on **Google Local** is, obviously, find a map. Here's how to do it, along with tips on what else you can do with your map, including linking to it from a blog or website.

1 Go to Google Local

In your browser's address bar, type **http://maps.google.com** to go to **Google Local**. You see a map of the United States with several controls on it, and the familiar search box at the top of the page. You can also get to **Google Local** by clicking the **Local** link at the top of any Google page.

2 Type a Location

If you know the precise location you want to map, type it in the search box. Make sure you include not only the street address and town or city, but also the state name. You can spell out the entire state name or use an abbreviation. After you've typed in the location, press **Enter**. You don't have to type an exact location; for example, you can type **hotels near LAX** and **Google Local** shows you hotels near the Los Angeles LAX airport. It recognizes major airports, and many locations such as tourist destinations. So you can type **Disneyworld** or **Yosemite National Park**, for example.

▶ NOTE

A handful of major cities, including San Francisco, New York, Chicago, and Boston, don't require that you type the state name. But to be safe, it's a good idea to always type the state name.

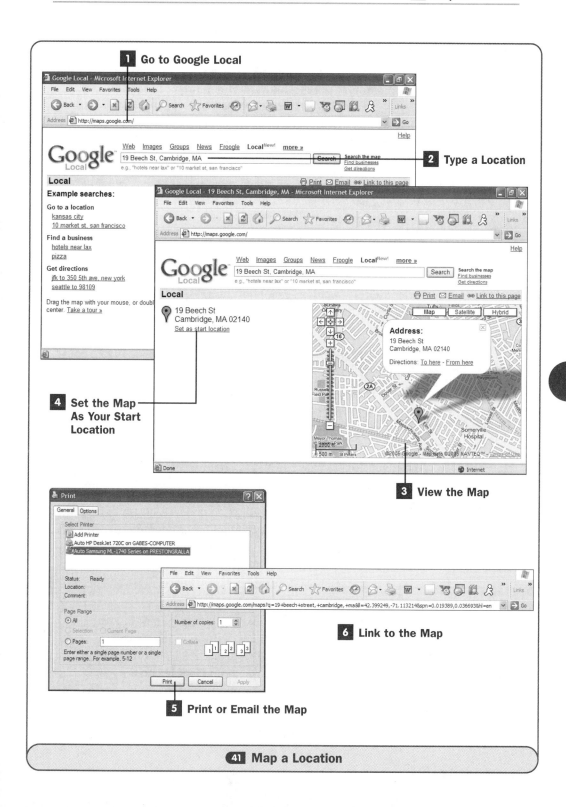

1 Go to Google Local

2 Type a Location

4 Set the Map As Your Start Location

3 View the Map

6 Link to the Map

5 Print or Email the Map

3 View the Map

A map of the location you specified appears, showing the surrounding streets, a pin-like icon representing the exact address, and a large cartoon-like balloon containing the street name. The balloon takes up a good portion of the map, so if you want to remove it, click the X in its upper-right corner. You can also click the **Satellite** or **Hybrid** button to get a different view of the area you're mapping. See **45 About Satellite Photos** for details.

To zoom in and out of the map and manipulate the map in other ways, see **42 Navigate Through Google Local**.

4 Set the Map As Your Start Location

If you'd like this location to appear every time you go to **Google Local**, click the **Set as start location** link on the left side of the screen. From now on, whenever you visit **Google Local**, this map location displays instead of the map of the United States that is normally displayed.

▶ TIP

41

If you set the currently displayed map as your start location, but the start location doesn't appear the next time you visit **Google Local**, you need to clear out your Internet cache, a folder of temporary files stored on your PC. To clear the cache in Internet Explorer, choose **Internet Options** from the **Tools** menu, click the **Delete Files** button, and then click **OK**.

5 Print or Email the Map

If you want to print the map, click the **Print** link at the top of the map and then print the map as you would any normal page.

To email the map, click the **Email** link. Your email program launches, and in the box of your email is a link to the map. You don't mail the map itself; just the link is sent, so the recipient can click it and go to the map.

6 Link to the Map

If you have a website or a blog, you can link to the map. Notice that the URL at the top of the page didn't change when you typed in a map location—it stayed at http://maps.google.com. If you included a link to that location on a website or blog, the link would go only to the main **Google Local** page. When you click the **Link to this page** link, though, the URL changes to a very long URL, like this one:

http://maps.google.com/maps?q=19+Beech+Street,+Cambridge,+MA&iwloc=
A&hl=en

You can use that link on your website or blog.

If you prefer, you can copy the link location to your computer's clipboard,
where you can easily paste it into your blog or into your website creation
tool. To do this in Internet Explorer, right-click the **Link to this page** link and
choose **Copy shortcut** from the context menu. That command copies the link
location to your Windows clipboard. Paste the link into whatever application
you want using the **Ctrl+V** keyboard shortcut or the **Edit**, **Paste** command.

42 Navigate Through Google Local

✔ BEFORE YOU BEGIN	→ SEE ALSO
41 Map a Location	**45** About Satellite Photos
	69 Navigate Through Google Earth

Mapping a location is useful, but more often than not, you're going to need to
navigate around—zoom in and out on the location and easily maneuver to
places near and far. This task shows you how to do this.

42

1 Use the Slider

You can zoom in and out on your map by using the vertical slider on the left
side of the map. Hold your mouse over the horizontal bar on the slider; the
mouse pointer turns into a hand. Hold down the mouse's left button and
drag the bar toward the top of the screen to zoom in; drag toward the bottom
to zoom out.

2 Use the Navigation Arrows

If you want to move north, south, east, or west on your current map, use the
four navigation arrows at the top of the slider. Click the arrow in the direction you want to move the map. When you click, you move half a screen's
worth of distance, at whatever zoom magnification you're currently viewing
the map.

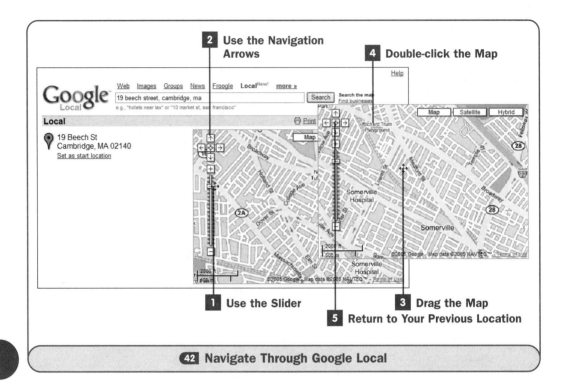

42   **④ Navigate Through Google Local**

③ Drag the Map

If you want to move the map in increments other than half a screen at a time, you can drag the map in any direction. Hold down the left mouse button anywhere on the map and drag the map in the direction you want to move. As you drag the map, a four-headed arrow appears to show that you are moving the map. When you want to stop, release the mouse button.

④ Double-click the Map

Instead of dragging or using the navigation arrows, you can double-click any location on the map, and you are immediately sent to that point. This is particularly useful when you're zoomed very far out because you can quickly and accurately go to a location a great distance away from your current one.

▶ **TIP**

Google Local works for more places than just the United States. You can get maps for many other countries by typing the address, including the city and country; for example, **Old Queen Street, London, UK**. If you don't know the street address, type the name of the city and country, and then zoom in to where you want to go using the navigational tools.

5 Return to Your Previous Location

If you've been looking at maps of various regions and you want to return to the location where you were previously, click the small box with four inward-facing arrows in the middle of the navigation arrows.

---

43 Find Local Information with Google Local

✔ BEFORE YOU BEGIN	→ SEE ALSO
1 Perform a Basic Google Search	**70** Find Local Information with
41 Map a Location	Google Earth

Perhaps **Google Local**'s most powerful feature is its capability to give you local information about anywhere you might want to visit. Want to find hotels near the Los Angeles airport; free wireless hot spots in Somerville, Massachusetts; zoos in Atlanta, Georgia; museums in Lincoln, Nebraska; or Thai restaurants in Cincinnati, Ohio? Those are just some of the things you can find with the **Local** feature of **Google Local**.

43

1 Type What You're Looking For

Ask and you shall receive: The simplest way to find a local business or resource is to type it into the search box at the top of the **Google Local** screen, such as **thai restaurants, Cincinnati, OH**; **WiFi, Somerville, MA**; **storage facilities Los Vegas, NV**; or **Hotels near Logan Airport**, and then click **Search**. A map appears with the results mapped and labeled with letters; a key to the map appears on the right side of the screen.

▶ **TIP**

Searching for hotels, restaurants, or other services near airports can be tricky, and if you're not careful, you get incorrect results. You get the best results if you use airport codes, such as **LAX** for Los Angeles' airport, or **BOS** for Boston's Logan airport. Oddly enough, if you use the airport's official name, you might get strange results or no results at all. If you don't know the airport code, type the name of the city, and the word airport—for example, **Hotels near Boston airport**—and you should get good results.

2 Click the Category

In some instances when you type a local search and click **Search**, you see a category listing at the left side of the screen in addition to your results. It might contain a category as well as several subcategories, for example, **Restaurants, Restaurant Thai**. Click the category or subcategory to see more related listings in the area where you're searching.

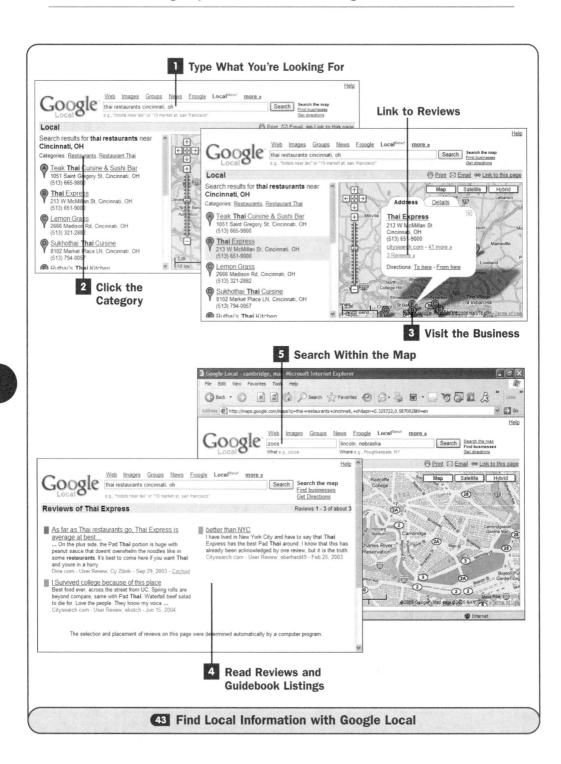

1 Type What You're Looking For

Link to Reviews

2 Click the Category

3 Visit the Business

5 Search Within the Map

4 Read Reviews and Guidebook Listings

43 Find Local Information with Google Local

3 Visit the Business

To get more information about any of the businesses on the map, click the location on the map itself (click its letter pin), or click the listing to the left of the map. The map moves to that location, and a balloon appears with information about the business, including the name, address, and links to reviews, directions, and more information.

The balloon has two tabs on it—an **Address** tab and a **Details** tab. Click both to get all the information you can find about the place of business. The **Details** tab has information such as what kind of payment is accepted, the business hours, and so on. Keep in mind that, oddly enough, the **Details** tab doesn't always have more information than the **Address** tab. So click them both.

▶ **NOTE**

Google Local gives the most detail about the United States and Canada, and the second most detail about the United Kingdom (that is, you might not get a **Details** tab for locations in the UK). At the moment, **Google Local** provides no details for locations elsewhere in the world, but that might change as Google updates the information it stores about cities across the world.

43

4 Read Reviews and Guidebook Listings

If the business (such as restaurant) or location has been reviewed by users, a **Reviews** link appears on the **Address** tab. Click the link, and you see the list of reviews that are typically from people who have visited the restaurant and are posted on sites such as www.dine.com and www.citysearch.com. You can read the summary of each review and click a link to read the full review.

If the location has been described or reviewed in any of a variety of guidebooks, such as www.mobiletravelguide.com, links to the descriptions or reviews appear on the **Address** tab. Because Google gets the reviews from many places, the site you are researching might have more than one link to a review. Click any of the links for details.

5 Search Within the Map

When a map is displayed on your screen, you can search that location and nearby locations for businesses without having to type the name of the location. For example, if you've done a search for restaurants in Cincinnati, Ohio, and that map is displayed, you can now search for hotels by just typing **Hotels** at the top of the screen; the map shifts to display the hotels in Cincinnati.

Be careful when you have a map displayed because searching can lead to very confusing results. No matter what you type in the search box, it searches only through the area of the currently displayed map and the nearby region. So, for example, if you have a map of Cambridge, Massachusetts, on your screen, and you type **Hotels in Cincinnati, OH** into the search box, you get no results because Google searches only through the Cambridge area. If you're viewing a map and want to search for businesses or resources in another part of the country, click the **Find businesses** link at the top of the page, and fill out that form.

---

44   **Get Directions to Anywhere with Google Local**

✔ BEFORE YOU BEGIN	→ SEE ALSO
41 Map a Location	**71** Use Google Earth to Get Directions
42 Navigate Through Google Local	

44

When you use **Google Local**, you're often primarily interested in finding directions to somewhere. As you'll see in this task, it's just as easy to find directions as it is to map a location.

1 Type Your Search Terms

In the search box at the top of the page, type your starting and ending destination, like this: **19 Beech St., Cambridge, MA to 10 Market St., San Francisco, CA**. Remember to include the state as well as the city and street. If you need directions only from city to city, you don't have to type street numbers.

Alternatively, click the **Get directions** link next to the search box, type your starting location in the left search box, and type your destination in the right search box. When you're done, click **Search**.

▶ CAUTION

Be aware that the directions **Google Local** gives are not always the most direct, and there is a chance that they might be outdated. It's a good idea to double-check the directions using another online map service, such as MapQuest at www.mapquest.com.

2 Read and Print the Directions

A map appears with the starting location pinpointed in green with a triangle in the pin and the ending location pinpointed in red with a square in the pin. Step-by-step directions are on the left side of the page, along with the distance in miles and the approximate driving time. Read the directions. To print them out, click the **Print** link above the map and print as you would any page.

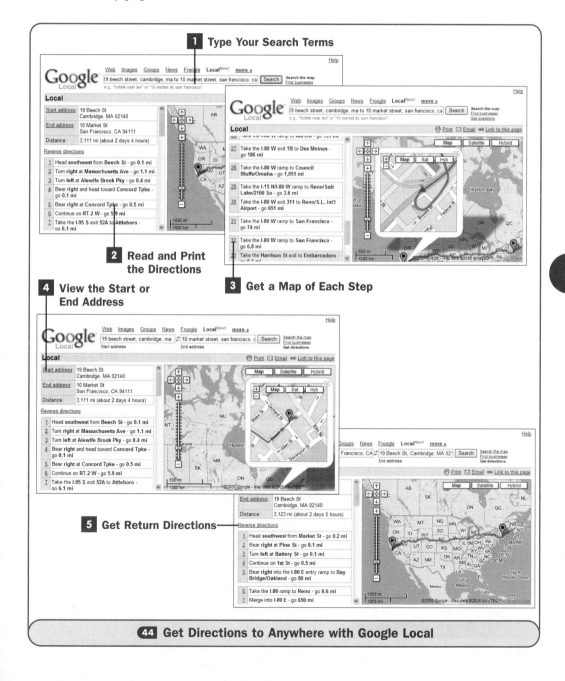

1 Type Your Search Terms

2 Read and Print the Directions

3 Get a Map of Each Step

4 View the Start or End Address

5 Get Return Directions

Note that you can navigate the map as you can any map by using Google's navigational tools, as described in **42** **Navigate Through Google Local**.

3 Get a Map of Each Step

The directions on the left side of the page are numbered. For a close-up map of any of the steps, click the number, and a close-up map of the directions for that step appears superimposed over the main map of directions. You can zoom in and out of the close-up map by clicking + to zoom in and – to zoom out. To close the close-up map, click the X in the upper-right corner of its window.

4 View the Start or End Address

To see a close-up map of the start address, click the **Start address** link on the left side of the page; for a close-up of the end address, click the **End address** link. The appropriate close-up map appears superimposed on the main map.

5 Get Return Directions

If you want return directions, you don't have to do another search—click the **Reverse directions** link on the left side of the page. Return directions appear. On the map, the start address and end address reverse (note the change in pin color and shapes).

---

45 | **About Satellite Photos**

✔ BEFORE YOU BEGIN	→ SEE ALSO
41 Map a Location	**69** Navigate Through Google Earth

One of the more amazing features of **Google Local** is its capability to show you actual close-up satellite photos of anywhere in the United States and of many places in the world.

To display a satellite photo of a particular area, first display a map location as you would normally. Then click the **Satellite** button to see a satellite photo of the location at the same zoom percentage as the original map. You can zoom in and out and navigate with satellite photos in the same way as you can with normal maps. Note that not all locations have satellite maps, and in some locations, the satellite maps are low-resolution or cannot be displayed at the zoom level in which your original map is currently displayed. Try zooming out several steps to determine whether a satellite map can be found for that area. (For more information about satellite photos, see Chapter 11, "Discovering the World with Google Earth.")

You can also view a hybrid map in which there is a satellite photo with the local street names superimposed over it. The nearby figures show you a map of New York City's Fifth Avenue and Metropolitan Museum of Art, a satellite map of the same location, and finally, a hybrid map of the same location.

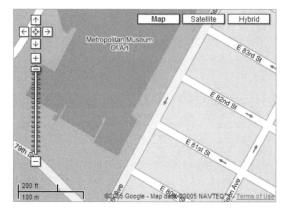

A Google map of New York's Fifth Avenue and the Metropolitan Museum of Art.

45

A satellite photo of New York's Fifth Avenue and the Metropolitan Museum of Art.

A hybrid map of New York's Fifth Avenue and the Metropolitan Museum of Art.

45

8

Create Your Own Google Home Page

IN THIS CHAPTER:

As you've seen throughout this book, Google is more than a mere search engine—it's practically an entire universe in which you can live when you're online.

At the center of that universe is what Google calls *Personalized Home*, a customized page you can build that includes links to a wide variety of information, including news, weather, stock information, blog and RSS feeds, and Google services such as **Gmail**. As time goes on, Google will add more links to its services on this page.

▶ KEY TERM

Personalized Home—A customized Google page that has links to your personalized news, weather, stock information, and other Google services, such as **Gmail**.

In this chapter, you'll learn how to set up and customize your own **Personalized Home** page.

46	**About Google Personalized Home**
✔ **BEFORE YOU BEGIN** **57** Set Up a Gmail Account	→ **SEE ALSO** **1** Perform a Basic Google Search

Think of **Personalized Home** as command central for Google. From this page, you can do normal Google searches and you can get links to all kinds of information and services.

As with a number of other Google services, you must have signed up for a Google account to use **Personalized Home**. For details, see Chapter 1, "Start Here."

To get to your **Personalized Home** page, head to www.google.com, and click the **Personalized Home** link (look in the upper-right corner of the screen). If you haven't already signed in to your Google account, you have to sign in now. After you do that, you come to a relatively bare page that you can begin customizing, as detailed in the rest of this chapter.

If for some reason you don't want to use **Personalized Home** and prefer the normal barebones Google page, click the **Classic Home** link at the top of the page, and you go back to old-fashioned Google.

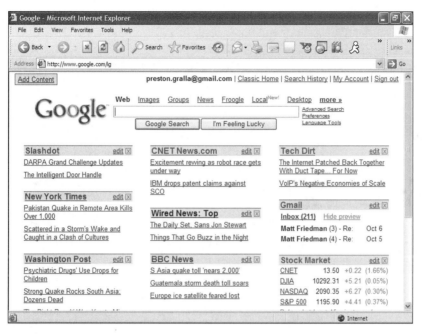

*The Google **Personalized Home** page.*

▶ **TIP**

You can make **Personalized Home** your browser's home page so that whenever you start your browser or click the **Home** button in your browser, you are sent to your Google **Personalized Home** page. In Internet Explorer, choose **Internet Options** from the **Tools** menu, type **http://www.google.com** into the **Address** box at the top of the screen that appears, and click **OK**.

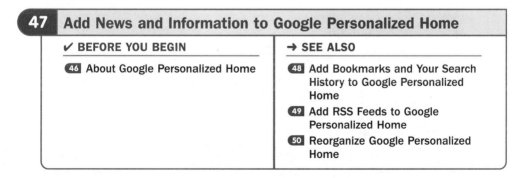

When you first visit it, your Google **Personalized Home** page isn't personalized at all. So the first thing you should do, after you sign in to Google, is to add sources of news and information to the page.

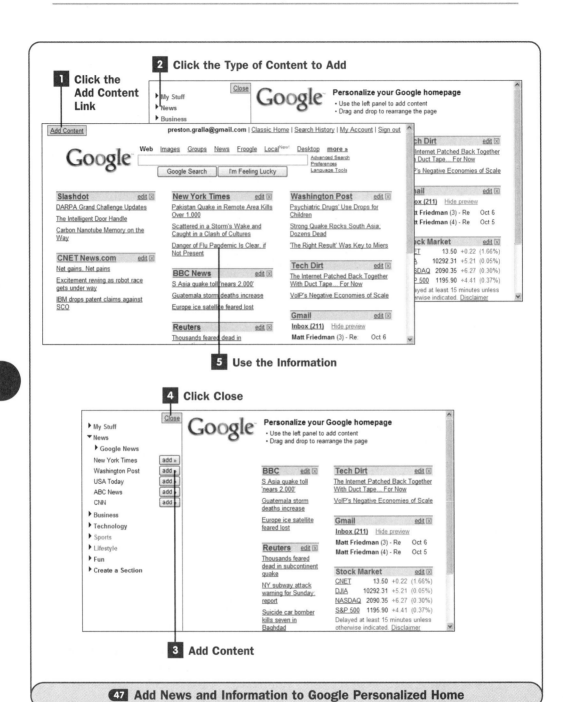

47 Add News and Information to Google Personalized Home

As you'll see in this task, you add them by choosing from a variety of sources provided by Google.

1 Click the Add Content Link

From the main Google page, click the **Personalized Home** link (look in the upper-right corner of the screen) to go to your own **Personalized Home** page. The **Add Content** link is in the upper-left corner of the page. When you click it, a pane opens on the left with a list of categories of news and content you can add to **Personalized Home**.

2 Click the Type of Content to Add

In the pane on the left side of the screen is a selection from a variety of content categories, including **News**, **Business**, **Technology**, **Sports**, **Lifestyle**, and so on. When you click a category, it expands to list individual sources of content you can then add to the page.

3 Add Content

Click **Add** next to any source of content you want to add to your page. After a moment or two, the content is added to the right side of the page. A heading appears for the source of content, and then beneath it, links to news stories or other sources of content.

▶ **TIP**

Google plans to add new sources of news and information for **Personalized Home**. You should regularly check for new sources by clicking the **Add Content** link and then clicking each category to see what's new.

4 Click Close

When you're done selecting all the sources of news and information you want on your page, click the **Close** button at the top of the left pane. Now you see the entire list of news and information you selected to appear on your page.

5 Use the Information

The page functions like any web page—click the links for stories and information you're interested in and you are sent to the site that has the information. To find out how to reorganize the content of your personalized home page, see **50** **Reorganize Google Personalized Home**.

48   Add Bookmarks and Your Search History to Google Personalized Home

✔ BEFORE YOU BEGIN	→ SEE ALSO
47 Add News and Information to Google Personalized Home	**49** Add RSS Feeds to Google Personalized Home
	50 Reorganize Google Personalized Home

Personalized Home does more than enable you to read news, stocks, weather, and other sources of information. It also gives you access to personal information, notably your Web bookmarks and your search history.

Why bother to include your bookmarks on the page when you can get to bookmarks from your browser? Because when you put them on the **Personalized Home** page, you can get to them even when you're not at your own computer—you are able to get to them anywhere you can get an Internet connection.

Your search history is useful as well. You might want to run the same search regularly, for example, if you are doing research and want to see whether new information about a topic is available somewhere on the Internet.

1 Turn on Personalized Search

Google doesn't automatically keep a record of your search history—you first have to tell it to do so. So before you can work with your search history, you have to enable a feature called *Personalized Search*.

▶ KEY TERM

Personalized Search—A feature of Google that keeps a record of all your searches and enables you to revisit your search history.

To turn **Personalized Search** on, click the **My Account** link at the top of a Google page; from the page that appears, click **Personalized Search**. You come to a login page. Type your username and password (your username might already be typed in for you) and sign in. When you sign in to **Personalized Search**, you turn it on. The next page gives information about the **Personalized Search** feature.

2 Return to Personalized Home

Now that you've turned on your search history, you can add it to your **Personalized Home**. Go back to the **Personalized Home** page by clicking the **Google Home** link at the top of your search history page.

1 Turn on Personalized Search

2 Return to Personalized Home

4 Add Bookmarks and Search History

3 Click the Add Content Link

5 Add URLs to Your Bookmarks

6 Save Your Bookmarks

Bookmarks

Search History

48

3 Click the Add Content Link

You add bookmarks and your search history to your **Personalized Home** page in the same way you add other types of content. Display the content pane by clicking the **Add Content** link in the upper-left corner of the screen.

4 Add Bookmarks and Search History

Your bookmarks and search history can be found in the **My Stuff** category. Click **My Stuff** to expand the list of subcategories. Then click the **Add** buttons next to **Bookmarks** and **Search History**. Click **Close**. Your search history and bookmarks are added to your **Personalized Home** page.

▶ **NOTE**

If you haven't done any searches after you've turned on **Personalized Search**, your **Search History** in **Personalized Search** is empty. Searches are added to that section after you do them.

5 Add URLs to Your Bookmarks

Google does not import bookmarks from your browser onto your **Personalized Home** page. You have to add them yourself. To do this, in the **Bookmarks** section of your page, type the URL into the **Add a favorite URL box** (for example, type **www.ebay.com**). If you want a name for this bookmark to be displayed on the page rather than the URL itself, type a name for the bookmark in the **Give it a name (optional)** box. Then click **Add**. Continue to add as many bookmarks as you want.

6 Save Your Bookmarks

When you're done adding bookmarks, click **Save** and all the bookmarks are permanently added to your page.

---

49 Add RSS Feeds to Google Personalized Home

✔ BEFORE YOU BEGIN	→ SEE ALSO
47 Add News and Information to Google Personalized Home	**48** Add Bookmarks and Your Search History to Google Personalized Home
84 About Google Reader and RSS Feeds	**50** Reorganize Google Personalized Home

1 Click the Add Content Link

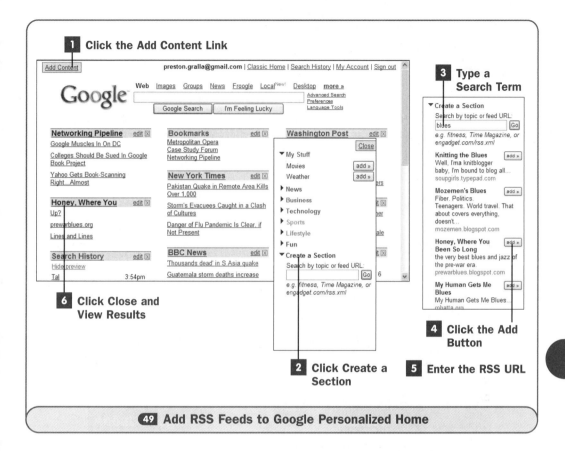

3 Type a Search Term

6 Click Close and View Results

4 Click the Add Button

2 Click Create a Section

5 Enter the RSS URL

49

49 Add RSS Feeds to Google Personalized Home

It's certainly useful to be able to add news and other information to your **Personalized Home** page. But the news and other sources are somewhat limited—after all, the Internet is a very big place and Google offers a choice of only a few information feeds.

You can, however, add your own sources of information to the page—you have the choice of literally thousands of them. There's only one caveat to what you can add—the information source must be in what's called a Really Simple Syndication (RSS) format, commonly called an RSS feed. (For more information about RSS feeds, see **84** **About Google Reader and RSS Feeds**.

Many thousands of RSS feeds are available—from big news sites to small bloggers and specialized sources of information—so there's plenty from which to choose.

To find sources of RSS feeds, you can visit several websites, including www. syndic8.com, www.2rss.com, www.blogstreet.com, and www.blogcatalog.com.

1 Click the Add Content Link

From the main Google page, click the **Personalized Home** link (look in the upper-right corner of the screen) to go to your own **Personalized Home** page. The **Add Content** link is in the upper-left corner of the page. As with adding all other kinds of content to your **Personalized Home** page, click this link to begin.

2 Click Create a Section

For some odd reason, Google calls adding an RSS feed "adding a section." So click the **Create a Section** category in the pane on the left side of the screen to add a feed.

3 Type a Search Term

Google makes it easy to find an RSS feed that matches what you're looking for. Just type a search term in the **Search by topic or feed URL** box and click **Go**. Google searches through RSS feeds and lists any that match the term(s) you've entered.

4 Click the Add Button

Add RSS feeds to your **Personalized Home** page the same way you add other content, by clicking the **Add** button.

5 Enter the RSS URL

An RSS feed has a URL, and you might know the exact URL for the feed. If you do, enter its URL, such as **http://www.networkingpipeline.com/blog/ movabletype/ntp.xml** in the **Search by topic or feed URL** box and click **Go**. When you do this, the feed is automatically added to your **Personalized Home** page; you won't have to click an **Add** button to add it to the page.

6 Click Close and View Results

When you're done adding RSS feeds to your page, click **Close** to return to your **Personalized Home** page. The RSS feed have been added.

49

50 Reorganize Google Personalized Home

✔ BEFORE YOU BEGIN	→ SEE ALSO
47 Add News and Information to Google Personalized Home	**48** Add Bookmarks and Your Search History to Google Personalized Home
	49 Add RSS Feeds to Google Personalized Home

You've added all the content you want to **Personalized Home**. But what if you want it ordered differently—you want the stock information to appear at the bottom of the page, you want the New York Times news front and center, and you want more news to be available from the New York Times than from other sources? And what if you want to delete content from the page?

As you'll see in this task, it's easy to organize **Personalized Home**.

1 Hover the Mouse over a Section

Select the section you want to move by hovering your mouse over the section. Hover it over the blue bar at the top of the section, not on individual entries within the section. A four-headed arrow appears.

2 Drag the Section

When the four-headed arrow appears, press the right mouse button and drag the section to where you want it to go by moving the mouse. When the section is where you want it to be, release the mouse button. The section is dropped in its new location.

3 Choose the Number of Items to Show

You can change the number of entries showing for any section. To do it, first click the **edit** link for that section (the link is in the blue bar at the top of the section). A **Show** drop-down box appears. Choose the number of items you want to appear for that section.

4 Click Save

After choosing the number of items, click **Save**. The section now has the new number of entries you've specified for it.

50

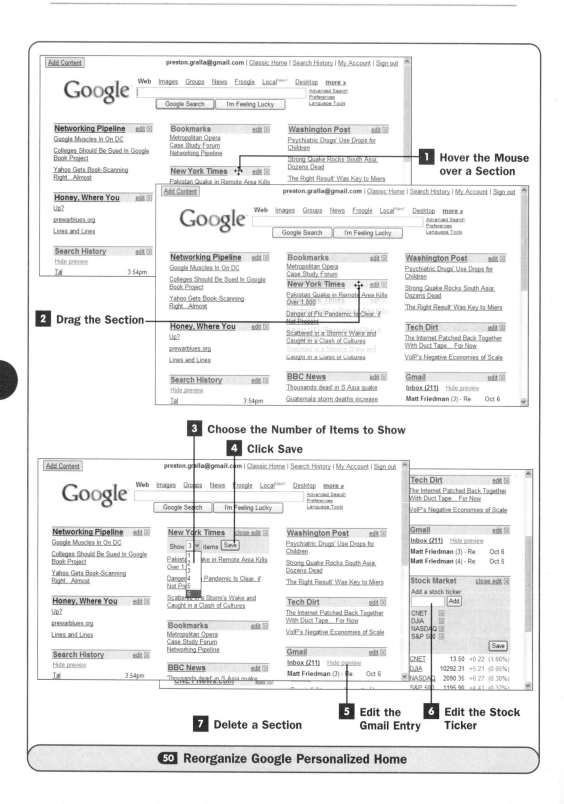

1 Hover the Mouse over a Section

2 Drag the Section

3 Choose the Number of Items to Show

4 Click Save

5 Edit the Gmail Entry

6 Edit the Stock Ticker

7 Delete a Section

50 Reorganize Google Personalized Home

5 Edit the Gmail Entry

If you have a **Gmail** account, you can show a preview of your most recently received emails or not show those emails. If the preview isn't showing and you want to see a preview, click the **Show Preview** link in the **Gmail** section. If you want to hide the entries, click **Hide Preview**. When you preview **Gmail** on your page, you see the sender and first several lines of the subject line of your most recent emails. You can show previews from one to nine emails, depending on your preferences. If you hide the preview, you don't see a preview of any **Gmail** messages and see only the link you can click to go to your **Gmail** account.

▶ **NOTE**

If you have a **Gmail** account, a link to it (including links to the most recent messages in your inbox) shows up automatically on your **Personalized Home** page. For details on how to get a **Gmail** account, see **57** Set Up a Gmail Account.

6 Edit the Stock Ticker

A *stock ticker* shows you updated stock prices. To add a stock you want to track to the **Stock Market** section, click that section's **edit** link. Type a stock symbol in the **Add a stock ticker** box and click **Add**. To remove a stock symbol, click the **X** next to its symbol in the list of entries. When you're done adding and deleting stocks tickers, click the **Save** button.

7 Delete a Section

To delete a section, click the **X** in the section's blue bar (next to the **edit** link). That section is immediately removed from your **Personalized Home** page. If you change your mind and want the section back, click the **Undo** link that appears at the top of the page. Only the most recent section you've deleted has the **Undo** link at the top of the page. So, for example, if you delete your **Stock Market** section, and then delete your **Gmail** section, there is an **Undo** link at the top of the page for **Gmail**, but not for **Stock Market**. To add the **Stock Market** section back to your home page, you must add it as explained in **47** Add News and Information to Google Personalized Home.

50

9

Googling Anywhere with the Google Toolbar

IN THIS CHAPTER:

Google is such a great and useful site that it's a shame you can use it only when you're on the Google site. If you use the *Google Toolbar*, though, you can use Google no matter where you are on the Internet. The **Google Toolbar** runs as a toolbar in your browser, and no matter where you are, you can type a search term, and **Google Toolbar** does a Google search.

▶ KEY TERM

Google Toolbar—A toolbar for your browser that enables you to search Google no matter where you are on the Internet.

The **Google Toolbar** also offers a variety of other features, such as digging deeper into each site to offer more knowledge about certain pieces of information and filling out web forms for you automatically. It might be the single most useful Google tool you'll ever use.

51 Use the Google Toolbar to Search from Anywhere	
✔ **BEFORE YOU BEGIN**	→ **SEE ALSO**
1 Perform a Basic Google Search	**56** Customize the Google Toolbar

51

The **Google Toolbar** has many benefits, but the biggest among them is this: You can use Google to search the Web from anywhere. No matter what site you're on, you won't need to go back to Google to do a search. Here's how to do it.

1 Download the Google Toolbar

Go to **http://toolbar.google.com**, click the **Download Google Toolbar** button, and follow the instructions for installation. For more details about downloading and installing Google tools, see Chapter 1, "Start Here."

▶ TIP

The **Google Toolbar** does not work with every browser. The Internet Explorer version of the **Google Toolbar** is what you get from http://toolbar.google.com. There is also a Firefox version of the **Google Toolbar**, available at http://toolbar.google.com/firefox. As of this writing, the **Google Toolbar** was not available for any other browsers, but check http://toolbar.google.com for links to versions for any other browser.

2 Display the Google Toolbar

After you install the **Google Toolbar**, it should automatically appear as a toolbar just beneath Internet Explorer's **Address** bar. If it doesn't, you need to display it. To do that, choose **View, Toolbars, Google**.

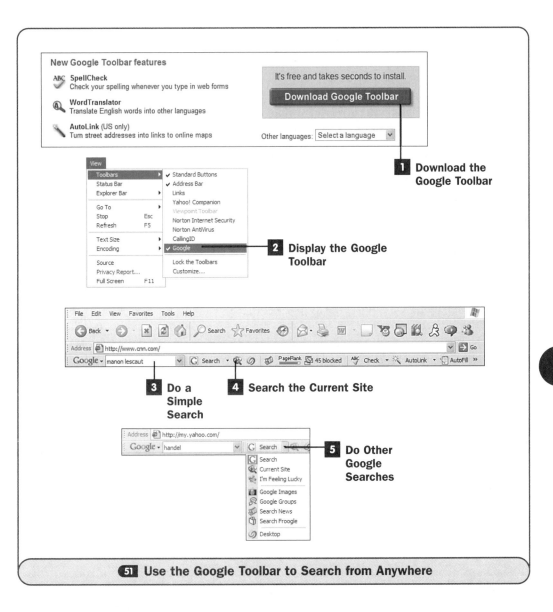

3 Do a Simple Search

To search with the **Google Toolbar**, type your search term(s) into the search box in the **Google Toolbar**, and press **Enter** or click the **Search** button. You do a Google search, just as if you were on Google. The search results pages are the same, as well.

4 Search the Current Site

Some sites you visit might not have their own search feature, and even if the site does have a search box, its search capabilities might not be especially powerful. The **Google Toolbar** enables you to use the power of Google to search the site you're currently visiting. Type in your search term(s), and then click the **Current Site** icon. It's the icon located to the right of the **Search** icon, and looks like a pair of eyes on a magnifying glass. If the **Current Site** icon isn't visible, you can make it appear on your **Google Toolbar**. For details, see **56** Customize the Google Toolbar.

5 Do Other Google Searches

The **Google Toolbar** enables you to use many Google search features, not just the basic search. As of this writing, you can use the **Google Toolbar** to search through **Google Images**, **Google Groups**, **Froogle**, **Google News**, and your own computer using the **Google Desktop** if you have that installed. (For details about the **Google Desktop** and how to install it, see **34** Search Your PC with Google Desktop.) You can also use the **I'm Feeling Lucky** feature (for details, see **1** Perform a Basic Google Search). To search other Google sites using the **Google Toolbar**, type your search term, and then click the down arrow next to the **Search** button. Choose the kind of search you want to perform, and Google automatically performs that search.

52

52	**Block Pop-ups with the Pop-up Blocker**	
✔ **BEFORE YOU BEGIN**		→ **SEE ALSO**
51 Use the Google Toolbar to Search from Anywhere		**56** Customize the Google Toolbar

Among the countless things that drive most people crazy about the Internet are *pop-ups*, those annoying small ads in browser windows that appear when you visit certain websites. **Google Toolbar** includes a pop-up killer, so it's a great, free way to kill these ads. Here's how to use the **Google Toolbar**'s **Pop-up Blocker**.

▶ **KEY TERM**

Pop-ups—Small browser windows that pop up over your current web page when you visit certain websites. Pop-ups usually offer advertisements or other promotional material.

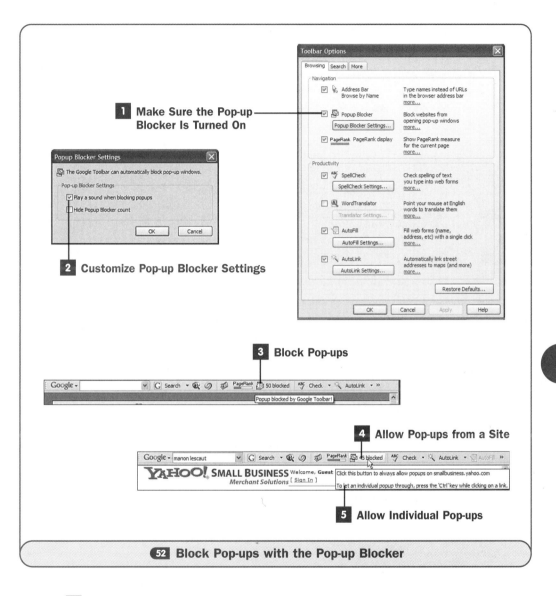

1 Make Sure the Pop-up Blocker Is Turned On

2 Customize Pop-up Blocker Settings

3 Block Pop-ups

4 Allow Pop-ups from a Site

5 Allow Individual Pop-ups

52 Block Pop-ups with the Pop-up Blocker

1 Make Sure the Pop-up Blocker Is Turned On

The **Pop-up Blocker** should be automatically turned on when you use the **Google Toolbar**. However, you might have accidentally turned it off, or it might be turned off for another reason. To turn it on, click the **Google** icon at the far left of the **Google Toolbar**, and choose **Options** from the menu that opens. From the **Toolbar Options** dialog box that appears, make sure that you are on the **Browsing** tab. Then check the box next to **Popup Blocker**.

2 **Customize Pop-up Blocker Settings**

You can control the behavior of the **Pop-up Blocker**. To do it, click the **Popup Blocker Settings** button in the **Toolbar Options** dialog box. To make the **Pop-up Blocker** play a sound whenever it blocks a pop-up, enable the **Play a sound when blocking popups** option. You can't change the sound Google plays when blocking pop-ups.

The **Pop-up Blocker** displays the number of pop-ups it has blocked. Whenever it blocks another pop-up, the number increases by one. If you don't want that number displayed, enable the **Hide Popup Blocker count** option.

When you're done, click **OK**.

3 **Block Pop-ups**

With the **Pop-up Blocker** turned on, you don't have to do anything to block pop-ups—the blocker automatically blocks pop-ups for you. When you visit a site that has a pop-up ad, you hear a click (if you've allowed sounds to play), and for a moment you get a message that the **Pop-up Blocker** has blocked a pop-up. The icon for the **Pop-up Blocker** changes and displays a red exclamation point inside a yellow starburst.

4 **Allow Pop-ups from a Site**

In some instances, you want pop-ups to be displayed. For example, some sites use pop-ups to give you extra information, such as more details about the site. To always allow pop-ups from a particular site, click the **Pop-up Blocker** icon in the **Google Toolbar**; from now on, the **Pop-up Blocker** allows all pop-ups from this site and also allows the last pop-up it blocked. To turn pop-ups off for the site, click the **Pop-up Blocker** icon again.

5 **Allow Individual Pop-ups**

Sometimes, a link leads to a pop-up, and you might want to let only that pop-up through—for example, if the link pops up a page in which you're interested. To allow that single pop-up, hold down the **Ctrl** key while clicking the link on the web page.

53

53	**Fill out Web Forms with AutoFill**	
✔ BEFORE YOU BEGIN		**→ SEE ALSO**
51 Use the Google Toolbar to Search from Anywhere		**56** Customize the Google Toolbar

Here's one more thing that drives many people crazy about the Internet—having to fill out web forms. You might have to fill them out when registering for a site or when buying at an online store. Having to retype the same information can get to be old very fast. The *AutoFill* feature from the **Google Toolbar** enables you to fill in any form automatically, with minimal, if any, typing.

▶ **KEY TERM**

AutoFill—A feature of the **Google Toolbar** that fills in web forms with text that you define.

1 Turn on AutoFill

The **AutoFill** feature should be automatically turned on when you use the **Google Toolbar**. However, you might have accidentally turned it off, or it might be turned off for another reason. To turn **AutoFill** on, click the **Google** icon at the far left of the **Google Toolbar** and choose **Options** from the menu that opens. On the **Toolbar Options** dialog box, make sure that you are on the **Browsing** tab. Then enable the **AutoFill** check box.

2 Enter Your Information into AutoFill

To fill in a form you encounter on the Internet with your information, you must first enter your personal information into **AutoFill**. Click the **AutoFill Settings** button on the **Toolbar Options** dialog box to open the **AutoFill Settings** dialog box. Fill in your personal information, including your name, email address, phone number, and mailing address.

You can add more than one address by selecting the **an alternate address** option, and clicking the **Add/Edit Alternate Address** button, filling out the form, and clicking **OK**. If you select **an alternate address** at the bottom of the **Primary Address** area, that alternate address is used when a page asks for a shipping address.

AutoFill can fill out many, but not all, pieces of information on web forms— for example, it does not fill in your income, social security number, and similar information. On any web form you want **AutoFill** to fill out for you, you can have **AutoFill** show you which fields of information it *can* fill out— enable the **Highlight fields on Web pages that AutoFill can update in yellow** check box in the **AutoFill Settings** dialog box.

When you're done making your selections, click **OK**.

53

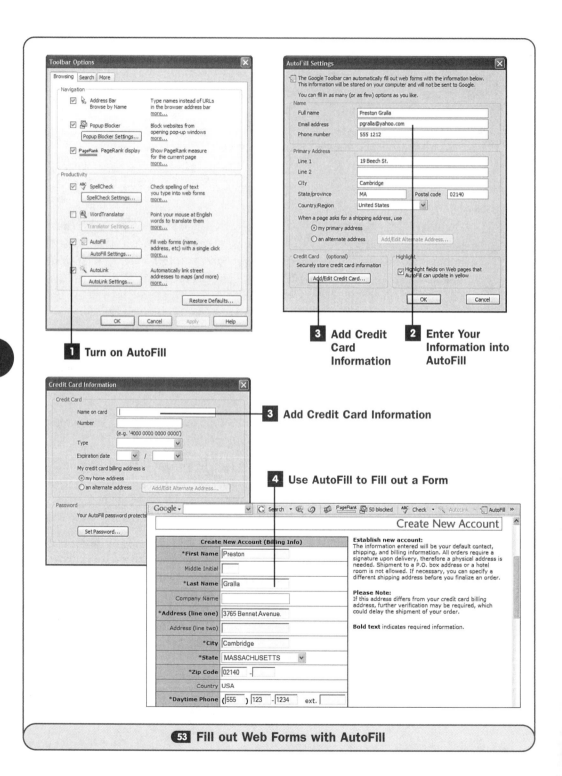

53

1 Turn on AutoFill

3 Add Credit Card Information

2 Enter Your Information into AutoFill

3 Add Credit Card Information

4 Use AutoFill to Fill out a Form

53 Fill out Web Forms with AutoFill

3 Add Credit Card Information

If you frequently buy online, you can speed things up by having AutoFill fill in your credit card information. In the **AutoFill Settings** dialog box, click the **Add/Edit Credit Card** button and then fill out the **Credit Card Information** dialog box that appears.

▶ **NOTE**

When you add your credit card information to **AutoFill**, anyone who uses your computer is able to buy online using your credit card information. Worse, they can *see* your credit card information. I recommend that you put your credit card information into **AutoFill** only if you are absolutely sure that no one will ever use your computer who might want to steal your credit card information. Furthermore, never use the credit card information feature of **AutoFill** on a laptop computer because a laptop can be easily stolen—along with your credit information.

Make sure you set a password so no one else can use your credit card information. When you go to a web page that has a field for your credit card, **AutoFill** asks for the password before it fills in the field. To create a password, click the **Set Password** button on the **Credit Card Information** dialog box, fill out the form, and click **OK** for each page that appears.

4 Use AutoFill to Fill out a Form

When you come to a web page with a form on it, the grayed-out **AutoFill** button on the **Google Toolbar** becomes colored. Fields on the form that AutoFill can fill out turn yellow. Click the **AutoFill** button to fill out the form.

54

---

54 Dig Deeper on Any Web Page with AutoLink

✔ BEFORE YOU BEGIN	→ SEE ALSO
51 Use the Google Toolbar to Search from Anywhere	**56** Customize the Google Toolbar

---

AutoLink is one of the more clever features of the **Google Toolbar**. It enables you to dig deeper into any page you're on and automatically creates links to information related to what's on the page. Specifically, it looks for addresses, books, and Vehicle Information Numbers (VINs) on any page it finds. It then creates links to each of those pieces of information that provide more data about the item, for example, showing you a map of any address on the page.

▶ **KEY TERM**

AutoLink—A feature of the **Google Toolbar** that automatically creates links on pages you visit so you can delve deeper into the information presented on the page.

1 **Make Sure AutoLink Is Turned On**

AutoLink should be automatically turned on when you use the **Google Toolbar**. However, you might have accidentally turned it off, or it might be turned off for another reason. To turn it on, click the **Google** icon at the far left of the **Google Toolbar** and choose **Options** from the menu. In the **Toolbar Options** dialog box that opens, make sure you are on the **Browsing** tab. Then enable the check box next to **AutoLink**.

2 **Customize AutoLink Settings**

To provide additional information about any link on the page, **AutoLink** needs to use information providers—services that provide maps, International Standard Book Number (ISBN) information, and VIN information. By default, **AutoLink** uses **Google Local** for maps, Amazon for ISBN information, and CarFax for VIN information. You can change those providers, though. To do this, click the **AutoLink Settings** button on the **Toolbar Options** dialog box. Then from the drop-down lists, choose the providers you want to use for maps, ISBN information, and VIN information.

You can also choose whether **AutoLinks** should be opened in new browser windows, or should instead be opened in the existing browser window. By default, **AutoLink** opens new links in the current window. To make the new pages of information open in a new window, enable the **Open AutoLinks in new window** check box.

When you're done, click **OK** to close the **AutoLink Settings** dialog box and return to the **Toolbar Options** dialog box. Click **OK** to close the **Toolbar Options** dialog box.

3 **Look for AutoLinks**

On any page you visit, click the **AutoLink** icon in the **Google Toolbar**. (It's the icon of a magic wand, and is labeled **AutoLink**.) If an **AutoLink** cannot be created for information on the page, you get the message **No items found**.

If a link or links *is* found, you get a message telling you how many links were found, and the links are created on the page itself as well as displayed in the **Google Toolbar**. In addition, the **AutoLink** text changes to reflect the links it found—for example, the link **Look for Map** appears next to the magic wand icon if **AutoLink** found a map. When you click the **Look for Map** link (or any of the other **AutoLinks**), you are sent to the place on the page where the link was created.

54

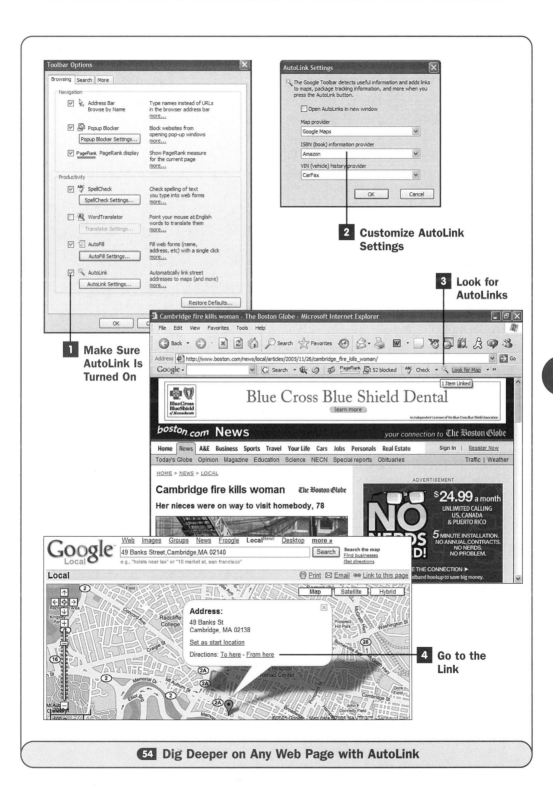

2 Customize AutoLink Settings

3 Look for AutoLinks

1 Make Sure AutoLink Is Turned On

4 Go to the Link

54 Dig Deeper on Any Web Page with AutoLink

4 Go to the Link

The **AutoLink** works like any other link: it's highlighted in blue on the page as well as underlined, and when you hold your mouse over the link, you see a ToolTip that explains it's an AutoLink. Click it to get more information. For example, when you click a map **AutoLink**, you are sent to a map of the location.

55	About PageRank
✔ **BEFORE YOU BEGIN**	→ **SEE ALSO**
51 Use the Google Toolbar to Search from Anywhere	56 Customize the Google Toolbar

PageRank is one of those small features that you either love or hate—there's rarely any in-between. What it does is incredibly simple: It provides a rank for the page you're visiting on a 1–10 point basis, with 10 as the top choice. The ranking is of a site's "importance," which is a measure of a site's popularity, as well as whether Google considers the site to be highly important.

55

▶ **KEY TERM**

PageRank—A Google feature that ranks the importance of the page you're currently visiting on a 1–10 point basis, with 10 as the top choice.

Whenever you go to a site, the bar associated with the **PageRank** icon in the **Google Toolbar,** shown in the nearby figure, changes. The further it moves to the right, the more highly ranked is the page. To see the exact ranking, hover your mouse pointer over the icon.

Google's PageRank result for the Yahoo! web page.

Don't try to figure out how Google decides on its **PageRank**—you'll never be able to do it. That's because **PageRank** goes to the very heart of how Google delivers search results, and so is made up of exceedingly complex algorithms that constantly change. Those algorithms are a closely guarded secret because when you do a Google search, Google takes into account the **PageRank** of the results it finds when deciding what results to show to you.

So what use is **PageRank** to mere humans? It can help you determine whether the site you're on is reputable, and so can help you determine whether to trust information you find on the page. If the site has a low **PageRank**, you should trust it less than if it has a high one.

To learn how to turn **PageRank** on or off, see **56** **Customize the Google Toolbar**.

---

56 | **Customize the Google Toolbar**

✔ BEFORE YOU BEGIN	→ SEE ALSO
51 Use the Google Toolbar to Search from Anywhere	**52** Block Pop-ups with the Pop-up Blocker
	53 Fill out Web Forms with AutoFill
	54 Dig Deeper on Any Web Page with AutoLink
	55 About PageRank

The **Google Toolbar** offers many services and features—and many ways to customize them. Because it's so complex, you can change how the **Google Toolbar** looks and works, and that's what you'll learn to do in this task.

56

1 Go to the Toolbar Options Dialog Box

You customize the **Google Toolbar** from the **Toolbar Options** dialog box. To get there, click the **Google** icon at the far left of the **Google Toolbar** and choose **Options** from the menu.

The **Toolbar Options** dialog box opens, with three tabs on it—**Browsing**, **Search**, and **More**.

2 Customize the Browsing Tab

The **Browsing** tab is divided into two sections: **Navigation** and **Productivity**.

In the **Navigation** section, check the box next to **Address Bar Browse by Name** if you want to be able to type the *name* of a website, rather than the entire URL, into the browser's **Address** bar to visit the site. For example, if you wanted to visit www.amazon.com, you could type in **Amazon** instead of **www.amazon.com**.

For details about customizing the **Pop-up Blocker**, see **52** **Block Pop-ups with the Pop-up Blocker**. To turn on the **PageRank** display, check the box next to **PageRank display** (as explained in **55** **About PageRank**).

1 Go to the Toolbar Options Dialog Box

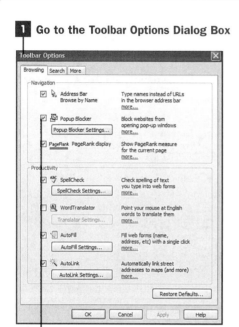

56

2 Customize the Browsing Tab

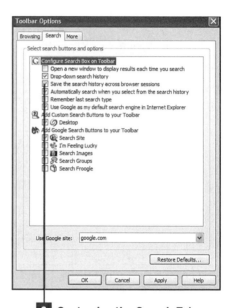

3 Customize the Search Tab

4 Customize the More Tab

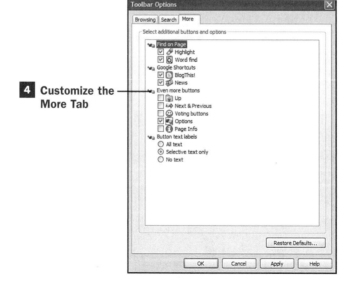

56 Customize the Google Toolbar

In the **Productivity** section, check the box next to **SpellCheck** if you want the **Google Toolbar** to check your spelling when you fill out web forms. To customize how it checks spelling—for example, whether it should ignore words in all capital letters—click the **SpellCheck Settings** button and fill out the dialog box that appears.

Also in the **Productivity** section, check the box next to **WordTranslator** if you want to be able to hold your mouse over an English word on any web page and translate it into other languages, including Spanish, German, Italian, French, Korean, Japanese, Traditional Chinese, and Simplified Chinese. Click the **Translator Settings** button and choose the language into which you want words translated.

For details about the **AutoFill** feature, see **53** **Fill out Web Forms with AutoFill**. For details about **AutoLink**, see **54** **Dig Deeper on Any Web Page with AutoLink**.

3 Customize the Search Tab

The **Search** tab of the **Toolbar Options** dialog box enables you to customize how the **Google Toolbar** performs searches, and what buttons to add to your toolbar. The top section of the tab controls how searches should work—for example, whether to open a new window to display search results, whether Google should remember the last search you typed, and so on. This section is self-explanatory, so check the boxes next to the search functions you want to use.

The bottom section enables you to add various search buttons to your toolbar, such as buttons for searching through the current site, for searching through Google Images, and so on. Check the boxes next to the buttons that you want to be displayed on the **Google Toolbar**.

▶ **NOTE**

If you'd like, you can have the **Google Toolbar** perform a search using a different search engine than Google's normal one. You can instead use any of the dozens of Google search sites from all over the world, from obvious places such as the Italy Google site to less well-known ones such as the Google Uzbekistan site. To choose a different search engine, choose it from the **Use Google site** drop-down list at the bottom of the **Search** tab.

4 Customize the More Tab

The **More** tab of the **Toolbar Options** dialog box enables you to customize a variety of features. The **Find on Page** section enables you to decide how the **Google Toolbar** should perform searches on the page on which you are currently located. Check the box next to **Word find** if you want an icon to

56

appear on the **Google Toolbar** which enables you to search for a word on the current page. Check the box next to **Highlight** if you want the word you're searching for to be highlighted when you search for it on the page.

The **Google Shortcuts** section enables you to put buttons on the **Google Toolbar** that allow you to use other Google features. Enable the **Blog This!** check box if you want the **Blog This!** button to appear on the **Google Toolbar**. When you click the **Blog This!** button, you can write a blog about the current page and have it appear on your **Blogger** blog. For details, see **82 Power Up Your Blogging with Blogger Add-ins**. Enable the **News** check box to display a **News** button on the **Google Toolbar**; click the **News** button to go straight to **Google News**.

The **Even more buttons** section enables you to put a variety of buttons on the **Google Toolbar**, as listed here. Check the boxes next to the buttons you want to appear in the **Google Toolbar**.

- **Up** brings you up a level on the domain in which you are currently. For example, if you were on the www.samspublishing.com/articles/article.asp?p=426767 page and you clicked the **Up** button, you would be sent to www.samspublishing.com/articles/. Click the **Up** button again, and you would go to www.samspublishing.com.

- **Next & Previous** bring you to the next page and the previous page you've visited.

- **Voting** buttons enable you to tell Google whether you think the page you are on is a good one or a bad one. Google uses this information when figuring out its **PageRanks**.

- **Options** enables you to jump to the **Toolbar Options** dialog box directly, without having to click the **Google** icon and select **Options** from the menu.

- **Page Info**, when clicked, provides more information about the current web page, such as showing what other pages are similar to the one you are currently viewing.

Finally, the **Button text labels** section enables you to decide whether the **Google Toolbar** buttons should display without text (that is, appear just as an icon), display all the text associated with each button, or display only the selected text that Google thinks is most applicable.

When you're done making choices on the **Toolbar Options** dialog box, click **OK** to put your choices into immediate effect.

56

10

Using Gmail, the Best Email on Earth

IN THIS CHAPTER:

Many people believe that *Gmail*, Google's email service, is the best email service on earth. To begin with, it offers what seems like an unlimited amount of storage—two gigabytes as of this writing, and possibly more being added as you read this.

▶ KEY TERM

Gmail—Google's email service, which you use by going to the Google **Gmail** page.

In addition to storage, **Gmail** has another benefit—it enables you to search through email using Google's search tools. Considering that most of us have serious problems finding specific email messages from a week ago, a month ago, or more, this search feature is a significant benefit. In addition, you can read your mail on the Web with **Gmail**, or you can read your mail with normal email software, such as Outlook or Outlook Express.

For all these reasons, even if you already have an email account, it's worthwhile getting a **Gmail** account as well—especially because it's free.

57

57 Set Up a Gmail Account

✔ BEFORE YOU BEGIN	→ SEE ALSO
67 About Gmail and Privacy	**58** Compose and Send Mail
	59 Read Mail and Attachments

Before you can use **Gmail**, you must first set up a **Gmail** account. **Gmail** has been in beta testing for a significant amount of time and is still in beta as of this writing. As explained in Chapter 1, "Start Here," however, that doesn't really mean that much because Google frequently keeps its services in beta for long periods of time, sometimes more than a year.

However, with **Gmail**, there's one more twist to things—as of this writing, the only way to set up a **Gmail** account is to receive an invitation from a **Gmail** user. That might change by the time you read this, but if it hasn't and you want a **Gmail** account, you should ask everyone you know if they have one, and ask them to send you an invitation.

1 Ask a Friend for an Invitation

In order to get **Gmail** as of this writing, you have to first be invited by someone who already has a **Gmail** account. (By the time you read this, that might have changed.) The person with an existing **Gmail** account has to

enter your name in the **Invite a friend** box on her **Gmail** inbox page, and
click **Send Invite**. You, of course, have to have an existing email account for
her to send you mail.

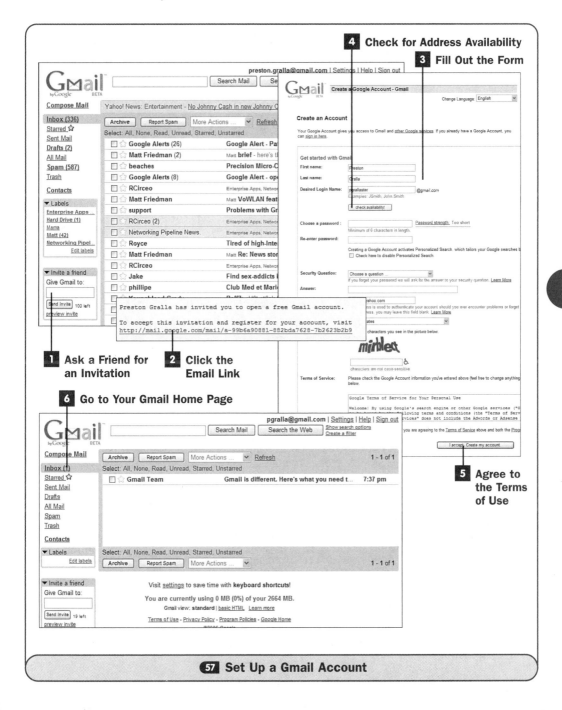

4 Check for Address Availability

3 Fill Out the Form

1 Ask a Friend for an Invitation

2 Click the Email Link

6 Go to Your Gmail Home Page

5 Agree to the Terms of Use

57

▶ **TIP**

You can also sign up for **Gmail** by using your cell phone. Make sure your cell phone is turned on. Go to www.gmail.com, and click on the **Sign up for Gmail using your mobile phone** link in the lower-right corner. Enter your cell phone number in the **Mobile phone number** text box, type the odd-looking characters into the next text box, and click **Send code**. In a few moments you receive a text message on your cell phone. Read the message, enter your invitation code into the **Invitation code** text box, and click **Next**. The **Create an Account** page appears. You can now follow the instructions of step 3 and onward of this task.

2 **Click the Email Link**

Your invitation is sent to your current email address. In the invitation is a link you can click to accept the invitation and set up your account. Click the link, and your browser launches, bringing you to a Google site that enables you to set up your account.

3 **Fill Out the Form**

On the form that appears, fill in your first and last names, your desired login name, an existing email address that can be used if your **Gmail** account doesn't work and Google has to get in touch with you, and similar information. Pay particular attention to the security question because if you forget your password, Google requires that you answer the security question properly before it provides you with your password.

4 **Check for Address Availability**

After you fill out the form, you should check whether the email address you want to use is available. What Google calls your **Login name** is also your email address that you'll give out to people. So after you fill in the **Designed Login Name** field, click the **check availability!** button.

▶ **TIP**

If you already have a Google account when you register for **Gmail**, the Google username you use to log into your account is changed from your old Google name to your new **Gmail** login. For example, if your existing Google username was **johnsmith@joesmith.com** and your **Gmail** log in is **john.smith@google.com**, your Google username is changed to **john.smith@google.com**. You get an email from Google alerting you to the change.

If the email address you specified is available, just below the **check availability!** button you see a message telling you that it is available. If it's not available, you get a message telling you that it's not available and suggesting other similar names that *are* available. Choose one of those alternatives,

57

or type another email address and click the **check availability!** button until you find an available name that you want.

5 Agree to the Terms of Use

At the bottom of the page are links to Google's terms of use and related policies. Click those links to read the policies. If you agree with them, click the **I have read and agree to the Terms of Use. Start using Gmail** button. If you don't agree with the terms of use, you are not able to open a **Gmail** account.

6 Go to Your Gmail Home Page

After you agree to the terms of use, you come to a page outlining the basics of how to use **Gmail**. Skim through the page, and then click **I'm Ready - show me my account** and you'll be sent to your **Gmail** inbox.

There is an email from the **Gmail** team, welcoming you to **Gmail**; this email message has links to more information about **Gmail**. Read the email, and click any links in the message that interest you.

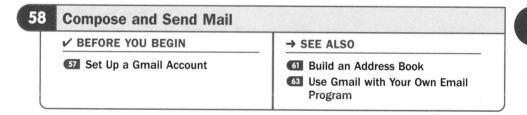

58	**Compose and Send Mail**
✔ **BEFORE YOU BEGIN**	→ **SEE ALSO**
57 Set Up a Gmail Account	**61** Build an Address Book
	63 Use Gmail with Your Own Email Program

Composing and sending mail with **Gmail** is quite straightforward—and despite its ease, you'll find that it includes all the features you've come to expect from a piece of email software on your PC, such as Outlook, as you'll see in this task.

1 Click Compose Mail

Log into your **Gmail** account by going to www.gmail.com and typing your username and password. Then in the upper-left corner, click the **Compose Mail** link.

2 Compose Your Message

The **From:** field is already filled in with your **Gmail** address. Type the email address of the recipient in the **To:** field. As you type, **Gmail** looks through people to whom you've sent a message, and pops up their addresses. For example, if you've already sent messages to Angelina@ballerina.com and Angryboy@big.isp.com, when you type the letter A, both those addresses pop up. To choose either one, scroll to it to select it and press **Enter**.

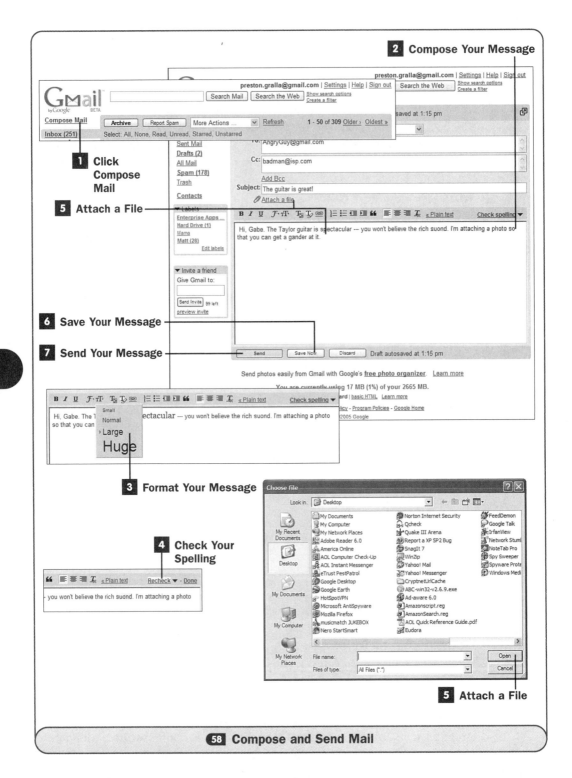

2 Compose Your Message

1 Click Compose Mail

5 Attach a File

6 Save Your Message

7 Send Your Message

3 Format Your Message

4 Check Your Spelling

5 Attach a File

58

58 Compose and Send Mail

As you keep typing, fewer matches appear. In this example, if you typed **Angel**, only the Angelina@ballerina.com address would appear for you to select.

If no address appears, type the complete email address in the **To:** field. If you're going to send the mail to multiple people, type in all their addresses, separated by commas. (See **61** **Build an Address Book** for details about how to build an address book in **Gmail**.)

You can also send copies of the message to others by clicking the **Add Cc** link, and filling in the email address of the person you want to copy on the email. And you can also send a blind copy to someone by clicking the **Add Bcc** link and filling in the email address of the person. For a blind copy, no one except you sees the address in the blind copy field.

▶ **NOTE**

Many people consider blind copies to be in bad form. They believe that it is inherently deceitful not to let people know that other people are getting and reading the email. (Using blind copies might also trigger spam filters that cause your mail to be considered spam.) Others say that is presents no problem at all. So decide for yourself whether to use the feature.

58

Make sure to enter the subject of your message in the **Subject** text box. Then, in the large text box, type the body of your email message. This is where you type the main text of the memo or letter.

3 Format Your Message

Google enables you to format the text of your message—you can change fonts, colors, make bulleted and numbered lists, and so on. To do it, use the formatting toolbar at the top of the large message text box. Highlight the text you want to format and then choose the appropriate tool from the toolbar.

Keep in mind, though, that only recipients who use an email program that reads HTML are able to see the formatting. Also, some people turn off HTML in their email, so even if they have software that can read HTML, they might not be able to see the formatting you apply.

If you'd prefer that your mail message contains only plain text and not have any formatting, click the **Plain text** link in the formatting toolbar. This option affects just this email message, and not all the email messages you send.

4 Check Your Spelling

An email message represents who you are to the world, so you want to make sure it goes out without spelling errors. To check your spelling, click the **Check spelling** link in the formatting toolbar above the main message text box. **Gmail** highlights any words that it considers misspelled. But as of this writing, it doesn't actually correct those misspellings, so you'll have to make the change yourself. After you make the spelling changes, click the **Recheck** link to make sure you've corrected the words properly. When all errors have been corrected, you'll receive the message **No misspellings found**.

5 Attach a File

To attach a file to a message, click the **Attach a file** link. The **Choose file** dialog box appears. Navigate to the file you want to attach, highlight it, and click **Open**. The filename appears beneath the **Subject** line in the header area of your message. Click **Attach another file** if you want to attach more than one file. Click the **Remove** link to remove a file. After about 30 seconds, the **Remove** link disappears, and you see a message box with the filename and a check box. To remove the file, disable the check box.

6 Save Your Message

If you don't want to send the message yet but want to save it for later, click the **Save Now** button at the top or the bottom of the screen. The message shows up in your **Drafts** folder, which you can access by clicking the **Drafts** link on the left side of the screen. If you want to discard the message without saving or sending it, click **Discard**.

7 Send Your Message

When you're ready to send the message, click the **Send** button. The message is sent to all the email addresses listed in the **To:**, **Cc:**, and **Bcc:** fields. A copy of the message is saved in your **Sent Mail** folder.

---

59 | Read Mail and Attachments

✔ BEFORE YOU BEGIN	→ SEE ALSO
57 Set Up a Gmail Account	60 Search Through Your Mail
58 Compose and Send Mail	62 Manage Your Mail with Labels and Filters

59

It's exceedingly easy to read your email in **Gmail**—and it might even be easier to read it in **Gmail** than in your regular email program, because **Gmail** is simpler to use than most email software. Here's how to do it.

▊1 Go to Your Inbox

After you log on to **Gmail**, click the **Inbox** link on the left side of the screen. Next to the link is a number in parentheses; this is the total number of messages in your inbox. When you get to your inbox, any messages you haven't yet read are in boldface.

For each email message listed in your inbox, you are able to see the sender, the subject, the first several words of the message, and the date the message was received (as well as the time, if the message was received today). Any messages that have attachments have a paperclip icon next to the date or time.

▶ NOTE

When you get an important message, click the **star** next to it. A yellow star appears next to the message to remind you that there's something special about this message. In addition to remaining in your inbox, all starred messages also show up in the **Starred** folder, which you can get to by clicking the **Starred** link just underneath the **Inbox** link on the left side of the page.

59

▊2 Read a Message

Click a message to read it. You see the text of the message, and if a picture has been attached, you can see a thumbnail of the picture attachment. If the attachment is a **.doc** file, you see a Microsoft Word icon; if it's a **.pdf** file, you see an Adobe Acrobat icon; and if it's a text file, you see an icon of a sheet of paper.

▊3 View and Download the Attachment

If there is an attachment to the email message you're viewing, you see the attachment name and size. To view the attachment, click the **View** link; the attachment opens in a new window in a viewer, if the file is viewable. To download the attachment to your PC, click the **Download** link next to the attachment. When the **File Download** dialog box opens, click **Save** to save the file to your PC's hard drive.

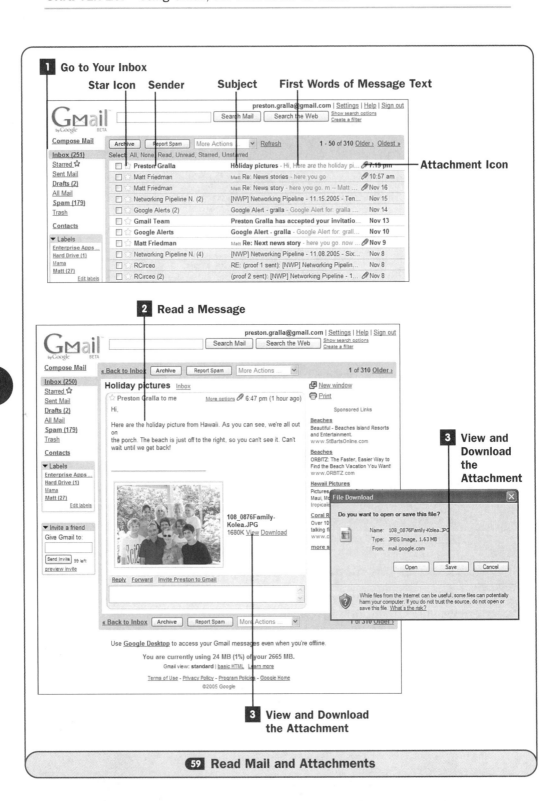

1 Go to Your Inbox

Star Icon   Sender   Subject   First Words of Message Text

Attachment Icon

2 Read a Message

3 View and Download the Attachment

3 View and Download the Attachment

59

5 Display and Use Options

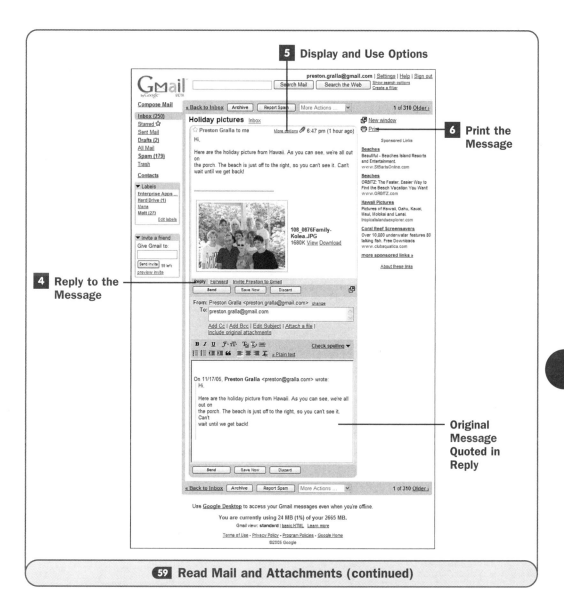

6 Print the Message

4 Reply to the Message

Original Message Quoted in Reply

59 Read Mail and Attachments (continued)

▶ **NOTE**

Gmail lacks one very useful feature—a simple **Delete** button. If you want to delete mail, first you have to select the message, and then select **Delete**. That command won't delete the message, though; it only puts it in the **Trash** folder. You then have to click the **Trash** link on the left side of the page, enable the check boxes next to each message you want to permanently delete, and then click the **Delete Forever** button. However, if you use the Firefox browser, you can put a **Delete** button right on the **Gmail** inbox, saving you all those steps. To do this, you must install a program called Greasemonkey and then use a special Greasemonkey script. For details, go to www.arantius.com/article/arantius/gmail+delete+button/.

4 Reply to the Message

To reply to the message, click the **Reply** link at bottom of the page. You are able to see the message you're responding to, above where you type your reply message. The message text box automatically quotes the complete text of the original message, but you can delete that text if you want. Click **Send** when you want to send the mail.

To forward the message to a new person, click the **Forward** link and fill in the email address of the person to whom you want to send the message.

5 Display and Use Options

You can do much more than just respond to an email message. You can trash it, or add the sender to your contact list (also called an address book), among other options. To see these options, click the **More Actions** drop-down menu at the top of the original message. Then choose the action you want to take. You can take any of these actions:

- **Mark as read**—Marks the message as being read.
- **Mark as unread**—Marks the message as unread.
- **Add star**—Stars the message as important.
- **Remove star**—Removes the star.
- **Delete**—Moves the message to the trash.
- **Apply label**—Applies a label to the message so you can more easily manage the message. (For details, see **62 Manage Your Mail with Labels and Filters**.)

6 Print the Message

With the message opened, click the **Print** link on the right side of the screen. The message prints to your default printer.

---

60 Search Through Your Mail

✔ BEFORE YOU BEGIN	→ SEE ALSO
1 Perform a Basic Google Search	**62** Manage Your Mail with Labels and Filters
6 About Google Search Operators	
59 Read Mail and Attachments	

One of the best reasons for using **Gmail** is that you can use Google's search technology to find mail fast. It's far superior to the searching you can do with your normal email software. And as you'll see in this task, in addition to normal Google searching, you can do email-specific searches, such as on the date you received the mail.

1 Do a Basic Search

From the main **Gmail** page at www.gmail.com, type in your search terms and click **Search Mail**. Note that you can use all the search tips and operators you use when searching the Web with Google (for details, see **1** **Perform a Basic Google Search** and **6** **About Google Search Operators**).

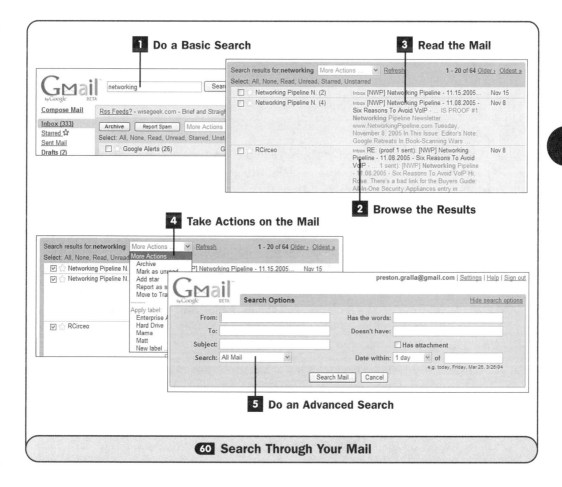

2 Browse the Results

After **Gmail** does the search, it presents a page or pages of results, listing the emails that match your search terms. For each piece of mail, you see who sent the mail, in what folder the mail is found, the subject line of the mail, the date the mail was sent or received, and the first several lines of the mail message.

▶ **NOTE**

Keep in mind that when you do a search, you search through *all* your email, including mail you've sent as well as mail you've received.

3 Read the Mail

To read any of the email messages listed in the results page, click the message. You read it in **Gmail**, just as you would read any other email message, and can do anything you normally could with the email, such as replying to it or forwarding it.

4 Take Actions on the Mail

You can perform actions on the mail you find—and not just to one piece of mail, but to groups of messages. Check the box next to every piece of mail on which you want to perform an action. Then click the **More Actions** drop-down menu, and choose which action to take:

- **Archive**—This option moves the mail out of your inbox. The messages aren't visible in your inbox, but they still live on **Gmail** and so can be found if you search for them. (For more information, see 62 **Manage Your Mail with Labels and Filters**.)

- **Mark as unread**—If you've read the mail but want it to show up in your inbox as unread, choose this option. If you've not yet read the message, this option is **Mark as read**.

- **Add star**—This option adds a star to the selected mail messages. (You can use the star symbol to identify messages that have importance to you for some reason.) In addition to a star showing up next to the messages in the inbox, the starred mail appears in the **Starred** mail folder.

- **Report as spam**—This option reports the message as spam to the **Gmail** spam filter, which helps **Gmail** determine in the future which messages are spam and which aren't.

60

- **Move to Trash**—This option moves the selected mail messages to the trash.

- **Apply label**—This option applies a label to the selected mail messages so the mail appears in a folder with that label. Note that the mail also remains in your inbox, and so is available in your inbox as well as in the labeled folder (see **62** **Manage Your Mail with Labels and Filters** for more information about labels).

5 Do an Advanced Search

Gmail offers a search option that has features specifically suited for email, such as being able to search by terms in the subject line, by the sender, and so on. At the top of the **Gmail** main page, to the right of the **Search the Web** button, click the **Show search options** link to display a **Search Options** page that enables you to search by sender, recipient, subject, date, and whether the mail has an attachment. You can also search for mail in only specific folders, and you can search for specific words—or you can search for mail that *doesn't* have specific words. When you're done typing your search terms, click the **Search Mail** button, and **Gmail** searches your mail. The results appear as they do for a standard email search, and you can perform any of the actions described in step 4 on the messages you find. The following is more information on the search fields:

- **From**—Type the email address of the person who sent you the mail message for which you are looking.

- **To**—Type the email address of the person to whom you sent the mail message for which you are looking.

- **Subject**—Type a word or phrase that exists in the subject line of the email message you sent or received.

- **Has the words**—Type a word that is found anywhere in the message.

- **Doesn't have**—Type a word that you *don't* want to be found in the message. To be effective, combine the **Doesn't have** option with other search fields.

- **Has attachment**—Enable this check box if the email message you are looking for has an attachment.

- **Date within**—Enables you to set the dates within which the message was sent.

60

61   Build an Address Book

✔ **BEFORE YOU BEGIN**

  58 Compose and Send Mail
  59 Read Mail and Attachments

Any good email program includes an address book, a list of people with whom you correspond. **Gmail** includes a very useful, lean address book, as you'll see in this task. The address book contains, at a minimum, the email addresses of those people with whom you correspond, and can contain much more information as well, such as phone numbers, physical addresses, and freeform text.

61

1   Check Your Contacts

Gmail calls your address book your **Contacts**, and the moment you start using **Gmail**, your **Contacts** begin to fill up. As you read and send messages, **Gmail** automatically adds names and addresses to your **Contacts**, without you having to do anything. To see your **Contacts**, click the **Contacts** link on the left side of the main **Gmail** page.

There are two links on the page—**Frequently Mailed** and **All Contacts**. Click the **All Contacts** link to see a list of everyone with whom you've exchanged email; click the **Frequently Mailed** link to see a list of only those people with whom you more frequently correspond.

2   Add Information About a Contact

Gmail automatically enters the email addresses of people with whom you communicate via email into your **Contacts**, but all it includes is the person's name and email address. You can, however, add more information about a person in your **Contacts** list, including address, phone number, and similar information.

In the **Frequently Mailed** or **All Contacts** list, click the contact for whom you want to supply more information. A page that includes more information than just the contact's email address opens. If **Gmail** could not determine anything about the contact other than the email address (that is, if this page contains no more information), click the **edit contact information** link to open the **Edit Contact** page. Type the person's name and add any relevant notes.

If you want to add more information about this contact, such as phone numbers and address, click **Add more contact information** and fill out the form.

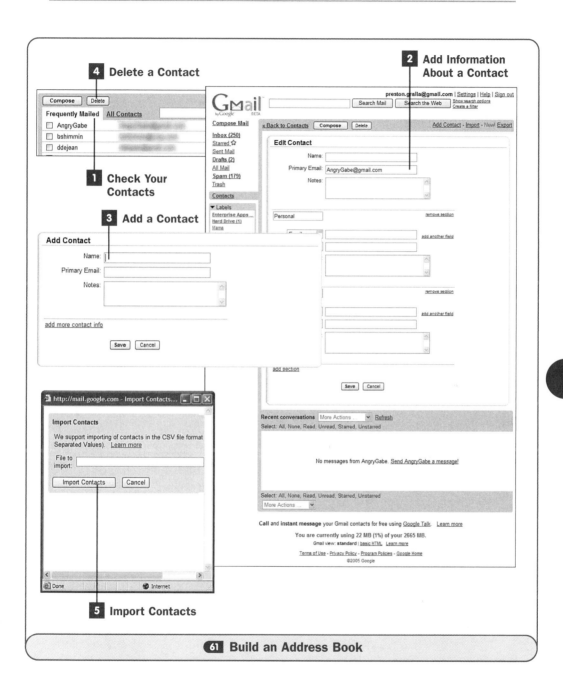

4 Delete a Contact

2 Add Information About a Contact

1 Check Your Contacts

3 Add a Contact

5 Import Contacts

61

61 Build an Address Book

Each contact form is made up of several sections; each section has a label (such as **Personal** or **Work**) and fields for email, phone, and address information. You can add an entire new section to the form by clicking the **add**

section link at the bottom of the form. To remove a section, click the **remove section** in the upper-right corner of the section you want to delete.

When you're done editing information about this contact, click the **Save** button. The contact is saved in your **Contacts** list, which is sorted alphabetically by first name or first letter of the email address. After you save the contact, you stay on the contact page.

▶ **NOTE**

At the bottom of the page of information about a contact is a list of all the recent email you've exchanged with this contact. It's a great way to get a quick review of recent conversations you've had with the contact.

3 Add a Contact

You don't have to wait to receive an email from someone or send an email to someone to add a contact to your **Contacts** list. To do it, click the **Contacts** link on the left side of any **Gmail** page, click the **Add Contact** link at the top of the list of contacts, and fill out the **Add Contact** form. If you want to add more information about this contact, click the **add more contact info** link and refer to step 2. When you're done filling in information about this contact, click **Save**.

4 Delete a Contact

To delete a contact, click the **Contacts** link on the left side of any **Gmail** page and click to display the **Frequently Mailed** or **All Contacts** list. Enable the check box next to each contact you want to delete and click the **Delete** button above and to the left of the list of contacts. Confirm the deletion to permanently delete the contact from the **Frequently Mailed** list and also from the **All Contacts** list.

5 Import Contacts

If you already have an email program, you probably have an address book in it. Your existing address book contains the email addresses of people you will want to communicate with using **Gmail**. If you'd like, you can import your existing address book and have all the entries in it show up in your **Gmail Contacts** list. Importing an existing address book is a two-stage process: First you export your contacts from your existing email program into what's called a comma-separated values (CSV) formatted file, and then you import that CSV file into **Gmail**.

How you export your address book from your old email program varies according to your email software. In Outlook, choose **File**, **Import and**

61

Export to launch the **Import and Export Wizard**. Choose **Export to a file**, click **Next**, and from the screen that appears, choose **Comma Separated Values (Windows)**. From the next screen, choose your contacts folder (the folder to which you want to save the file you're creating).

On the next screen, give the CSV file you're about to create a name (the **.csv** file extension is automatically added to the filename you specify here), browse to the folder where you want to save the file, click **Next**, and then click **Finish**. Outlook exports the information in its address book to a CSV-formatted file, with the filename and location you specified.

Now that the CSV file is ready, go to **Gmail** and click the **Contacts** link on the left side of the page. Then click the **Import** link at the top of the page. The **Import Contacts** window pops up. Type in the full path of the .csv file and its name (the directory information for the folder in which you saved the CSV file as well as the filename you specified), such as **C:\GContacts\ mycontacts.csv**. Then click **Import Contacts**. After a minute or more, depending on the speed of your Internet connection and how many contacts you're importing, you receive a message telling you that your contacts have been imported and listing the total number of contacts you've imported. Click the **Close** button. The address book entries from your old email application are now available in **Gmail**. To see them, click the **All Contacts** link at the top of the **Contacts** screen.

62

▶ NOTE

You can also export your contacts from **Gmail** to another email program. To do this, click the **Export** link located at the top of the **Contacts** list in the **Contacts** screen. From the screen that appears, choose to export your address book entries to **Outlook CSV** if you're going to import them into Outlook or another email program, or choose **Gmail CSV** if you're going to import your address book entries to another **Gmail** account. After you save the CSV file, you can then import it into your other email program (read the email program's documentation for details on how to do so). To import the CSV file into another **Gmail** account, follow the instructions in this step.

---

62 **Manage Your Mail with Labels and Filters**

✔ BEFORE YOU BEGIN	→ SEE ALSO
58 Compose and Send Mail	**60** Search Through Your Mail

What's the biggest problem that most people have with their email? Managing it. Many of us live in email, and we send and receive hundreds of messages a day.

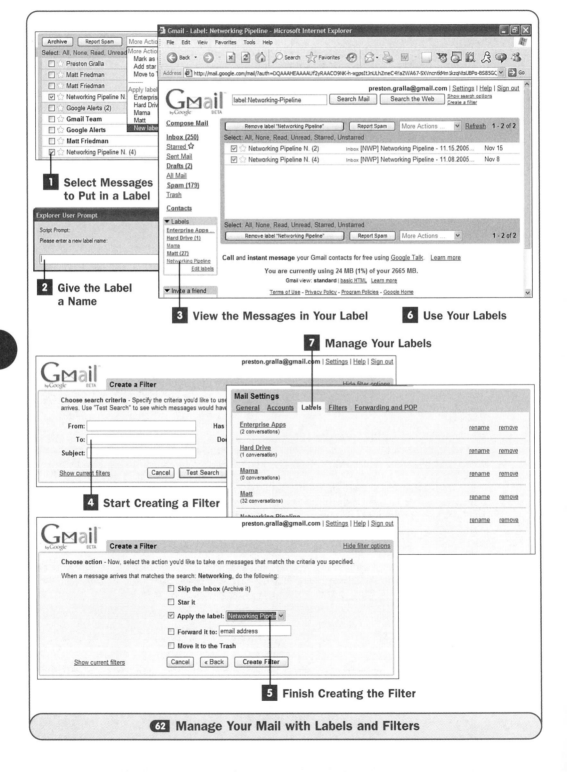

1 Select Messages to Put in a Label

2 Give the Label a Name

3 View the Messages in Your Label

6 Use Your Labels

7 Manage Your Labels

4 Start Creating a Filter

5 Finish Creating the Filter

62 Manage Your Mail with Labels and Filters

To help you control it all in **Gmail**, you use what **Gmail** calls *labels* and *filters*. Here's one area where **Gmail** is more confusing than most email programs because it's not obvious how to use these features. So follow the steps in this task to master them.

▶ KEY TERMS

Labels (Gmail)—A way to organize your mail in **Gmail**. Labels function much like folders in email programs.

Filters—A rule that is applied to incoming mail—for example, to move it to a certain label.

1 Select Messages to Put in a Label

Labels in **Gmail** are used much like folders are used in email programs such as Outlook—you use labels to organize your mail. One difference between **Gmail** and other mail programs, however, is that a single piece of mail can show up in many labels, as well as in your inbox. Think of each label as a particular search; email in that label matches certain search terms.

To create a label, enable the check boxes next to the messages in your inbox that you want to be put into the label you're about to create. To create a label for the messages, select **New label** from the **More Actions** drop-down menu.

2 Give the Label a Name

In the **Please enter a new label name** text box that pops up, type a name for the label and click **OK**. The label is created and you receive a notice at the top of your inbox telling you that your label has been created and how many email messages (which **Gmail** calls *conversations*) are in the label.

3 View the Messages in Your Label

To view the messages in your label, click the **Labels** link on the left side of the **Gmail** page to see a list of all the labels you've created; then click the name of the label you want to view. You see all the messages contained in that label. Each message has a check box next to it; you can take actions on the messages by choosing the desired action from the **More Actions** drop-down menu.

4 Start Creating a Filter

When you create a label, you're essentially creating a placeholder. The label contains the messages you've told **Gmail** to put into it. But no new incoming

62

messages are automatically included in the label, even if those messages have the same subject lines or sender information as other messages in the label (all incoming mail, by default, appears only in the inbox).

You can, however, create a filter that automatically places appropriate incoming messages in a specific label. A filter is essentially a rule that is applied to all incoming messages; the filter tells **Gmail** how to handle specific messages. You can create a filter to tell **Gmail** to make certain messages appear in certain labels. You can, for example, create a label named **Mother** and then have all incoming messages from your mom show up in that label.

To create a filter, click the **Create a filter** link at the top of the main **Gmail** page (to the right of the **Search the Web** button). From the page that appears, tell **Gmail** what information it should filter on. You can tell it to create a filter based on the subject's email address, on the email address to whom the email is being sent, on the subject line, on whether the incoming email message has an attachment, whether it has certain words, and whether it doesn't have certain words. When you're done filling out the criteria for filtering incoming email messages, click **Next Step**.

62 ▶ **NOTE**

If you want to see what results the filter criteria you have specified will create, click **Test Search** before you click **Next Step**. You'll then see what messages in your inbox will be filtered.

5 Finish Creating the Filter

The next page of the filter-creation process enables you to tell **Gmail** what action to perform on the filtered mail. You can select multiple actions so the filter can perform multiple actions on the filtered mail.

Enable the check boxes next to each action you want the filter to take. You can have the filter skip the inbox; star the message (that is, enable the star icon next to the message in the inbox to identify the message as having some significance); have the mail show up in a certain label (you can choose from the list of labels you have already created, as explained in steps 1–3); forward the message to another email address; or move the filtered mail to the trash. When you're done specifying the actions to be taken on the filtered mail, click the **Create Filter** button.

The **Mail Settings** page opens to the **Filters** tab, which shows all the filters currently in use. (You can also access this page by clicking the **Settings** link in the top-right corner of the main **Gmail** page.) From the **Filters** tab, you can edit any of the filters, delete any filters, and create a new filter.

6 Use Your Labels

To see all the messages contained in any label, click the **Labels** link on the left side of the **Gmail** page to display a list of all the labels you've created. Click the name of the label for which you want to view messages. You can then take the normal actions on those messages.

To apply a label to a single message when you read the message, select the label you want applied from the **More Actions** drop-down list.

7 Manage Your Labels

You can delete, rename, and create new labels. To do it, click the **Edit labels** link at the bottom of the **Labels** list on the left side of the **Gmail** page. The **Mail Settings** page opens to the **Labels** tab; click the **rename** link next to a label to rename a label, or click the **remove** link next to a label to remove a label. Note that the messages still remain in your inbox.

To create a new label, type the label name in the **Create a new label** text box and click **Create**.

► **NOTE**

You can archive your mail by putting it into **Gmail**'s Archive in two way. To archive a single message when you're reading it, click the **Archive** button. When you're in the inbox, enable the check boxes next to mail you want archived, and then click the **Archive** button.

63

63 Use Gmail with Your Own Email Program

✔ BEFORE YOU BEGIN

57 Set Up a Gmail Account

Not everyone is a fan of web-based email, such as **Gmail**. One problem with web-based mail is that you can't read messages you've received except when you're online. Another is that you can't compose messages except when you're online. And some email programs, such as Outlook, integrate into desktop software in ways that web-based mail can't. For example, Outlook can use Microsoft Word as its editor for creating messages and shares a clipboard with other Microsoft Office applications.

Gmail, though, gives you the best of both worlds. In addition to working as web-based mail, it also gives you the option of working with your normal email software so you can use **Gmail** just as you do the email you normally receive through your ISP. Follow the instructions in this task so that any email program that runs on your PC as a separate program, such as Outlook, Eudora, Outlook Express, and others, can send and receive messages through your **Gmail** account.

▪ Go to Gmail Settings

To use your normal email software with **Gmail**, you have to change settings related to a *POP3* mail server. You first have to configure **Gmail** to use your email software's POP3 server, and then add settings in your email software to retrieve the mail from the server.

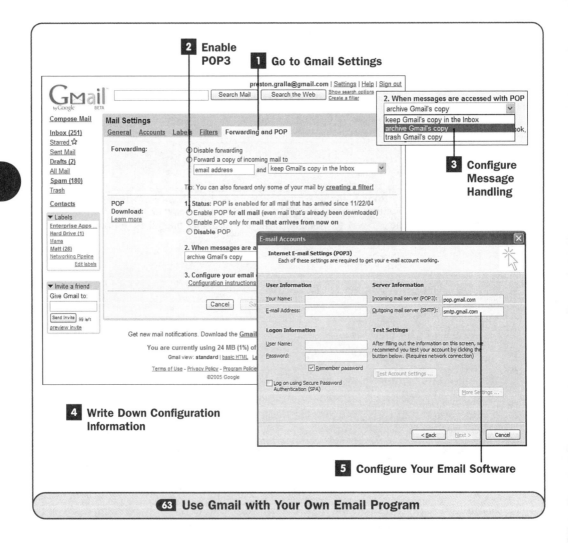

63 Use Gmail with Your Own Email Program

▶ KEY TERM

POP3 (Post Office Protocol 3)—A communications protocol that governs the receiving of email. A POP3 mail server receives mail; you then connect to the POP3 server and retrieve mail from the server using your email software.

To configure **Gmail** to allow you to use its POP3 server with your email software, first click **Settings** on the top of the **Gmail** main page, and then click the **Forwarding and POP** link at the top of the page. The **Mail Settings** page opens to the **Forwarding and POP** tab.

2 Enable POP3

This **Forwarding and POP** screen enables you to configure exactly how you want to use POP3. If you want your email software to retrieve all the email you've ever received on **Gmail**, choose **Enable POP for all mail**. Be very careful before making this selection. Remember, **Gmail** gives you several gigabytes of storage, so if you've received a lot of mail, you could end up downloading hundreds of megabytes of mail when you make your first connection to **Gmail** using your email software. Also keep in mind that even if you have only a little mail in your **Gmail** inbox, that's not all the email you have in your **Gmail** account. Much of your mail might be in the **Archive** folder, and you might have hundreds or thousands of messages there, even if they're not currently showing in your inbox.

If you choose **Enable POP only for mail that arrives from now on**, only those messages you receive after this point are downloaded to your email software. This is a much safer choice than the **Enable POP for all mail** option. If you want some old mail downloaded, you can always go into your **Gmail** account and forward the mail to yourself. That way, the forwarded mail is treated as new mail and downloaded, while all the rest of your old mail isn't downloaded.

3 Configure Message Handling

Next, make your choice about what should happen to your **Gmail** messages after your other email software accesses those messages. Should they be kept on the **Gmail** server, and if they are, should they be kept in the inbox or in the **Archived** mail folder? You make this choice from the **When messages are accessed with POP** drop-down menu. Here are your choices:

- **Keep Gmail's copy in the Inbox**—This option leaves all new mail on the **Gmail** server, and also leaves it in your **Gmail** inbox. Even after you download your **Gmail** mail to your PC, it stays in the **Gmail** inbox on the Web, as if you hadn't read it.

63

- **Archive Gmail's copy**—This option leaves all new email on the **Gmail** server, but instead of putting it into your **Gmail** inbox, it moves it to your **Archived** mail folder. So, whenever you visit **Gmail** on the Web, click **All Mail** to see all your mail, both archived and non-archived.

- **Trash Gmail's copy**—This option moves all the messages to your **Trash** folder, where it is cleaned out by **Gmail** on a regular basis.

4 Write Down Configuration Information

Now it's time to configure your email program to get your **Gmail** mail. You set up your email program to access **Gmail** as you do to access any other new mail account. You'll need to know a few things about the **Gmail** service: the address of **Gmail's** POP3 server, the address of **Gmail's** *SMTP* server, and whether to use a secure connection. For your POP3 server, use **pop.gmail.com**, and for your SMTP server, use **smtp.gmail.com**. When setting up this new account, make sure to tell your software to use a secure connection (SSL) for both SMTP and POP3. Write down the settings before you begin configuring your email software, so you don't forget them before you're asked to type them into the setup screens.

63

▶ KEY TERM

SMTP (Simple Mail Transfer Protocol)—A communications protocol that governs the sending of email. When you send email, you send it to an SMTP server, which in turn sends the mail towards its destination.

5 Configure Your Email Software

Now it's time to configure your email software to work with **Gmail**. How you do this varies according to your email software. The following instructions cover how to do it in the most recent version of Outlook.

▶ NOTE

For instructions on how to configure other email software, click the **Configure instructions** link on the **Forwarding and POP Gmail** page.

Launch Outlook and choose **E-mail Accounts** from the **Tools** menu. Click **Next**. Choose **Add a new e-mail account** and click **Next**. From the **Server Type** screen that appears, choose **POP3** and click **Next**. On the screen that appears next, enter your name, your email address, and your **Gmail** username and password. In the **Incoming Server (POP3)** text box, type **pop.gmail.com**, and in the **Outgoing mail server** text box, type **smtp.gmail.com**. Enable the check box next to **Remember password**.

Click the **More Settings** button and then choose the **Advanced** tab. In both the POP3 and SMTP sections, enable the check boxes next to **This server requires an encrypted connection (SSL)**. When you do that, the port numbers for the servers change. For POP3, the port number should change from 110 to 995. If it doesn't, type **995** in the **Incoming Server (POP3)** text box. For SMTP, type **465** into the **Outgoing Server (SMTP)** text box. Now click the **Outgoing Server** tab. Enable the check box next to **My outgoing server (SMTP) requires authentication** and select **Use same settings as my incoming mail server**. Click **OK**. From the screen that appears, click **Next** and then click **Finish**.

---

64 | **Get Mail Notifications with Gmail Notifier**

✔ BEFORE YOU BEGIN	→ SEE ALSO
57 Set Up a Gmail Account	**59** Read Mail and Attachments
	99 Create a Google Talk Account

Web-based email, such as **Gmail**, can be annoying to use because to find out whether you have new mail, you need to constantly check the website.

Gmail has a simple solution: **Gmail Notifier**, which constantly checks your **Gmail** account to see whether there is new mail, and shows you the subjects, senders, and snippets from the mail. This task shows you how to use it.

1 Download and Install Gmail Notifier

From the **Gmail** main page, click the **Gmail Notifier** link at the bottom of the page; alternatively, go to http://toolbar.google.com/gmail-helper. Click the **Download Gmail Notifier** button, and download and install **Gmail Notifier**. (For information about how to download and install software, see "How To Download and Install Google Tools" in Chapter 1, "Start Here."

▶ NOTE

If you've installed **Google Talk**, you don't need to install **Gmail Notifier** because **Google Talk** includes the functionality of **Gmail Notifier**. For more details, see **105** About Browsing and Reading Gmail from Google Talk.

During installation, you are asked whether you want to run **Gmail Notifier** when you start your computer, and whether you want to use **Gmail** to send email whenever you click a **mailto:** link on the Web. Enable the appropriate check boxes if you want **Gmail Notifier** to run on startup, and if you want **Gmail** to send email when you click **mailto:** links; disable the check boxes if you don't.

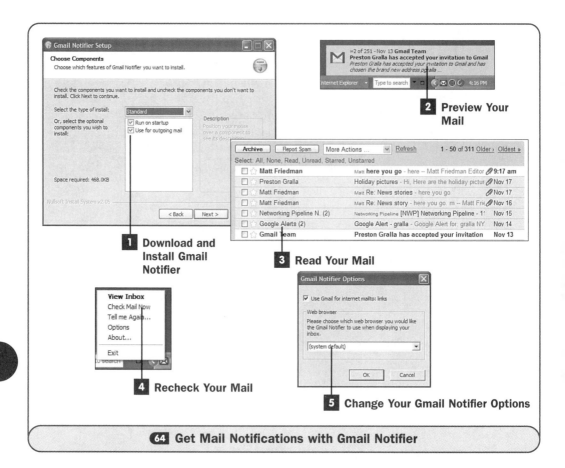

64 Get Mail Notifications with Gmail Notifier

2 Preview Your Mail

As soon as you install **Gmail Notifier**, it begins checking your **Gmail** inbox and issues an alert for each piece of new mail **Gmail** receives. **Gmail Notifier** runs as a small envelope icon in the **Notification** area at the bottom-right corner of your Windows desktop. Just above that icon it issues its alerts. When you get a new piece of mail, **Gmail Notifier** shows you the subject matter and a snippet of text from the message. It also tells you how many total pieces of mail you have in your inbox.

3 Read Your Mail

To read your mail, double-click the **Gmail Notifier** icon. You are sent to your **Gmail** inbox, where you can read your mail as you would normally.

4 Recheck Your Mail

If you want **Gmail Notifier** to recheck your entire mailbox or if you want it to check for new mail, right-click the **Gmail Notifier** icon and select **Check Mail Now** to check for new mail; click **Tell me Again** to have **Gmail Notifier** go back to your inbox and show you your most recent mail.

5 Change Your Gmail Notifier Options

You can change the browser that **Gmail Notifier** uses to display your **Gmail** inbox, and you can change whether you want to use **Gmail** for **mailto:** links. Right-click the **Gmail Notifier** icon in the **Notification** area and choose **Options** from the context menu. In the **Gmail Notifier Options** dialog box that appears, enable the check box next to **Use Gmail for internet mailto: links** if you want to use **Gmail** for them; disable the check box if you don't want to use **Gmail** for **mailto:** links.

From the **Web browser** drop-down list, choose the browser you want to use to display your **Gmail** inbox. If you want to use your default browser, choose **(system default)**. When you're done, click **OK**.

65

65 About Gmail and Spam

✔ BEFORE YOU BEGIN

57 Set Up a Gmail Account
59 Read Mail and Attachments

To use email is to be victimized by spam, and that's no different for **Gmail** than when you use other email programs. It's this simple: When you use **Gmail**, you receive spam.

Gmail does its best to filter out spam before it reaches you, and routes what it considers spam to the **Spam** folder. Click the link to the **Spam** folder on the left side of the **Gmail** screen to view the spam messages you have received. Most likely, **Gmail** is right—everything you find there is spam. But if you find mail that isn't spam, check the box next to the message you want to retrieve and click the **Not spam** link at the top of the screen The selected messages are moved to your inbox, and **Gmail** remembers this sender as a valid address so that it doesn't put any more messages from this sender into the **Spam** folder.

Similarly, if you find a piece of spam in your inbox, enable the check box to the left of the message and click the **Report Spam** button. The selected mail is moved to your **Spam** folder.

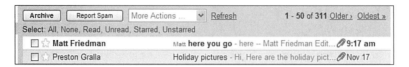

*Enable the check box next to a mail message and click **Report Spam** to move the mail to your **Spam** folder.*

66   Customize Gmail

✔ **BEFORE YOU BEGIN**

57 **Set Up a Gmail Account**

66

Don't like the way **Gmail** works? No problem—you can change it. You can customize the number of messages **Gmail** shows per page, whether to include a *signature*, and similar aspects of **Gmail**.

▶ **KEY TERM**

Signature—Text that is automatically appended to the bottom of all your outgoing email, often including your contact information.

1 Go to the Settings Page

To customize **Gmail**, you need to go to the **Settings** page. To get there, click the **Settings** link at the top of a **Gmail** page.

2 Change the Language and Page Size

At the top of the page is a drop-down list of all the languages you can use for **Gmail**. By default, this option is set to **English (US)**. Choose another language if you want. The language you select is used to display the **Gmail** command names and interface words, not the actual text of the messages you send and receive.

From the **Maximum page size** setting, you can choose **25, 50,** or **100** from the drop-down list to determine the maximum number of messages (which **Gmail** calls conversations) to display on each page.

3 Use Keyboard Shortcuts

If you want **Gmail** to allow you to use keyboard shortcuts to perform common tasks such as creating **Gmail**, select the **Keyboard shortcuts on** option.

To turn keyboard shortcuts off, select the **Keyboard shortcuts off** option. Table 10.1 shows the keyboard shortcuts you can use, taken straight from the Google Help page.

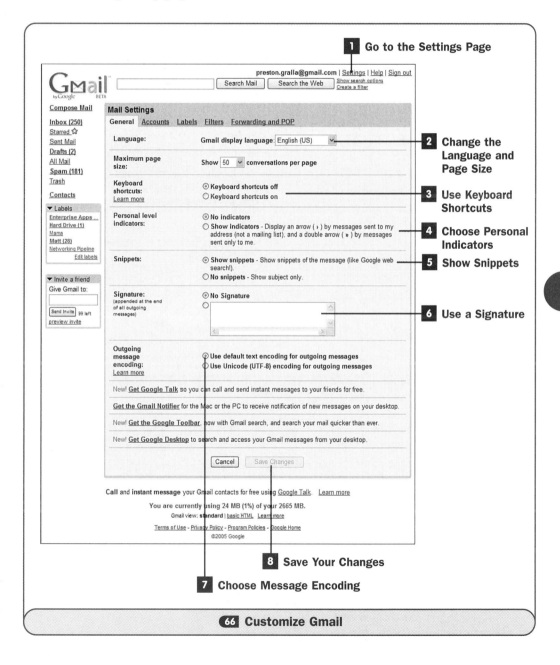

1 Go to the Settings Page

2 Change the Language and Page Size

3 Use Keyboard Shortcuts

4 Choose Personal Indicators

5 Show Snippets

6 Use a Signature

7 Choose Message Encoding

8 Save Your Changes

66

TABLE 10.1   Gmail Shortcuts

Shortcut Key	Definition	Action
C	Compose	Allows you to compose a new message. **Shift+C** allows you to compose a message in a new window.
/	Search	Puts your cursor in the search box.
K	Move to newer conversation	Opens or moves your cursor to a more recent mail message (conversation). You can press **Enter** to expand a message (conversation).
J	Move to older conversation	Opens or moves your cursor to the next oldest message (conversation). You can press **Enter** to expand the message (conversation).
N	Next message	Moves your cursor to the next message. You can press **Enter** to expand or collapse a message. (Only applicable in Conversation View.)
P	Previous message	Moves your cursor to the previous message. You can press **Enter** to expand or collapse a message. (Only applicable in Conversation View.)
O or Enter	Open	Opens your conversation. Also expands or collapses a message if you are in Conversation View.
U	Return to conversation list	Refreshes your page and returns you to the inbox, or list of messages (conversations).
Y	Archive*, or remove from current view	Automatically removes the message or conversation from your current view.
X	Select conversation	Automatically checks and selects a message (conversation) so you can archive, apply a label, or choose an action from the drop-down menu to apply to that message or conversation.
S	Star a message or conversation	Adds or removes a star to a message or conversation. Stars allow you to give a message or conversation a special status.
!	Report spam	Marks a message as spam and removes it from your inbox or conversation list.
R	Reply	Replies to the message's sender. **Shift+R** allows you to reply to a message in a new window. (Only applicable in Conversation View.)
A	Reply all	Replies to all message recipients. **Shift+A** allows you to reply to all message recipients in a new window. (Only applicable in Conversation View.)

66

TABLE 10.1 Continued

Shortcut Key	Definition	Action
F	Forward	Forward a message. **Shift+F** allows you to forward a message in a new window. (Only applicable in Conversation View.)
Esc	Escape from input field	Removes the cursor from your current input field.
Tab, and then **Enter**	Send message	After composing your message, use this key combination to send the message automatically. (Supported only in Internet Explorer.)
Y, and then **O**	Archive and next	Archive your current message or conversation and move to the next one.
G, and then **A**	Go to All Mail	Takes you to **All Mail**, the storage site for all the mail you've ever sent or received (and have not deleted).
G, and then **S**	Go to Starred	Takes you to the **Starred** folder, where you can see all messages or conversations you have starred.
G, and then **C**	Go to Contacts	Takes you to your **Contacts** list.
G, and then **D**	Go to Drafts	Takes you to the **Drafts** folder, where you can see all drafts you have saved.
G, and then **I**	Go to Inbox	Returns you to the inbox.

*From the **Inbox** folder, **Y** means **Archive**. From the **Starred** folder, **Y** means **Unstar**. From the **Trash** folder, **Y** means **Move to inbox**. From any label, **Y** means **Remove the label**. **Y** has no effect if you're in the **Spam**, **Sent**, or **All Mail** folders.

4 Choose Personal Indicators

Gmail can tell you when a message is sent specifically to you rather than to a mailing list (a list of multiple email addresses), and can tell if you are the only recipient of a message. Gmail calls these *personal indicators*. On the **Gmail Mail Settings** page, select the **Show indicators** option if you want an arrow (>) shown next to messages sent specifically to your address rather than to a mailing list, and a double arrow (>>) shown next to messages sent only to you. Select **No indicators** if you don't want any indicators to appear in your inbox or other views of your mail.

▶ **KEY TERM**

Personal indicators—In **Gmail**, an indication of whether mail has been sent to your specific address or to a mailing list.

5 Show Snippets

If you want **Gmail** to show the first snippet of the text in the body of the email message in addition to the subject line of a message, select **Show snippets**. If you don't want snippets displayed, select **No snippets**, and only the subject line is shown.

6 Use a Signature

You can append a signature to the bottom of all your outgoing email messages. The signature can be any text you want. Many people include their contact information, and some people also include a famous quotation.

To append a signature, type the text you want to use as your signature in the **Signature** box, and select the radio button next to the text box.

7 Choose Message Encoding

Whenever you send an email, **Gmail** selects the encoding method that matches the language in which you've created your mail. Encoding tells browsers and software how to display characters and letters.

The **Outgoing message encoding** area enables you to choose that default encoding or to instead use a special coding method called Unicode (UTF-8). If people to whom you send **Gmail** email have no problems reading it, you should choose **Use default text encoding for outgoing messages**. If people have had problems reading some characters, try choosing **Use Unicode (UTF-8) encoding for outgoing messages**.

8 Save Your Changes

When you're done, click the **Save Changes** button at the bottom of the **Settings** page to apply the changes immediately. If you decide you don't want to make the changes, click **Cancel** instead.

---

67 About Gmail and Privacy

✔ **BEFORE YOU BEGIN**

57 Set Up a Gmail Account

In some of your incoming email, you might notice sponsored links on the right side of the page—these links are essentially advertising. These ads are not random; they are related to the content of the message itself. Not all emails have sponsored links. A message from your friend about his ten-year-old son's grades might not have sponsored links, while a message from someone about buying office equipment might have links to sites that sell office furniture. The nearby figure shows an example of those links.

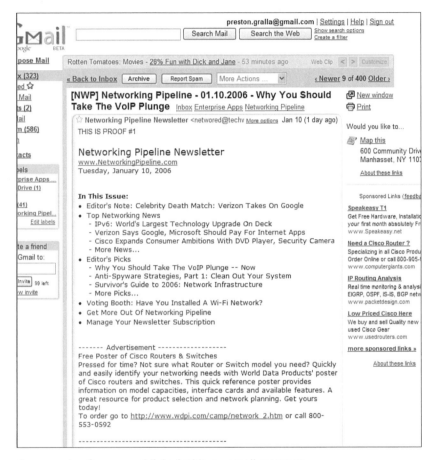

An example of sponsored links inside an email message.

How do those sponsored links end up there? Google examines all your incoming email, and if it finds certain words, it places sponsored links in your email messages. This works in the same way Google searches do—when you do a Google search, Google looks at the search terms, and if it finds certain words, it places sponsored links in your search results.

At first blush, it might seem as if having Google examine your mail is an invasion of your privacy. But there's less here than meets the eye. First of all, no people read your mail; software parses through it looking for search terms. Secondly, Google isn't doing anything that different from what your normal email ISP does.

In order to filter out spam before it reaches you, ISPs have software examine email, and then discard spam.

So **Gmail** isn't really an invasion of your privacy. But if the idea of Google software examining your software still bothers you, there's a simple solution—don't use **Gmail**.

67

11

Discovering the World with Google Earth

IN THIS CHAPTER:

One of man's greatest desires has been to fly...and **Google Earth** enables you to fly anywhere in the world without leaving your chair. It does much more than that as well. It shows you 3D satellite photos of places throughout the world, enables you to take guided flying tours, shows you local information along the way, and more, as you'll see in this chapter. Use **Google Earth** when you want to see a satellite map of anywhere on Earth or when you want to get driving directions—and a 3D tour of the drive. **Google Earth** is similar to **Google Local**, except that it includes real satellite photos—and you can take a virtual flight as well.

Google Earth also includes two for-pay versions: **Google Earth Plus** and **Google Earth Pro**. These versions of the application offer extra features, such as high-resolution printing and the capability to import and export data.

To get started with **Google Earth**, go to http://earth.google.com for details about running the **Google Earth** application. Click the **Download** link (or go to http://earth.google.com/download-earth.html) to download and run the installation file. For details about how to download and install software, see Chapter 1, "Start Here."

After you install **Google Earth**, launch it by double-clicking the desktop icon.

68

68 Fly to a Location

✔ **SEE ALSO**

69 Navigate Through Google Earth
70 Find Local Information with Google Earth

You don't need wings to fly. As you'll see in this task, you can fly from place to place in seconds with **Google Earth**. You are able to view satellite photos of any place on Earth by clicking the location on a globe, and you then take a virtual flight to get there. After you are at your destination, you can view the map and navigate through it.

1 Click the Fly To Button

When you first launch **Google Earth**, you should already be in the **Fly To** area, but if you're not, click the **Fly To** button in the upper-left corner of the **Google Earth** screen.

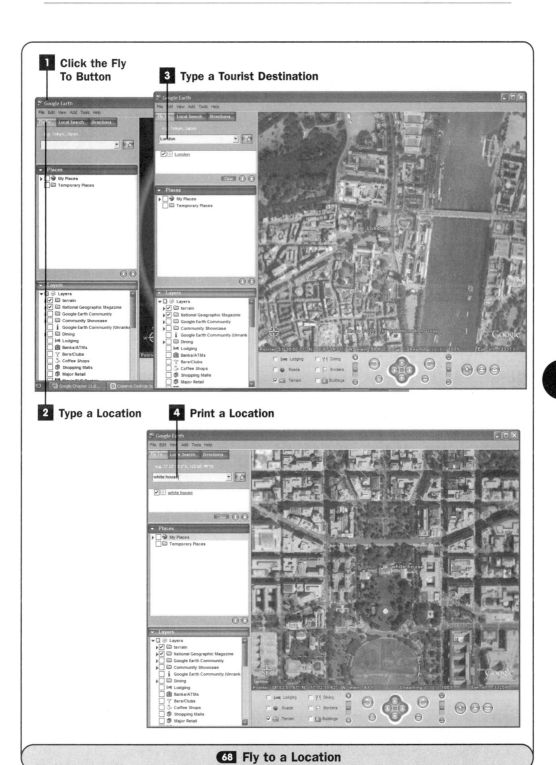

1 Click the Fly To Button

3 Type a Tourist Destination

2 Type a Location

4 Print a Location

▶ NOTE

Google Earth requires a lot of computing power, and if you don't have a relatively new and powerful computer, it is extremely sluggish. You are best off if you use Windows XP; have a computer that runs at 2.4GHz or better and has at least 512MB of RAM, 2GB of hard disk space, and a 3D graphics card; and a screen with a resolution of at least 1280×1024 at 32-bit color.

▣ Type a Location

In the input text box just under the **Fly To** button, type a location. You can type an exact address, such as **51 Main Street, Cambridge, Massachusetts,** or you can type a city or a country, such as **London, England**. After you type the location you want to view, press **Enter** or click the **Search** button. You can also type the exact longitude and latitude coordinates (you don't have to enter the superscripted degree sign °). Or you can enter the intersection of two streets, a ZIP Code, or any other location-identifying string of characters. Searching by street address works only in the United States, the United Kingdom, and Canada.

After you type the desired location, **Google Earth** "flies" you to that location by moving the Earth in 3D animation, and then zooming in on the location.

68

▶ TIP

To get back to the initial view of the globe, type **globe** into the search box and press **Enter** or simple drag the **Zoom** slider down to zoom back out. If you've already typed in the search box the destination to which you want to return, click the down arrow next to the search box, choose the destination, and press **Enter**.

▣ Type a Tourist Destination

Type a tourist destination, for example, **White House** or **Great Wall of China**, and you immediately zoom to that destination.

▣ Print a Location

To print an image of the location you're viewing, choose **File, Print** from the menu bar. A dialog box appears, with options for **Quick Print** and **Medium (1000 pixels)**. The **Quick Print** option prints a low-resolution picture, and the **Medium** option prints a higher-resolution picture. (If you want to print high-resolution photos, you have to buy **Google Earth Plus** or **Google Earth Pro**.)

▶ NOTE

Not all locations you travel to have high-resolution maps. Some parts of the world only have low-resolution maps, so they are blurry and cannot be zoomed into.

69 Navigate Through Google Earth

✔ BEFORE YOU BEGIN	→ SEE ALSO
68 Fly to a Location	**72** About Customizing Your View by Adding and Removing Layers

Flying to a location by typing in its address is just one way to move around **Google Earth**. What happens when you get to a location and want to move around? How can you control how you zoom or tilt the view? That's what you'll learn how to do in this task.

1 Use the Flying Controls

When you're at a location, you can move around using the controls at the bottom of the screen. Click any of the four arrows to move you in the direction they point. Use the counterclockwise and clockwise arrows to rotate the view in the direction shown. You can also click any point on the screen, and drag with your mouse to move around.

2 Zoom In and Out

You can zoom in or out at any location. Drag the **Zoom** slider (located on the left side of the flying control pad) toward the + sign to zoom in; drag it toward the – sign to zoom out.

69

▶ NOTES

If your mouse has a scroll button, click the area on the screen you want to zoom into and roll the button down to zoom out; roll the button up to zoom in.

You can double-click the area on the screen into which you want to zoom and you zoom slowly into that area. When the zoom factor is where you want it, click once to stop zooming.

3 Tilt the View

Drag the **Tilt** slider (located on the right side of the flying control pad) to tilt the view forward or backward. If you tilt the view so you are looking at the terrain as if you were hovering just above the surface, you can then use the **Zoom** slider to "fly" across the surface of the area you're viewing.

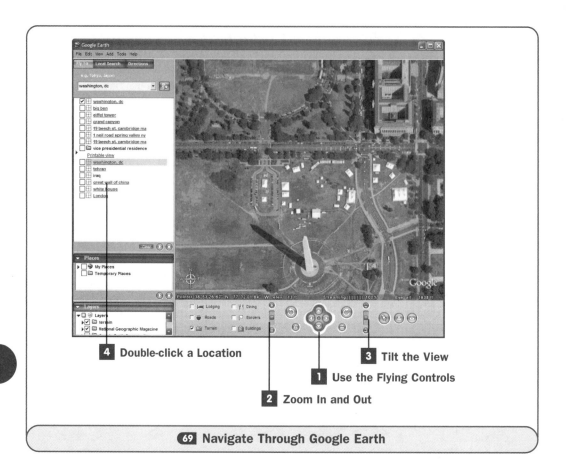

4 Double-click a Location

3 Tilt the View

1 Use the Flying Controls

2 Zoom In and Out

69 Navigate Through Google Earth

69

▶ NOTE

The two small buttons to the right and left of the flying control pad arrows serve related but different purposes. If you've rotated the screen using the counterclockwise or clockwise arrows, click the **Reset North** button to the left of the flying control pad to return the alignment to true north. If you've tilted the view, click the **Reset Tilt** button to the right of the flying control pad to return the tilt of the screen so you are looking directly down on the view.

4 Double-click a Location

As you travel around the world, **Google Earth** keeps a running list of every place you visit on the left side of the screen. Double-click any location to immediately fly to it. For any location, you can layer information on top of the map, including roads, buildings, terrain, and so on. For details, see

72 About Customizing Your View by Adding and Removing Layers.

If you want to start fresh with your touring, click the **Clear** button at the bottom of the list of locations to delete all previously visited locations from the list.

To fly to any place you've already visited, click the place you want to visit on the map, and then click the **Tour** button next to the **Clear** button at the bottom of the locations list. To stop the tour, click the **Stop** button next to the **Tour** button. **Google Earth** also includes a worldwide tour you can take, in which you fly all over the world—from Paris to London to the Grand Canyon to the Forbidden City in China and beyond. Click the **Sightseeing** link in the location list, and then click the **Tour** button.

70 | Find Local Information with Google Earth

✔ BEFORE YOU BEGIN	→ SEE ALSO
68 Fly to a Location	**43** Find Local Information with Google Local
69 Navigate Through Google Earth	**71** Use Google Earth to Get Directions

70

Flying around Earth and zooming in and out is certainly entertaining, but you can use **Google Earth** for more than entertainment. You can use it to find local information, such as restaurants, museums, cafes, and more near a location, as you'll see in this task. The actual information you are able to get is much the same as the information you can get using **Google Local**, as detailed in **43** **Find Local Information with Google Local**. But with **Google Earth**, of course, you get detailed satellite photos, the capability to fly, and more.

1 Click Local Search

From any place in **Google Earth**, click the **Local Search** button in the upper-left corner of the screen. (If you haven't downloaded and installed **Google Earth** yet, turn to the beginning of this chapter for help.) This brings you to a screen that enables you to search for local information.

▶ **NOTE**

As of this writing, **Google Earth** doesn't include local information from all over the world; it includes local information from only the United States, Canada, and the United Kingdom.

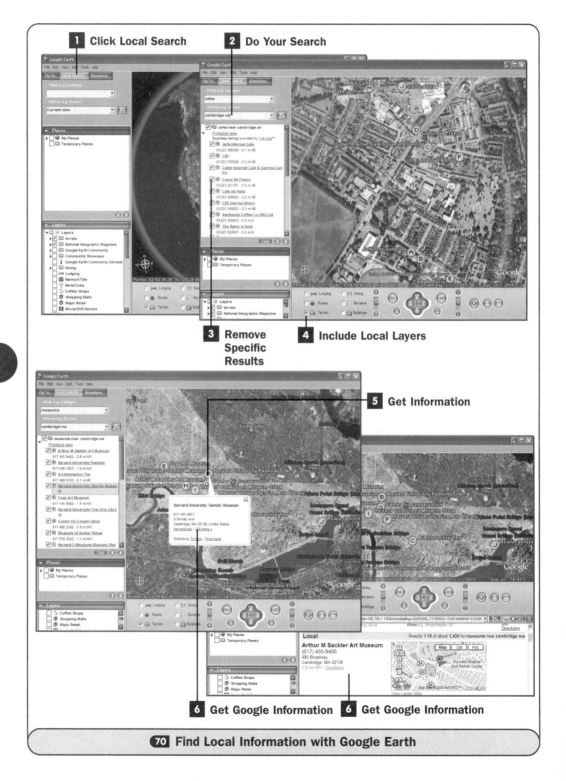

1 Click Local Search

2 Do Your Search

3 Remove Specific Results

4 Include Local Layers

5 Get Information

6 Get Google Information

6 Get Google Information

70 Find Local Information with Google Earth

70

2 Do Your Search

In the **What** text box at the top of the search form, type what you're looking for, such as **restaurants**, **cafes**, **colleges**, **museums**, and so on. Be as specific as possible—for example, if you're looking for an Indian restaurant, type **Indian restaurants**.

In the **Where** text box at the bottom of the form, type in the location. For major cities, you won't have to include the country, state, or county. But for smaller locations, include these identifiers. When you've filled in the two text boxes in the form, press **Enter** or click the **Search** button. You fly to the location, and the local search results are displayed and labeled over the view on the screen. In addition, on the left side of the screen, you see a list of all the results.

3 Remove Specific Results

If you want to remove one or more results, uncheck the box next to that result in the list on the left side of the screen.

4 Include Local Layers

The bottom-left side of **Google Earth** includes icons for basic local information—for local lodging, roads, terrain, dining, borders (country borders, for example), and buildings. Check the box next to any of these elements that you want displayed. (For more information about layers, see **72** **About Customizing Your View by Adding and Removing Layers**.)

70

5 Get Information

To get information about any of the places displayed, click the letter next to the label on the screen; a balloon box pops up. Depending on the location and the place, the pop-up includes a variety of information, such as the address, possibly its website, and links to reviews and more information about it. You can also get information by clicking the place in the left side of the screen.

6 Get Google Information

If more Google information is available about the place, the pop-up box includes a link, such as **778 More>>**. Click that link, and at the bottom of the **Google Earth** screen (or a completely new browser window opens), a **Google Local** page appears with more information about the location, taken from Google search results. The page also includes a map of the location. You can scroll through the results, and use them just as you would use regular Google search results. To make the page disappear, click the **X** on the upper-right side of the Google information page.

71 Use Google Earth to Get Directions

✔ BEFORE YOU BEGIN

70 Find Local Information with
Google Earth

→ SEE ALSO

44 Get Directions to Anywhere with
Google Local

71

Google Earth doesn't just show you locations—it gives driving directions as well. What makes it unique among mapping sites is that it also takes you on a guided tour of the path in 3D animation, as you'll see in this task.

1 Click Directions

From any place in **Google Earth**, click the **Directions** button in the upper-left corner of the screen. (If you haven't downloaded and installed **Google Earth** yet, turn to the beginning of this chapter for help.) This brings you to a screen that enables you to get driving directions. As of this writing, **Google Earth** doesn't include driving directions from all over the world; it only includes directions in the United States, Canada, and the United Kingdom.

2 Get Driving Directions

In the **Start** text box, type your starting location. In the **End** text box, type the ending location. Then press **Enter** or click the **Search** button. **Google Earth** displays a satellite map of the directions in the right part of the screen, and a list of the directions in the left part of the screen. If you enter towns or cities rather than street addresses, **Google Earth** uses downtown post offices as the source and destinations when computing mileage, driving time, and directions. If you instead enter specific street addresses, **Google Earth** uses those street addresses for computing all that data. So it's best to give as specific location information as possible.

▶ NOTE

Both **Google Earth** and **Google Local** (formerly called **Google Maps**) enable you to find local information and directions. So when should you use one, and when another? Because **Google Local** is Web-based, rather than a separate program, it loads more quickly and is also directly integrated into Google. If you're looking for a quick local search, **Google Local** is the way to go. **Google Earth** includes animations and extras, such as the capability to actually view the locations in 3D, or fly along the driving route. So if you need those features, use **Google Earth**.

1 Click Directions

2 Get Driving Directions

3 Get a Printable View

4 Take a Flying Tour of Your Directions

5 Go to Any Step

3 Get a Printable View

If you want a printable view of the driving directions, click the **Printable view** link at the top of the driving directions in the left pane. A web page appears at the bottom of the **Google Earth** screen (or a completely new browser window opens) with the printable directions—the same ones you would get if you did a search for directions on **Google Local**. To print the directions, click the **Print** link on the page.

▶ **NOTE**

In some instances, when you click **Printable view**, you might get an error message in the page that appears, saying that the driving directions cannot be calculated. If that happens, type the beginning and starting points on the page that appears, including the states. For most locations, **Google Local** requires that you enter a state, but **Google Earth** does not. So **Google Local** cannot always properly retrieve the information if you did not enter a state.

4 Take a Flying Tour of Your Directions

You can get a 3D, animated, flying tour of your directions. Click the VCR-like **Play** button at the bottom of the directions on the left side of the page, and you take a flying tour of your directions. Use the **Pause** and **Play** buttons to start and stop the tour as you travel. To change the speed of the entire tour, refer to **74** **Change Google Earth Options**.

5 Go to Any Step

If you want to view any particular step of the directions, double-click the link in the left side of the screen, and you zoom straight to that step. The flying tour stops, and you cannot continue from that point—if you click the **Play** button again, the tour starts over from the beginning.

72	**About Customizing Your View by Adding and Removing Layers**
✔ **BEFORE YOU BEGIN**	→ **SEE ALSO**
68 Fly to a Location	**70** Find Local Information with Google Earth
	71 Use Google Earth to Get Directions

One of the most powerful features of **Google Earth** is its capability to layer destinations and information on the top of satellite maps. On the lower-right side of the screen, beneath the map itself, are several layers you can add, such as lodging, dining, and roads, among others. (When you add the **Roads** layer, for example, the actual street names of roads are added to the map.) You turn on and off layers by checking the box next to them. You can also add 3D buildings by turning on the **Buildings** layer, show borders between countries and counties by turning on the **Borders** layer, and show a 3D topographical map by turning on the **Terrain** layer, among other options.

But those layers are just the beginning of the kinds of layers you can add to the map. At the bottom-left corner of the screen is the **Layers** pane, which has countless types of information you can layer on top of maps. Want to see volcanoes or earthquakes? There are layers for those. How about shopping malls or DVD rental stores? Yes, those are there as well. So are golf courses, schools, city borders, postal code borders, Congressional districts…I won't go on because the list seems to be endless. (Note that some information, such as the **Crime Stats** layer, is available for only some locations.) Try them out, but be forewarned that layers are addictive, and you might find yourself spending more hours than you want zooming around the world, finding bars, volcanoes, and ATM machines.

---

73 | **Save Your Favorite Locations**   **73**

✔ **BEFORE YOU BEGIN**	→ **SEE ALSO**
68 Fly to a Location	**72** About Customizing Your View by Adding and Removing Layers

---

No doubt you have some favorite places in the world. **Google Earth** enables you to save those places in a convenient location so you can immediately fly to them with a double-click, as you'll see in this task.

1 Go to a Location

Visit any location on **Google Earth** as you would normally.

2 Save the Location

From the **Edit** menu, choose **Save to My Places** to save the currently displayed location as a favorite. You can also save a location if the location is in the list of places in the left pane. To do it, highlight the location in the top-left part of the screen and choose **Edit, Save To My Places** from the menu bar.

73

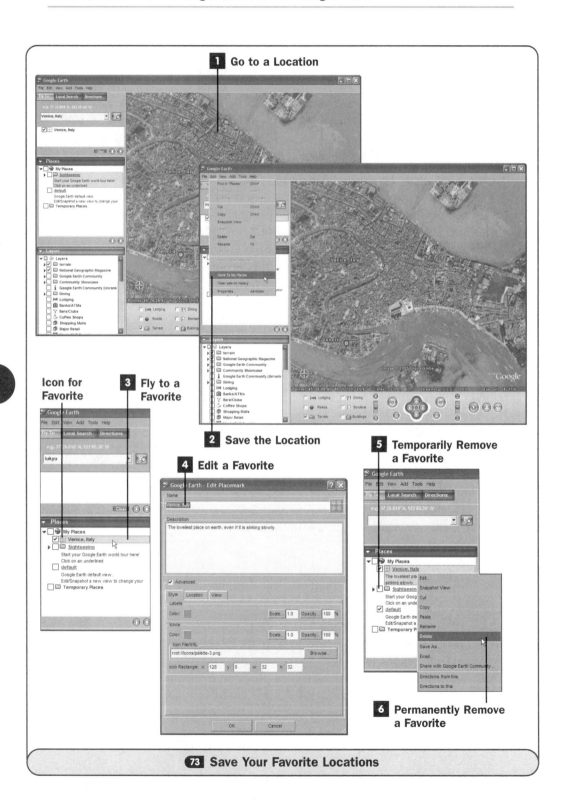

1 Go to a Location

Icon for Favorite   **3** Fly to a Favorite

2 Save the Location

4 Edit a Favorite

5 Temporarily Remove a Favorite

6 Permanently Remove a Favorite

73 Save Your Favorite Locations

The location vanishes from the top part of the screen and is instead displayed in the **Places** panel on the left side of the screen, underneath **My Places**. An icon is also displayed next to the name of that location on the map on the right side of the **Google Earth** screen, with the name of the place next to it. If necessary, zoom out a little to see the icon.

3 Fly to a Favorite

No matter where you are in the world, you can immediately fly to one of your favorite locations. In the **Places** panel on the left side of the screen, locate the favorite destination to which you want to fly, and double-click it. You immediately fly to that location.

4 Edit a Favorite

You can edit and annotate your favorite locations by changing a location's name, adding notes about it, and changing the icon that appears next to it in the **Places** panel and on the map in **Google Earth**. Right-click the favorite location in the **Places** panel on the left side of the screen and choose **Edit**. In the **Edit Placemark** dialog box that opens, you can change the name and add a description. Click **OK** when you're done. The description shows up next to the favorite in the **Places** panel.

73

▶ **TIP**

To change the icon that displays next to your favorite location in the **Places** panel, enable the **Advanced** check box; the **Edit Placemark** dialog box expands to show three tabs. Click the **Style** tab and choose the color and size of the icon you want to display. You can also change the color of the text label in this tab. Alternatively, click the icon to the right of the **Name** field at the top of the **Edit Placemark** dialog box and choose a new icon from the list that appears.

5 Temporarily Remove a Favorite

In the **Places** panel, favorite places have check boxes next to them. If you temporarily don't want a favorite to show up on the map in **Google Earth**, uncheck the box. The favorite still shows up in the **Places** panel, but it won't be labeled on the map section of **Google Earth**. You can still fly to that location by double-clicking it in the **Places** panel.

6 Permanently Remove a Favorite

To permanently remove a favorite, right-click it and select **Delete** from the contextual menu. The favorite is removed from the **Places** panel and from the map in **Google Earth**.

---

74 Change Google Earth Options

✔ BEFORE YOU BEGIN	→ SEE ALSO
68 Fly to a Location	**72** About Customizing Your View by Adding and Removing Layers

---

Google Earth is a complex program, and it offers innumerable ways you can customize it. Covering all those options is beyond the scope of this book, but this task shows you the basic ways to change its main options.

1 Open the Google Earth Options Dialog Box

Choose **Tools**, **Options** from the menu bar to open the **Google Earth Options** dialog box.

2 Customize the View Options

Click the **View** tab to change how **Google Earth** is displayed. Some of the options are complex, and aren't covered in this book, but here are the most important options:

- **Detail Area**—This option enables you to change the size of the window devoted to the mapping area. You can choose from **Small** (256×256 pixels), **Medium** (512×512 pixels), or **Large** (1024×1024 pixels). The best compromise is **Medium**, unless you have a monitor 19" or larger.

▶ NOTE

The **Detail Area** setting frequently does not work, and has no effect on the display size, so don't be frustrated if it doesn't make a difference on your system.

- **Texture Colors**—This option enables you to choose between **High Color** (16 bits) and **True Color** (32 bits) for the textured areas of the **Google Earth** map. The **True Color** selection gives a much richer visual experience, but it might slow down your system significantly. Try using the **True Color** option, and if your system is sluggish, change to **High Color**.

- **Labels/Icon Size**—This option enables you to choose between **Small**, **Medium**, and **Large**. This choice affects the size of all the icons on the screen—those in the mapping area as well as those in the **Places** panel. If you edited the size of an icon in the **Edit Placemark** dialog box (as explained in **73 Save Your Favorite Locations**), the customized icon size overrides this **Labels/Icon Size** setting.

74

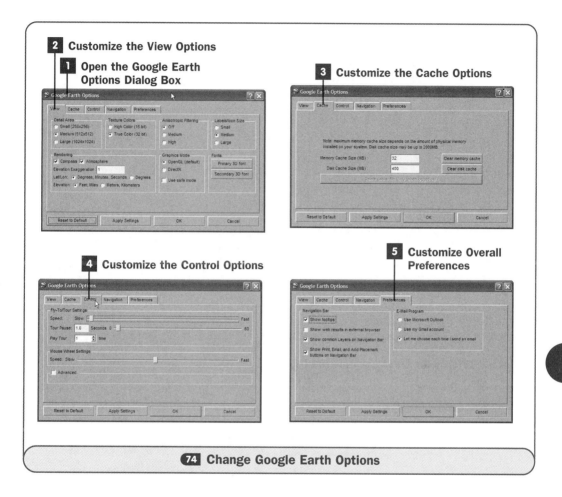

74 Change Google Earth Options

- **Fonts**—This option enables you to choose the fonts used to display the labels and other text in **Google Earth**. Click either the **Primary 3D Font** or the **Secondary 3D Font** button (both control the same font options, although this might change when **Google Earth** is updated), and choose the font style, size, and color.

Click the **Apply Settings** button when you're done making your choices.

3 Customize the Cache Options

A *cache* is a section of memory or a hard disk used to save data. When data is saved to **Google Earth**'s cache, it speeds up operations because **Google Earth** can grab the information from the local cache, rather than having to go out to the Internet. Click the **Cache** tab to customize how much of a cache to devote to **Google Earth** data. The default values are 32MB of RAM and

400MB of hard disk space. If you have 512MB or more of RAM, and more than 2GB of hard disk space free, considering increasing the numbers on this tab of the **Google Earth Options** dialog box.

4 Customize the Control Options

Click the **Control** tab to change options related to flying and the automated tour. The **Fly-To/Tour Settings** control the flying and tour options. The **Speed** slider controls the speed with which you fly, and at which the tour plays. The **Tour Pause** setting controls how long **Google Earth** should pause before starting a tour after you click the button. The **Play Tour** setting enables you to control how many times the tour should play.

The **Mouse Wheel Settings** slider enables you to control how fast the mouse wheel should zoom in and out of **Google Earth**.

▶ **NOTE**

The **Navigation** tab is supposed to control things such as the zoom level and the size of the **Google Earth** map. But I have yet to get those settings to work.

74

5 Customize Overall Preferences

Click the **Preferences** tab to customize the **Navigation Bar** and how **Google Earth** interacts with your email software. The navigation bar is the bar that appears at the bottom-right side of the **Google Earth** screen, under the mapping window, and controls how you navigate through **Google Earth**. This tab enables you to change these options:

▶ **NOTE**

You can email the current satellite photo you're viewing to a friend. Choose **File, Email View** from the menu bar or press **Ctrl+E**. Then choose **Email Location** if you want to email just the location, or choose **Email Image** if you want to email the image itself. From there, follow the onscreen directions to complete the email message. If you email a location, the person to whom you send the message must have **Google Earth** installed in order to view the location. They can download the file you sent, and that file jumps them to the location.

- **Show tooltips**—Enable or disable this check box to specify whether to show tooltips, which are the small balloons that contain explanatory text.

- **Show web results in external browser**—This option controls **Google Earth**'s actions when it needs to display information from Google, such as when you click a link in a location. You can have the results display in a separate browser window or at the bottom of the navigation bar.

- **Show common Layers on Navigation Bar**—When enabled, this option displays the six most common layers as check box options on the navigation bar. Disable the check box to turn them off.

- **Show Print, Email, and Add Placemark buttons on Navigation Bar**—This option controls whether the **Print**, **Email**, and **Add Placemark** buttons should appear on the navigation bar.

The **E-Mail Program** setting controls which email program **Google Earth** should use when you send an email from within the program. Google Earth searches your hard disk to discover the email applications you might have loaded on your computer; from the list it compiles, choose the email application you want to use.

Click the **Apply Settings** button when you're done specifying options. Then click **OK** to close the dialog box.

75

---

75 | About Google Earth Plus and Google Earth Pro

✔ **BEFORE YOU BEGIN**

68 Fly to a Location

Google Earth, like most Google tools, is free. But Google also has two for-pay versions of the software, Google Earth Plus and Google Earth Pro, each of which includes substantial extra features. Most people won't need to use either of the for-pay versions of **Google Earth**, but some people and businesses might find them useful. Here's what each offer:

- **Google Earth Plus** costs $20, and can import Global Positioning Satellite (GPS) data, offers higher-resolution printing than you can achieve with regular **Google Earth**, allows for animations, and includes customer support via email. To buy it, run **Google Earth**, select **Upgrade to Plus** from the **Help** menu, and follow the directions. For more information, go to http://earth.google.com/earth_plus.html.

- **Google Earth Pro** cost $400 for a one-year subscription, and is targeted at businesses rather than individuals, especially businesses that do location research and presentation. **Google Earth Pro** includes high-resolution imagery and data for the entire world (not just sections of it as **Google Earth** does), can import site plans and property lists, can import data from spreadsheets, and much more. Extra specialized modules are available for $200 each. For more information and to buy, go to http://earth.google.com/earth_pro.html.

75

12

Creating Your Own Blog with Google's Blogger

IN THIS CHAPTER:

Blogging, the act of writing a kind of online diary, has become a hobby for many and a preoccupation for some. Blogs enable you to write about anything you want, whether it be gardening, sleeping, playing guitar, politics...name it, and you can write about it.

Blogging has become part of the United State's political discourse, and has become extremely influential in campaigns and normal daily political life. But you don't have to be a honcho in order to blog. Anyone can do it.

Google's **Blogger** is probably the easiest way to create your own blog. It's free, it's simple, and it won't take you long to get started. Spend as much or as little time as you want; you can easily create a constantly changing blog if you spend only 10 minutes a day. **Blogger** is a Google-owned website. You don't need to download any software to use it to create your own blog. Just visit the site and follow the steps outlined in this chapter.

If you've always wanted to join the blog world, this chapter will show you how to do it.

76   Create a Blogger Account

→ SEE ALSO

27 Search Through Blogs with Google
77 Create a Blog Entry

Before you can create your blog, you need to create a **Blogger** account. Even though Google owns the **Blogger** website, creating a Google account won't help you here. Your Google account and **Blogger** account are completely separate. So you have to set up an account on **Blogger** before you can start your own blog.

1   Go to www.blogger.com

To start blogging with Google, go to www.blogger.com. This is Google's **Blogger** blogging site, and it's where you create your blog entries.

2   Click Create Your Blog Now

On the main page of the **Blogger** website, click the **Create Your Blog Now** button to get started with registration. You have to create an account before you can build your first blog.

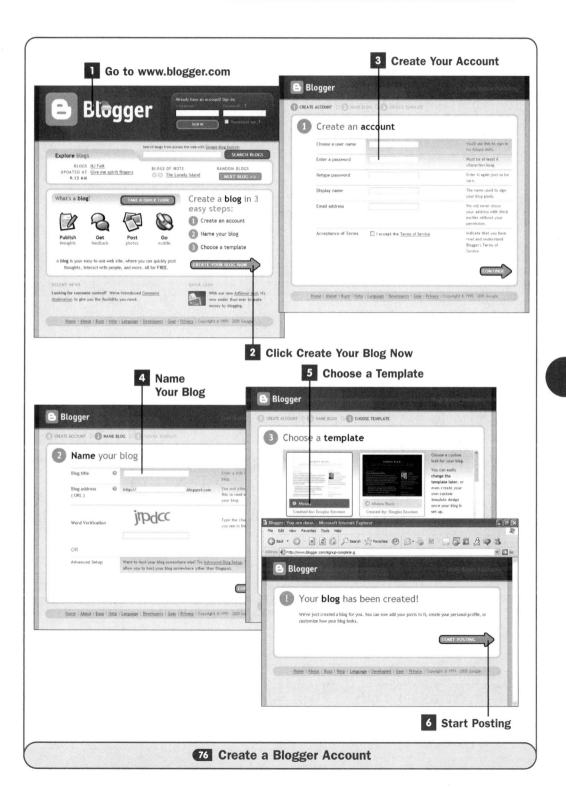

1 Go to www.blogger.com

2 Click Create Your Blog Now

3 Create Your Account

4 Name Your Blog

5 Choose a Template

6 Start Posting

76

③ Create Your Account

On the **Create an account** page that appears, type a username, password, your display name (the name you want to appear on your blog), and your email address. Click the **Terms of Service** link and read the legal agreement that appears in a new window; when you've finished reading, close the window to return to the **Create an account** page. Check the box next to **I accept the Terms of Service** and then click **Continue**.

④ Name Your Blog

On the **Name your blog** page that appears, enter a title for your blog and a blog address (a URL). The blog address ends in **blogspot.com**. So if you type the URL **prestonblog**, the complete URL at which people can find your blog is **www.prestonblog.blogspot.com**. After you type your preferred URL, type the **Word Verification** letters you see on the screen and click **Continue**. If the URL you enter is already taken, you get the notification, **Sorry, this blog address is not available**. Type a new URL and continue.

77

▶ **NOTE**

If you want to have your blog on a domain other than **blogspot.com**, click the **Advanced Blog Setup** link. You need to know the details of the domain you plan to use, such as the FTP server you use to upload files. Check with your hosting service for details.

⑤ Choose a Template

From the **Choose a template** page that appears, choose the template you want to use for your blog. Scroll down the page to see all the available templates. Don't worry if you end up choosing the wrong one. You can change the template later and even create a custom template if you want. When you've made a choice, click **Continue**.

⑥ Start Posting

Blogger takes a few moments to build your basic blog site. When it finishes, it displays a page telling you that your blog has been created. Click the **Start Posting** button to create your first post, as explained in **77** **Create a Blog Entry**.

---

77 **Create a Blog Entry**

✔ **BEFORE YOU BEGIN**

76 Create a Blogger Account

After you create your blog, you can begin posting. When you create a new post, the Post Editor opens a form in which you type the text of your post. Creating new posts for your blog is easy.

1 Go to Your Dashboard

Command central for your blog is what **Blogger** calls the **Dashboard**, so get there to create a post. To get to the **Dashboard**, go to www.blogger.com and type your username and password at the top of the screen. You log in and are sent to your **Dashboard** for your blog—the title of the blog you created is on the **Dashboard**.

▶ **NOTE**

If you create your first blog entry after creating your **Blogger** account, as outlined in **76** **Create a Blogger Account**, you won't have to first log into your **Dashboard**. When you click **Start Posting** at the end of creating your account, you are sent to the posting screen.

2 Enter a Title for the Post

To create a new post, click **New Post** next to your blog name. The Post Editor opens a new screen, which you fill out to create your post. At the top of the screen, next to **Title**, type the title of your post (you named the blog itself when you created your **Blogger** account). It's best to be pithy, descriptive, and to write a title that might draw readers in.

3 Write Your Post

After writing your title, write the body of your post. Make it witty, moving, mundane...anything you want. The point of the blog is to write and express yourself.

4 Format the Text

The toolbar just above your post enables you to format your text by using bold, italic, changing the font and size, adding color, and similar features. Highlight the text you want to change and select your action from the toolbar.

5 Add Pictures

Blogger enables you to add pictures to your blog, choosing images either from files you have on your computer or from elsewhere on the Internet. Position the insertion point in the body of your post where you want to insert the picture and then click the image icon on the toolbar. A dialog box appears that enables you to insert the image and control its look and placement.

77

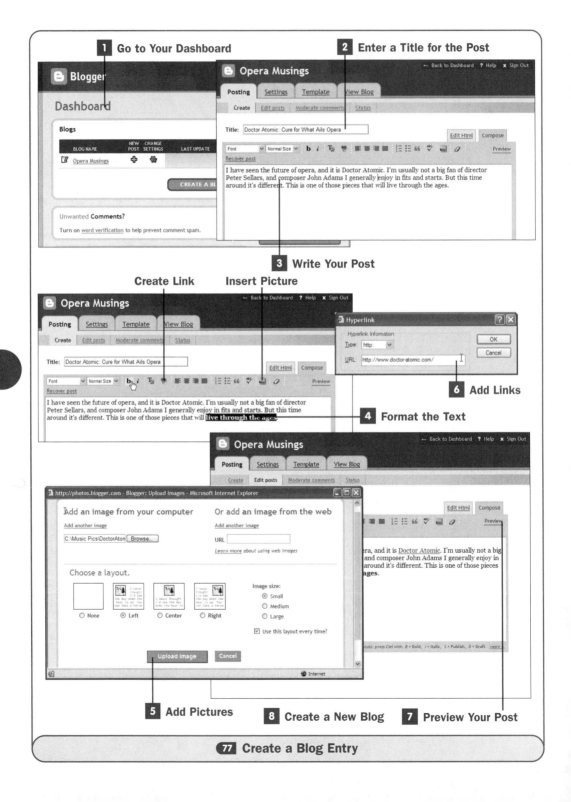

In the dialog box, click the **Browse** button, go to the folder where the image you want to use is stored, and select it. From the **Choose a layout** section of the dialog box, select how text should wrap around the image (if you'll have text wrapping around it). Next, choose the size in the **Image size** area at which you want the image displayed—small, medium, or large.

If you plan to use this same layout every time you include a picture, check the box next to **Use this layout every time?**

If you're not uploading the image from your computer, and instead are pointing to an image that's already on the Web, type its location in the **URL** text box. Provide the entire URL, including the image name, like this: **http://sfopera.com/images/2005/05-DoctorAtomic.jpg**.

When you're done specifying image information, click **Upload Image**. The specified image is uploaded from your computer (if the image is already on the Web, Blogger creates a link to the image on the Web). When it's done, a screen appears telling you that the image has been sent (or the link created). Click the **Done** button to return to the post-creation page.

6 Add Links

Blogger makes it easy to add links to your blog. Highlight the text you want to turn into a link and click the link icon in the toolbar. In the **Hyperlink** dialog box that opens, type the URL to which you want to link and click **OK**.

77

▶ NOTE

If you're comfortable editing HTML yourself, you can edit the HTML directly on the page and add HTML tags. To do it, click the **Edit HTML** link on the post-creation page.

7 Preview Your Post

Before posting, it's a good idea to preview your post so you can see what it looks like and test its links. Click the **Preview** link in the upper-right corner of the post-creation page. You see a preview of what your post will look like. If you want to publish what you see, click **Publish Post**. **Blogger** uploads all your files and tells you when the post is complete. To view your blog, click **View Blog**.

If you don't want to publish the post you are previewing, and instead want to edit it, click **Save as Draft**. You are brought back to your **Dashboard** page, and you see your post there. Click **Edit**. You are brought back to the page where you compose the post. Continue to edit it until it's what you want, and then publish it.

After your post is published, people can make comments about it by clicking **Post a Comment** underneath your post in the blog.

8 Create a New Blog

You're not limited to having just a single blog with **Blogger**. You can create multiple blogs if you have multiple interests. So you might want to create one about knitting, another about your Godzilla fascination, and yet another about your love of opera.

To create another blog in addition to one you've already created, go to the **Dashboard** and click the **Create a Blog** button. You go through the same steps you did from step 4 onward in **76** **Create a Blogger Account**.

---

78 Create a Blogger Profile

✔ BEFORE YOU BEGIN	→ SEE ALSO
76 Create a Blogger Account	**77** Create a Blog Entry

78

When you blog, you share your thoughts with the world. Many people create profiles of themselves on the blog so their lives as well as their thoughts can be shared with others. There's another good reason for creating a profile: If people understand your life and background, it helps them better understand your posts. When you create a profile, a link appears on your blog that reads **View my complete profile**. When someone clicks that link they can view your profile, with the information in it that you've chosen to provide.

1 Click the Edit Profile Link

Log into **Blogger** at www.blogger.com. When you do, you are sent to your **Dashboard**. To create a profile, click either the **Edit Profile** link or the **Add your photo here by editing your profile** link.

2 Fill out the Privacy Section

The top part of the page concerns your privacy. It enables you to choose whether your profile should be seen by others, whether your real name is shown with your blog rather than your display name, and whether your email address is shown on your blog. You can also provide links to other blogs you write. To link to another one of your blogs, click the **Select blogs to display** link, choose the blogs you want to display, and click **Save settings**. The links to your other blogs appear in your profile.

3 Fill out the Identity Section

The **Identity** section of the **Edit User Profile** screen enables you to include your username, email address, display name (the name visitors to your blog see), as well as your real first and last names.

1 Click the Edit Profile Link

2 Fill out the Privacy Section

3 Fill out the Identity Section

4 Include a Photograph and Audio Clip

78

78 Create a Blogger Profile

78

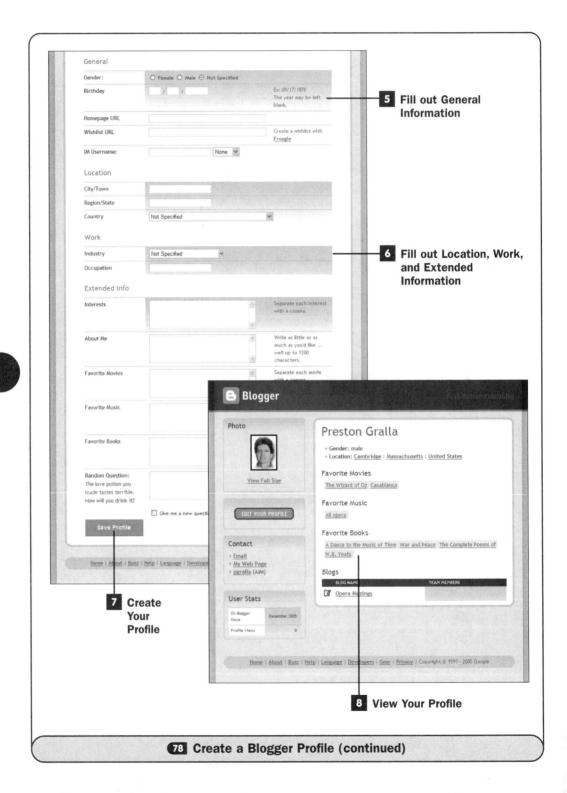

5 Fill out General Information

6 Fill out Location, Work, and Extended Information

7 Create Your Profile

8 View Your Profile

78 Create a Blogger Profile (continued)

4 Include a Photograph and Audio Clip

You can include a photograph of yourself and an audio clip you've made. You can't upload them, however, to the site from your computer. Instead, the files have to live in the Web somewhere. **Blogger** includes links to several free services that will host the files for you. Click the **photo hosting** link next to the **Photo URL** text box for information on how to get free hosting of your picture; click the **audio clips** link next to the **Audio Clip URL** text box to get free hosting for audio files.

5 Fill out General Information

The **General** portion of the **Edit User Profile** page enables you to fill in a variety of personal information, including gender; birth date; a home page URL if you have one; a *wishlist* URL, which you can create using **Froogle**; and an instant messenger username. To create a wishlist, click the **Froogle** link.

▶ KEY TERM

Wishlist—A list of items you are interested in having bought for you for a birthday or holiday, for example.

78

6 Fill out Location, Work, and Extended Information

The final parts of your profile concern your location, work, and a series of questions, such as your favorite movies and books.

7 Create Your Profile

When you're done, click **Save Profile**. Your profile is saved, and you're sent back to the **Edit User Profile** screen. Near the top, the screen has the message **Your settings have been saved**, and a **View Updated Profile** link. To view your profile, click the **View Updated Profile** link. If you've chosen to make your profile public, people are able to see it when they click the **View my complete profile** link on your blog page.

8 View Your Profile

There are two ways to see your profile. You can visit your blog and click **View my complete profile**, or you can go to your **Dashboard** and click the **View** link next to **Edit Profile**.

79 **Customize Your Blog Settings**

✔ BEFORE YOU BEGIN

76 Create a Blogger Account

→ SEE ALSO

80 Change Your Blog Template

Don't like the way your blog works or looks? No problem—you can easily change it. The **Blogger** application gives you considerable control over how you publish your blog, and how it looks and works, as you'll see in this task.

79

▮ Click Change Settings in the Dashboard

Log into **Blogger** at www.blogger.com; when the **Dashboard** appears, click the gear icon in the **Change Settings** column to open the screen that enables you to change your settings.

▮ Change Your Basic Settings

The **Basic** tab of the **Settings** pages, which you are sent to when you click the **Change Settings** gear icon, enables you to change these options:

- **Title**—Change the title of your blog.

- **Description**—Change the description of your blog.

- **Add your Blog to our listings**—Add your blog to the public **Blogger** directory. If you select **No**, the blog is still available on the Internet, but it won't be published or searchable in the **Blogger** directory.

- **Show Quick Editing on your Blog**—When you're viewing your blog, this option enables you to click an icon to edit a post. (The icon is located just beneath each post, and looks like a small pencil.) Only you can see the icon, and you have to be logged in to see it.

- **Show Email Post links**—This option puts an email link on your blog so people can easily email your posts to others by clicking the link.

- **Show Compose Mode for all your blogs**—This option displays the **Compose** tab that you use to create your blog posts. If the **Compose** tab isn't displayed, you have to enter HTML tags to format the text of the post yourself.

- **Delete Your Blog**—If you decide you no longer want to update your blog, it's a good idea to delete it so you no longer get comments from readers. The **Delete Your Blog** option enables you to delete your blog. You have to choose which blog to delete if you have more than one.

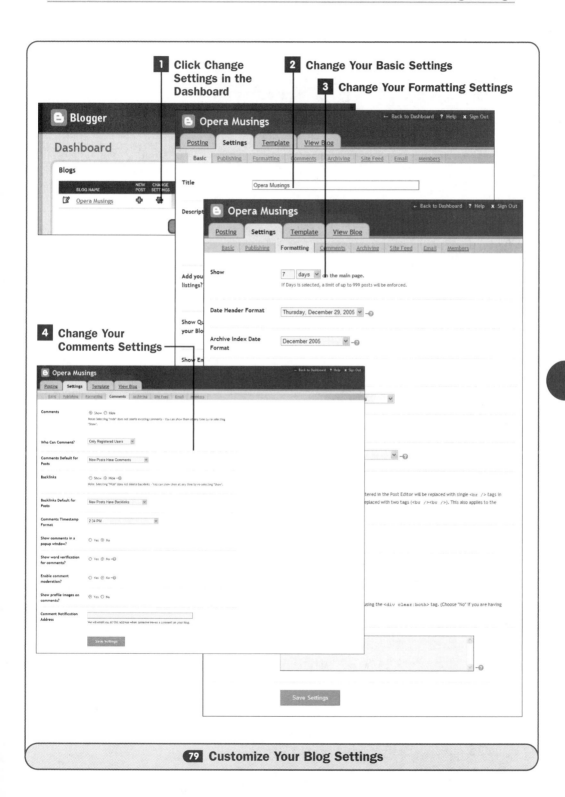

1 Click Change Settings in the Dashboard

2 Change Your Basic Settings

3 Change Your Formatting Settings

4 Change Your Comments Settings

79

79 Customize Your Blog Settings

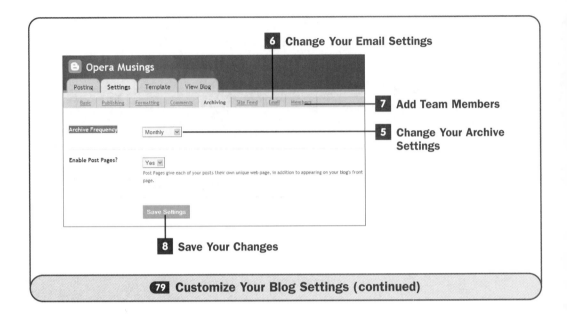

6 **Change Your Email Settings**

7 **Add Team Members**

5 **Change Your Archive Settings**

8 **Save Your Changes**

79 **Customize Your Blog Settings (continued)**

79

▶ **NOTE**

Use the settings on the **Publishing** tab (located at the top of the **Settings** page) if you want to change the URL of your blog. Before you change that setting, make sure the URL you want is available.

3 Change Your Formatting Settings

Blogger enables you to change how your blog is formatted. Click the **Formatting** tab at the top of the **Settings** page to change these settings:

- **Show**—Change how many days of posts to show on your main blog page, or how many individual posts to show. Whether you choose the number of days or the number of posts, you can show a maximum of 999 posts.

- **Date Header Format**, **Archive Index Date Format**, and **Timestamp Format**—Choose which date formats to use for those options; for example, December 2006 or 12/2006.

- **Time Zone**—Choose the time zone in which you live or create your posts.

- **Date Language**—Choose the language for the date on the blog (the language in which you type the text of the blog itself is unaffected by this selection).

- **Encoding**—Choose the language (actually, the character set) in which you want to publish your blog. The default is UTF-8, a form of character encoding that supports all languages. But if you publish in another language and are having display problems, choose the proper language from the drop-down list.

- **Convert line breaks**—Determine whether single hard returns entered in the Post Editor are replaced with single **
** tags in your blog, and two hard returns are replaced with two tags (**

). This also applies to the comment-posting form. Selecting **Yes chooses this option. If you select **No**, you have to add the HTML tags yourself.

- **Show Title field**—Enables you to create titles for your blog posts. If you choose **No** for this, your posts will not have titles, which means that you will not be able to include a title when you create a post.

- **Show Link Field**—Enables you to highlight a link to another page or blog on the Web. Enable this option by selecting **Yes**, and then paste this HTML code just above the "posted by" line in your blog:

  <BlogItemURL>

  <a href="<$BlogItemURL$>">Link</a>

  </BlogItemURL>

  So, for example, if you wanted to include a link in your blog to the site **Networking Pipeline** with the URL http://www.networkingpipeline. com, you'd add this HTML:

  <BlogItemURL>

  <a href="http://www.networkingpipeline.com">Networking Pipeline</a>

  </BlogItemURL>

- **Enable float alignment**—Choose how to align images with text on your blog.

- **Post Template**—Enables you to add HTML code to the top of every post so you don't need to add it manually each time. Only choose this option if you're experienced with HTML. The HTML you add would give your entire blog a different look than what is created by **Blogger**—the HTML would literally create a design template.

4 Change Your Comments Settings

To change how your blog handles comments, click the **Comments** tab at the top of the **Settings** page. As explained earlier, people can make comments to your blog by clicking the **Comment** link in each post. You can change these settings:

- **Comments, Who Can Comment,** and **Comments Default for Posts**— These options control your basic comments settings. The **Show** and **Hide Comments** radio buttons enable or disable the display of comments. The **Who Can Comment** option enables you to determine whether registered users, anyone, or only members of the blog can post. The **Comments Default for Posts** option controls whether or not all new posts have the **Comment** link enabled. Some people prefer to have the most interactivity with readers possible; others prefer none or limited contact with readers, so choose your comment preferences according to how much feedback you want.

- **Backlinks** and **Backlinks Default for Posts**—*Backlinks* appear whenever another blog or page on the Web has linked to your post. You can show or hide backlinks, and choose whether new posts should have them.

▶ **TIP**

Backlinks appear on the blog page and can be seen by a visitor to your blog. One problem with backlinks is that spammers and pornography sites have found a devious way to get their URLs in the public eye—they create backlinks (often in an automated way) on many sites. So if you are worried about that happening on your blog page—or if spam backlinks have already started appearing on your blog—turn off backlinks.

▶ **KEY TERM**

Backlinks—A method of keeping track of other blogs and pages on the Web that link to your blog.

- **Comments Timestamp Format**—Control the time format used to show when a comment was made; for example, **12/29/2005 2:33 PM** or **December 29, 2005 2:33 PM**.

- **Show comments in a popup window**—Choose whether comments should appear normally or in a popup window.

- **Show word verification for comments**—This option forces people to type a word displayed as a graphic on their screen before they can post a comment. This is done for security reasons—blog spam has become a big problem, and automated programs post pornographic and inappropriate comments to people's blogs. Forcing people to type the word stops the automated spam.

- **Enable comment moderation**—If you select **Yes** for this option, no comments are posted to your blog unless you first view them and allow them to be posted. This option cuts down on inappropriate comments.

- **Show profile images on comments**—If you choose **Yes** for this option and someone posts a comment to your blog who also has a blog on **Blogger** and has a profile that contains her photograph or another image, that image is displayed next to her comments on your blog.

- **Comment Notification Address**—If you enter your email address in this text box, a notification is sent to you every time someone makes a comment on your blog.

▶ **TIP**

Some of the options can be confusing. To get help, tips, and explanations about options you aren't sure about, click the question mark icon next to an option.

5 Change Your Archive Settings

When people want to see your previous blogs, they do it by reading through your archives—your blog postings organized on a daily, weekly, or monthly basis. To change your archive settings, click the **Archiving** link. To change archive frequency, select **Daily**, **Weekly**, **Monthly**, or **No Archive** from the drop-down list. When you archive posts, they move off the main blog page and onto their own archive page. So, for example, if you choose to archive weekly, **Blogger** moves the posts off the main page of your blog every week and makes those old posts accessible via links on your main blog page. If you post frequently, it's a good idea to archive frequently; if you rarely post, archive less frequently.

If you want to create a *post page*, which is a page that contains your post, by itself (in addition to the post living on your blog), select **Yes** next to **Enable Post Pages**. Visitors to your main blog page can then click a link to view the selected post on a separate page.

▶ **KEY TERM**

Post page—A separate web page that contains an individual post from your blog. The post also lives on your main blog page.

6 Change Your Email Settings

To change the way in which you interact with your blog via email, click the **Email** tab at the top of the **Settings** pages. If you want your blog mailed to you each time you publish, enter your email address in the **Blog Send Address** box. If you want to be able to create posts via email, enter a "secret name" in the **Mail-to-Blogger Address** box. You can then send an email to the secret address you create, and that email is posted as a blog entry.

79

▶ **NOTE**

The **Site Feed** section of your **Settings** options is used to create an RSS feed so people can read your blog in an RSS reader. For details, see **81** **Create a Site Feed**.

7 Add Team Members

Blogs don't have to be maintained by individuals; you can have a group blog in which multiple people can post. To do it, click the **Members** tab at the top of the **Settings** page, click **Add Team Member(s)**, and follow the instructions for adding a member to your blog.

8 Save Your Changes

When you've made your changes to your blog settings, click the **Save Settings** button at the bottom of a page, and your changes go into effect. The **Members** page does not have a **Save Settings** button, so if you're on that page, return to another page, such as the **Email** page, and click **Save Settings**.

80

80 **Change Your Blog Template**	
✔ **BEFORE YOU BEGIN**	→ **SEE ALSO**
76 Create a Blogger Account	**79** Customize Your Blog Settings

When you first signed into **Blogger**, you chose a blog template. A template changes the way your blog looks—it changes the layout, font, background colors, and so on. The actual content of your blog remains the same, regardless of the template you apply to your blog, but the template changes the look and feel of the blog. **Blogger** has dozens of templates from which you can choose. You don't need to continue using the first template you chose—you can change it any time you want. Here's how to do it.

1 Click Template in the Dashboard

Log into **Blogger** at www.blogger.com; when the **Dashboard** appears, click the gear icon in the **Change Settings** column to open the **Settings** screen. Click the **Template** tab at the top of the screen to open the **Template Settings** screen.

2 Click Pick New

Click the **Pick New** tab at the top of the page to open a page that enables you to select a new template for your blog.

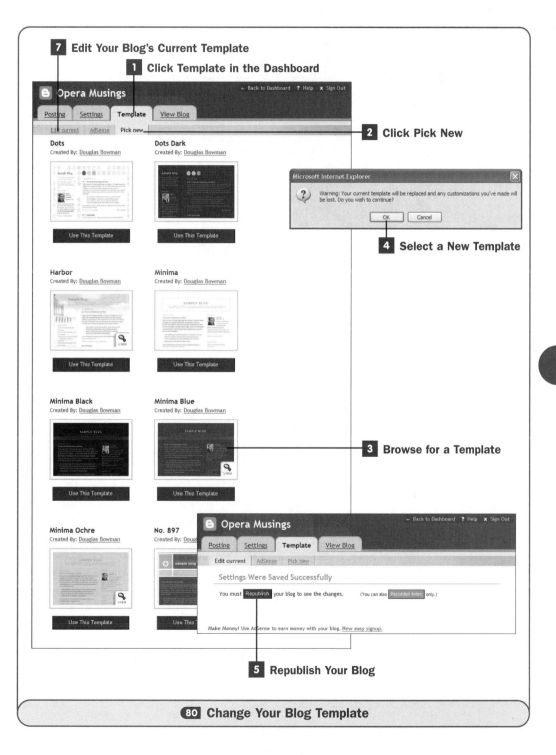

7 Edit Your Blog's Current Template

1 Click Template in the Dashboard

2 Click Pick New

4 Select a New Template

3 Browse for a Template

5 Republish Your Blog

80 Change Your Blog Template

Preview the Template

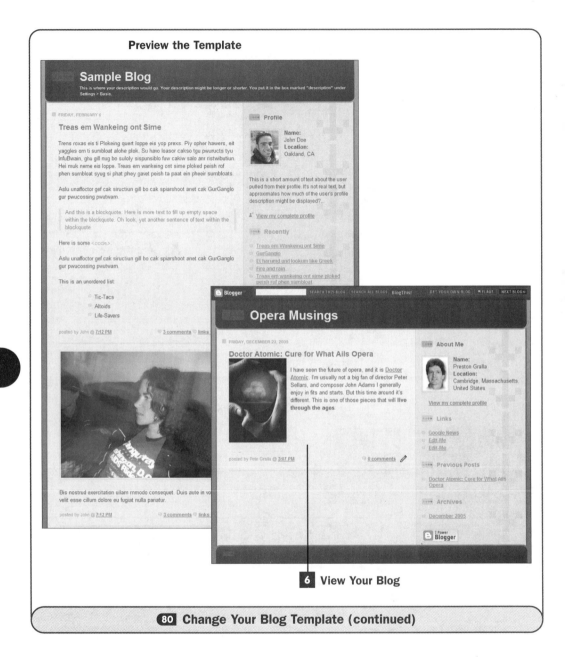

80

6 View Your Blog

80 Change Your Blog Template (continued)

3 **Browse for a Template**

Scroll through the templates, looking for one you want to use. When you see one in which you are interested, click the **View** button in the lower-right corner of the template thumbnail to see a full-page preview of the template page.

▶ **NOTE**

Not all templates have a **View** button that enables you to preview them.

4 Select a New Template

When you find a template you want to use, click the **Use This Template** button beneath the template thumbnail. A dialog box appears, warning that when you switch to a new template, any customizations you have made to your existing template will be lost. Click **OK** to continue and apply the new template, or click **Cancel** to cancel the change.

5 Republish Your Blog

You are sent to a page that tells you your template change was successfully made. But for the new settings to go into effect, you must republish your blog. When you republish your blog, you take all the existing posts and content and publish it in your new template. Click the **Republish** button to republish the blog and put the new template into effect. A page appears, telling you that your blog was successfully republished.

6 View Your Blog

Click the **View Blog** link to see your blog with the new template applied.

7 Edit Your Blog's Current Template

If you're comfortable with HTML, you can make changes to your blog's template yourself by using HTML tags. To do it, click the **Template** tab at the top of the **Settings** screen to open the **Template Settings** screen. Then click the **Edit Current** tab at the top of the page. Make the changes in the HTML input box. Then click **Save Template Changes**, and follow the directions for republishing your blog.

▶ **TIP**

The **AdSense** link at the top of the **Template** tab at on the **Settings** screen enables you to sign up for a Google-run advertising program. The program places context-sensitive links on your blog. You are paid each time someone clicks an ad link. After you sign up for **AdSense**, you are sent to a preview version of your template that shows how your blog will look with the **AdSense** ads. The template also includes drop-down boxes that enable you to change the size and placement of the ads.

80

---

81 | Create a Site Feed

✔ BEFORE YOU BEGIN	→ SEE ALSO
76 Create a Blogger Account	**49** Add RSS Feeds to Google Personalized Home
79 Customize Your Blog Settings	**84** About Google Reader and RSS Feeds

People lead busy lives, and the odds are that a great many of them are not going to take the time to visit your blog every day. So how to get people to read it? One of the best ways is to create a site feed that feeds the contents of your blog straight to people's computers. All they need is an RSS reader (a piece of software or a website that can accept and display site feeds). Your blog entries appear right in their RSS reader. Google also has an RSS reader, called **Google Reader**. For details about RSS feeds and RSS readers, see **84** **About Google Reader and RSS Feeds**. Creating a site feed, as you'll see in this task, is surprisingly easy.

1 Go to the Site Feed Page

Log into **Blogger** at www.blogger.com; when the **Dashboard** appears, click the gear icon in the **Change Settings** column. From the **Settings** page that opens, click the **Site Feed** link at the top of the page.

2 Turn on Your Site Feed

Choose **Yes** from the **Publish Site Feed** drop-down list. This option creates your feed.

▶ NOTE

Blogger creates its site feed in a format called Atom, which is a different feed format from the better-known RSS. But most, if not all, RSS readers can read Atom feeds as well as RSS feeds.

3 Choose Full or Short Descriptions

From the **Descriptions** drop-down box, choose either **Full** or **Short**. If you choose **Full**, the entire content of your posts appear in the site feed. If you choose **Short**, only the first paragraph, or approximately 255 characters (whichever is shorter), appears in the feed.

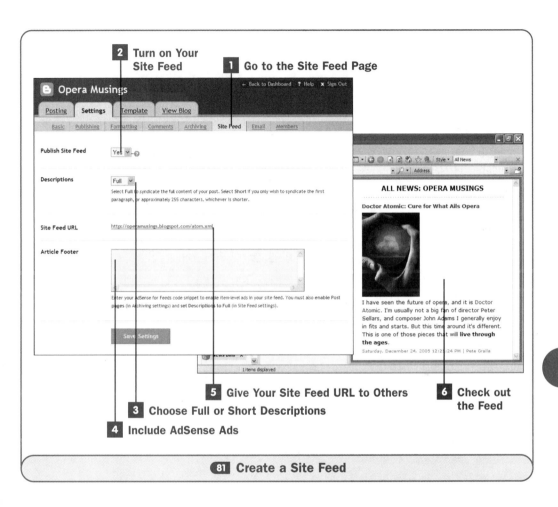

2 Turn on Your Site Feed

1 Go to the Site Feed Page

5 Give Your Site Feed URL to Others

6 Check out the Feed

3 Choose Full or Short Descriptions

4 Include AdSense Ads

81

81 Create a Site Feed

4 Include AdSense Ads

If you use the Google AdSense program and include ads on your site, you can include ads in your feed as well. When you sign up for AdSense, you are given an HTML code snippet. Copy the snippet into the **Article Footer** text box. You also have to enable the **Post pages** option on the **Archiving Settings** page and set the **Descriptions** option to **Full**, as noted in step 3. For details on how to enable the **Post pages** option, see **79** **Customize Your Blog Settings**.

5 Give Your Site Feed URL to Others

The page displays the URL of your site feed, for example, **http://operamusings.blogspot.com/atom.xml**. Give that URL to other people so they can read your site feed in an RSS reader.

6 Check out the Feed

To make sure that the feed is working properly, use an RSS reader to view it. If there are any problems with the URL and the site feed, go back over the steps in this task.

▶ **TIP**

You can use the free **Google Reader** to read the feed. The reader is Web-based, so you don't need to download additional software to read RSS with it. Go to it at www.google.com/reader. If you instead want to use downloadable software, you can download FeedDemon for $29.95 at www.feeddemon.com. A good free reader is SharpReader, available at www.sharpreader.net.

---

82 **Power Up Your Blogging with Blogger Add-ins**

✔ BEFORE YOU BEGIN	→ SEE ALSO
76 Create a Blogger Account	**56** Customize the Google Toolbar
51 Use the Google Toolbar to Search from Anywhere	

82

After blogging becomes a way of life for you, you'll want an easier way to create posts. Having to constantly navigate back to **Blogger** and go through the posting process can be unnecessarily time-consuming.

Two great **Blogger** add-ins make it much easier for you to post to your blog. **Blogger for Word** enables you to use Microsoft Word to post to your blogs, and **Blog This!** enables you to create a blog post from anywhere on the Web.

1 Download and Install Blogger for Word

Blogger for Word is a free add-in to Microsoft Word that enables you to create a blog post from directly within Word—you won't have to actually go to your blog posting page to create a post. To get the software ad-in, go to http://buzz.blogger.com/bloggerforword.html and download and install the add-in.

2 Edit Settings

After you install **Blogger for Word**, four new buttons appear on your Word toolbar—**Blogger Settings, Open Post, Save as Draft,** and **Publish**. If these buttons don't appear, click the **View** menu, choose **Toolbars,** and select **Blogger**.

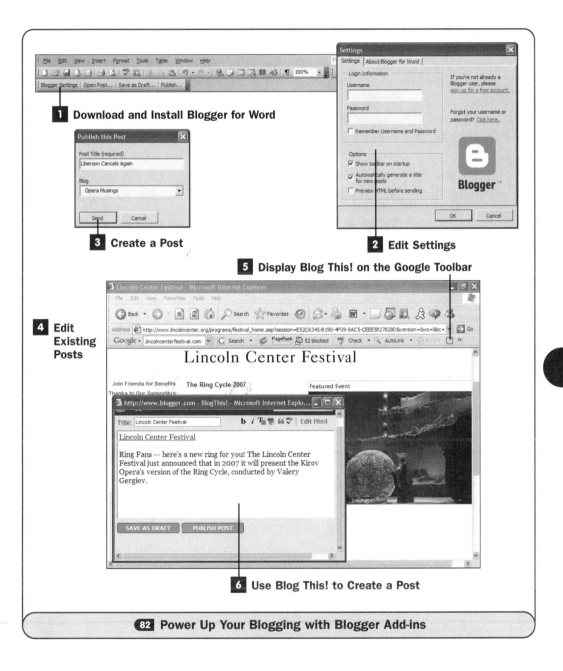

1 Download and Install Blogger for Word

3 Create a Post

2 Edit Settings

5 Display Blog This! on the Google Toolbar

4 Edit Existing Posts

6 Use Blog This! to Create a Post

82 Power Up Your Blogging with Blogger Add-ins

For **Blogger for Word** to post to your blog, it needs information such as your username and password. Click the **Blogger Settings** button in the **Blogger for Word** toolbar and fill out the form. In addition to specifying your username and password, you can also use the form to customize your **Blogger for Word** settings. Check the box next to **Show toolbar on startup** if you want the **Blogger for Word** toolbar to appear every time you start Word. If you want **Blogger for Word** to automatically create a title for your new posts, check the box next to **Automatically generate a title for new posts**. When you do this, **Blogger for Word** takes the first several words of your post and creates a title from them. (You can edit the title before you post.) And if you want to examine the HTML before you post it, enable the **Preview HTML before sending** check box.

▶ **NOTE**

When you're not using **Blogger for Word**, you can turn off its toolbar in Microsoft Word. Choose **View, Toolbars, Blogger** to take away the check mark next to the **Blogger** option. To turn on the **Blogger for Word** toolbar, choose **View, Toolbars, Blogger** again to put a check mark next to the **Blogger** option.

82

③ Create a Post

Write your post in Microsoft Word as you would any other document. You can format your text using boldface, italic, fonts, and colors, if you want. **Blogger for Word** automatically creates the HTML for the formatting for your blog.

To save your post so you can edit it later, click the **Save as Draft** button in the **Blogger for Word** toolbar. To publish your post, click the **Publish** button in the toolbar. From the form that appears, choose the blog to which you want to post this message (if you have more than one blog on your **Blogger** account). Edit the title of the post if you want and then click **Send**. You get a confirmation that the post has been sent. After a few moments, the post is made live. (You, of course, have to be connected to the Internet to publish your posts.)

④ Edit Existing Posts

You can also use **Blogger for Word** to edit existing posts. Click the **Open Post** button in the **Blogger for Word** toolbar and select the post or posts you want to edit. (You can choose up to 10.) After editing them, click **Publish** and then **Update**, and the posts you edited are updated. (You, of course, have to be connected to the Internet to edit your posts.)

⑤ Display Blog This! on the Google Toolbar

Frequently, blogs comment on current events, websites, or on other blogs. When creating a post that comments on a website or blog, you should put a link to the original blog or website at the top of your post.

To make it easy to comment on websites and blogs, you can use the **Blog This!** feature of the **Google Toolbar**. This option enables you to write a blog entry and create a link to a web page without having to go to your **Blogger** account—you can do it when you're on any web page.

Download and install the **Google Toolbar** if you haven't already. (For details, see **51** **Use the Google Toolbar to Search from Anywhere**.) Then make the **Blog This!** icon visible by clicking the **Toolbar Options** button, clicking the **More** tab, checking the box next to **Blog This!**, and clicking **OK**.

6 Use Blog This! to Create a Post

When you're on a web page about which you want to write a blog, click the **Blog This!** icon on the **Google Toolbar**. A window appears, at the top of which is the name of the page you're on and a link to the page. Write your blog post about the page. If you want to format the text, use the formatting toolbar in the **Blog This!** window. You can also edit the HTML directly by clicking the **Edit HTML** link. When you're done, click **Save As Draft** to save the post as a draft, or click **Publish Post** to publish the post directly to your **Blogger** account. After you publish the post, you get a screen telling you the post has been published. If you save the post as a draft, the post is saved to your blog, just as if you had created the post directly on **Blogger** and saved it there as a draft. You can open the draft post from your **Blogger Dashboard** and edit and publish it.

83

▶ TIP

If you use the alternative browser, Firefox, there's an excellent *extension* (Firefox's name for an add-in) that enables you to see any blog posts made about a web page. The **Blogger Web Comments** extension shows you all the **Blogger** posts about a particular web page and enables you to click straight to them. It even includes a **Blogger** posting form so you can blog about the page yourself. Get the extension from www.google.com/tools/firefox/webcomments. Note that the **Blogger Web Comments** extension works only with version 1.5 of Firefox or above.

83	**About Advanced Blogger Features**

✔ **BEFORE YOU BEGIN**	→ **SEE ALSO**
79 Customize Your Blog Settings	**82** Power Up Your Blogging with Blogger Add-ins

---

This chapter has given you a good start on setting up and creating a blog. But **Blogger** has so many features and blogging can be such a complex endeavor that an entire book could be written about creating blogs with **Blogger**.

▶ **TIP**

If you want to keep up on the latest news, power tools, and tips for using Blogger, check in regularly to the Blogger Buzz page at http://buzz.blogger.com.

A great way to take advantage of advanced features is to use HTML in your blogs. **Blogger** can use any HTML you can throw at it, so study up on HTML and then start using it. But make sure not to add too many fonts and special effects. The point of blogging is simplicity and your words; special effects can get in the way.

An excellent way to make your blog stand out is to create your own template. **Blogger** has only a limited number of precreated templates available, and so blogs can often seem similar to one another because of their look. But creating your own template in HTML makes your blog stand out from other blogs. To create your own template, go to your **Dashboard**, click the gear icon under the **Change Settings** column, click the **Template** link at the top of the **Settings** page, and then click **Edit Current**.

83

13

Reading News, Blogs, and More with Google Reader

IN THIS CHAPTER:

Really Simple Syndication (RSS) feeds are fast becoming one of the Internet's most popular new types of services. If you're in search of the latest news and information, you don't have to hop from website to website when you use them; you don't even have to do searches—feeds can be delivered straight to you.

One of the most common uses of RSS feeds are for reading blogs, but RSS feeds are not limited to blogs alone. News sites and services, such as the *New York Times*, *Washington Post*, *Reuters*, and many others now have feeds as well, so you can have breaking news delivered to you the instant it happens. And other sites are taking up RSS as well.

In this chapter, you'll learn how to use **Google Reader**, Google's free RSS reader.

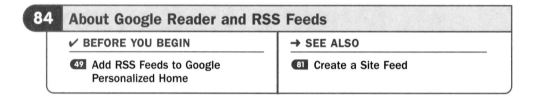

84 | **About Google Reader and RSS Feeds**

✔ **BEFORE YOU BEGIN**

49 Add RSS Feeds to Google Personalized Home

→ **SEE ALSO**

81 Create a Site Feed

RSS is a way of delivering information to your PC without you having to go out and visit a website to get that information. It is a special format used by websites and blogs to, in essence, broadcast information. Because the information is sent in a special format, you need a special reader to read the information. You view the information in the reader itself. The reader software enables you to choose which RSS feeds you want to read out of the many thousands available. Choosing an RSS feed is commonly called *subscribing to the feed*.

You can read RSS feeds in two primary ways. One way is to buy a special RSS reader or download a free one. An especially good for-pay reader is FeedDemon (available at www.feeddemon.com for $29.95). A good free reader is SharpReader (available at www.sharpreader.net). Downloadable RSS readers tend to be very powerful, with many features. The drawback is that they require installation, and if you're on a computer other than your own, you won't be able to read your RSS feeds. If you use a Web-based reader, such as the one Google offers, you can view your feeds by logging into the Web-based reader on any computer.

The other way to read RSS feeds is to use a website that enables you to read the feeds. Google offers several ways to read RSS feeds. Its **Personalized Home** page enables you to read the feeds—for information about how to do it, see **49** **Add RSS Feeds to Google Personalized Home**.

The **Personalized Home** RSS reader is simple to use, but it doesn't have many features. Essentially, it enables you to subscribe to feeds, and that's it.

Google Reader, on the other hand, offers far more features and rivals download-able RSS readers. It's easy to manage your RSS subscriptions, navigate through them, mail RSS items, and write your own blog entries about those RSS items when you use **Google Reader**.

So if you're just looking for a quick-and-dirty way to read RSS feeds, **Personalized Home** is the way to go. If you need more features, use **Google Reader**.

---

85 | **Subscribe to Feeds**

✔ BEFORE YOU BEGIN	→ SEE ALSO
84 About Google Reader and RSS Feeds	**49** Add RSS Feeds to Google Personalized Home
	81 Create a Site Feed

Subscribing to RSS feeds is easy—all you need to know is a topic in which you're interested, and you'll be able to find a feed, subscribe to it, and then read it. This task shows you how to do it.

1 Go to Google Reader

In your browser's address bar, type **www.google.com/reader** and press **Enter**.

2 Search for a Feed

In the search box at the top of the screen, type a term or terms that describe the kind of feed for which you're looking. Then click the **Search for new content** button. Google searches the Internet for any RSS feeds that match the search string you typed. If you click **Search the Web**, you instead do a normal Google search, so if you're specifically looking for RSS content, don't click that button. When you search for a feed, you search through an overall description of that feed, not through every individual item in the feed. So, for example, if you search for **Iraq**, you only get results of those feeds that include the word **Iraq** in the description of the feed itself—you won't get feeds in which individual items in the feed have the word **Iraq** in them.

3 Browse the Feeds

You are given a list of feeds. Each feed entry includes its name, a brief description, the site from which the feed comes, and the actual URL of the feed: for example, http://www.nytimes.com/services/xml/rss/nyt/ HomePage.xml. You don't need to know the URL of the feed to subscribe to it, but if you have a third-party RSS reader, such as FeedDemon, you can use

85

that URL to subscribe to the feed in the RSS reader. Click the blue link heading to check out the most recent page of the feed to see whether it is something to which you want to subscribe.

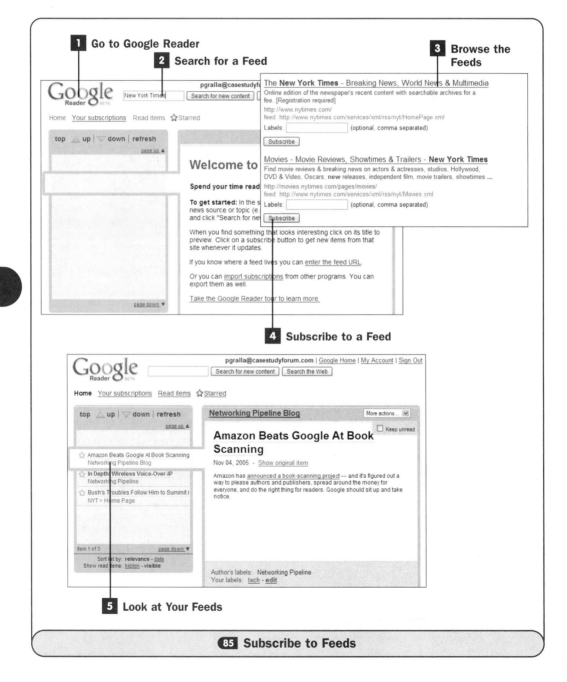

85   Subscribe to Feeds

4 Subscribe to a Feed

To subscribe to any feed, click the **Subscribe** button. You can also apply a label, or more than one label, to any feed by typing the label name or names in the **Labels** box. If you use more than one label, separate them with commas. There's no limit on the length of the label you specify.

Labels are useful if you subscribe to many feeds because they help you organize your feeds. If you don't apply labels now, you can at some later point, and you can also change the names of the labels later.

▶ TIP

If you know the URL of the feed to which you want to subscribe, type it into the search box and click **Search for new content**. The feed you specified is automatically added to your list of feeds in the **Google Reader**. Many sites post their RSS feed URLs. You can also find out the URL of a feed easily: If you see a small orange **RSS** icon on a page, that site has an RSS feed. Right-click the icon in Internet Explorer and choose **Copy Shortcut**. That action copies the RSS feed's URL into the Clipboard. You can now paste it into the **Google Reader** search box or into any other RSS reader.

You have to subscribe to each feed individually—in other words, you have to click the **Subscribe** button next to each feed to which you want to subscribe.

86

5 Look at Your Feeds

Go back to the main page of **Google Reader** by clicking the **Return to Home** link at the top of the search results page. To read your feeds, see **86** **Read Your Feeds**.

---

86 | Read Your Feeds

✔ BEFORE YOU BEGIN	→ SEE ALSO
85 Subscribe to Feeds	**87** Sort Your Feeds
	88 Manage Your Subscriptions

The whole point of subscribing to RSS feeds is to read them—and **Google Reader** makes it quite easy to do. After you've subscribed to your first feed(s), here's how to read them.

1 Read an Item

Go to the main page of **Google Reader**. You see a list of feed items on the left, and the most recent feed item on the right. If you're not logged in to your Google account, you are presented with a login screen. If you haven't yet created an account, you have to create one now. For details, see Chapter 1, "Start Here."

To view any item, click its title in the list on the left, and you see the title for the entry and a summary on the right side of the screen.

2 Browse the Items

To browse through your entire list of items, use the **up** and **down** buttons at the top of the left column to move through your list of feeds one item at a time. If you have more feeds than can fit in a single page in the left column of the **Google Reader**, use the **page up** and **page down** links at the top and bottom of the left column.

▶ TIP

Google Reader allows you to do more than read RSS feeds—you can also take a variety of actions for any item you read. From the **More Actions** drop-down list at the top-right corner of the **Reader** window, choose **Gmail this** if you want to send the item to someone using your **Gmail** account; choose **Blog this** if you want to write a blog posting in your **Blogger** blog about the item. You can also unsubscribe to the feed by choosing **Unsubscribe** from the **More Actions** drop-down list.

86

3 Read the Full Items

The entry you see on the right side of the screen is only the first section of the item—the first sentence or the first paragraph. To read the full item, click the **Show original item** link just above the entry on the right side of the screen. A new browser window opens up, and you are sent to the full item on the site that created the feed.

▶ NOTE

You can't search for archived feeds. The nature of an RSS feed is that it is always current.

4 Browse Using Labels

As explained in **85 Subscribe to Feeds**, you can assign labels to the feeds when you subscribe to them to make it easier to read your feeds. Click the **Your Subscriptions** link located just under the **Google Reader** title area, and you see a list of all the labels you've assigned to your feeds. Click any label, and you see the list of feeds to which you've assigned that label on the right side of the page. Click any feed to see the items in that feed.

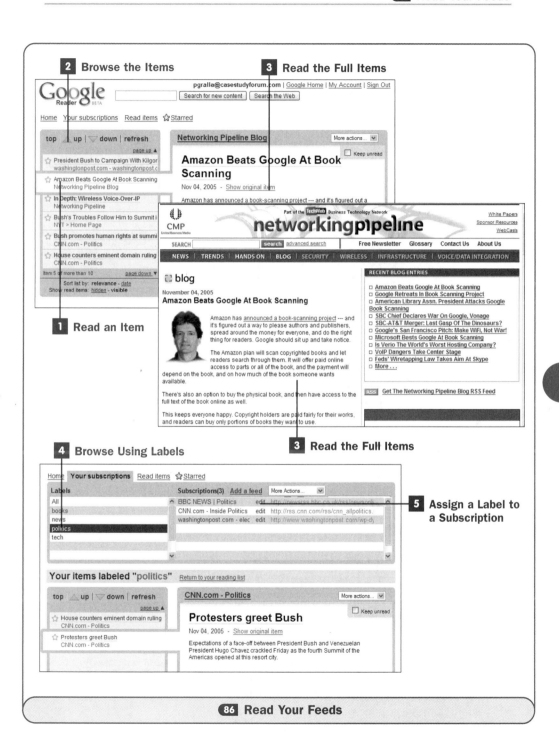

5 Assign a Label to a Subscription

To assign a label to one of your subscriptions, click the **Your Subscriptions** link, and then click **Edit** next to the subscription to which you want to add a label. In the **Labels** text box that appears, type the name or names of the labels you want to add to the subscription and click **Save**.

To edit a label for one of your subscriptions, click the **Your Subscriptions** link, and then click **Edit** next to the subscription whose label you want to edit. In the **Labels** text box that appears, change the name or names of the labels you want to edit and click **Save**.

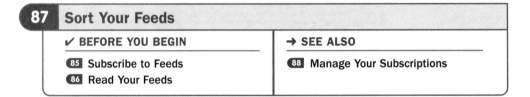

87   Sort Your Feeds

✔ BEFORE YOU BEGIN	→ SEE ALSO
85 Subscribe to Feeds	88 Manage Your Subscriptions
86 Read Your Feeds	

87

If you subscribe to and read a good number of feeds, very soon you can become overwhelmed by them. To make your feeds easier to use, you can use **Google Reader**'s capability to sort feeds. Start by signing into your Google account and opening **Google Reader**.

1 Star Important Items

As you read, you might want to keep a list of items that you want to re-read. To do that, you can put a star next to those items. Click the grayed-out star next to an entry, and the star turns bright yellow to remind you to come back to those entries.

2 Read Your Starred Items

To view all your starred items, click the **Starred** icon or link at the top of the page. You see a list of all your starred items from all your feeds. Read them as you would your normal feeds.

3 Review Read Items

To re-read items that you've already read, click the **Read items** link at the top of the page. You see a list of all the items you've read. Read them as you would your normal feeds.

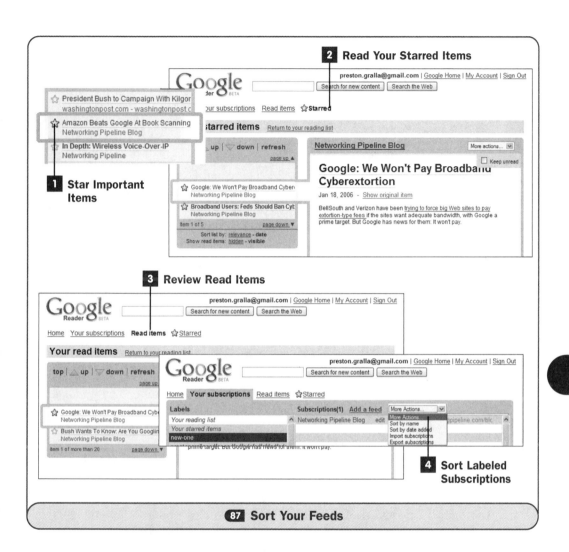

4 Sort Labeled Subscriptions

The best way to sort your entries is in the **Your subscriptions** area. Click the **Your subscriptions** link at the top of the page, and at the top of the new page that opens, click the **More Actions** down arrow. A drop-down box appears with a list of actions. By choosing from the list of options, you can then sort your items by the name of the feed and by the date you added the feeds to your subscription list. The **Import** and **Export** options enable you to import or export the link for a feed. For details, see **88** **Manage Your Subscriptions**.

88 Manage Your Subscriptions

✔ **BEFORE YOU BEGIN**

85 Subscribe to Feeds
86 Read Your Feeds
87 Sort Your Feeds

RSS has become so popular that every day there are new RSS feeds. Odds are that you'll constantly be adding feeds to **Google Reader**. But doing this can quickly make your subscription list unwieldy. You need some way to manage all your subscriptions—and **Google Reader** offers plenty of tools for doing that. Start by signing into your Google account and opening **Google Reader**.

1 Click Your Subscriptions

At the top of the main **Google Reader** page, click the **Your subscriptions** link to open a page with a list of all the feeds to which you've already subscribed. From here, you have all the tools you need to manage your subscriptions.

2 Filter Your Subscriptions

A simple way to view only a select group of your subscriptions is to filter them by name. In the **Filter** box, type the word by which you want to filter. (When you start typing the first letters of your filter word, Google starts to filter your subscriptions immediately. For example, if you have many subscriptions with labels such as **network** and **negative**, and you entered **ne** in the filter text box, both those labels would appear. When you continue typing **neg**, only the **negative** label appears.) Only those subscriptions whose names match the filter term you specified are now displayed. Note that the filter applies to *entire subscriptions*, but not to items within a subscription. So only those subscriptions that match the filter term appear, but every item in that subscription is displayed.

To display the list of all your subscriptions again, clear the filter text box.

3 Unsubscribe from a Feed

At first glance, there appears to be no way to unsubscribe from a feed. You would expect that a button or link for this would appear in the area near the **Filter** box in the **My subscriptions** tab, but it doesn't. Instead, you unsubscribe from a feed in the area where you actually read the item, in the bottom half of the page. To unsubscribe from a feed, click the **More actions** drop-down list box in that portion of the screen (not the **More actions** list box in the **Your subscriptions** area at the top of the page) and select **Unsubscribe**.

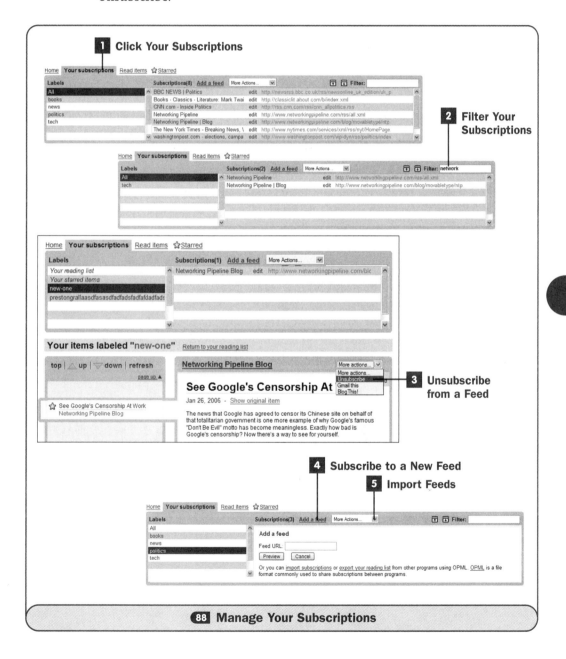

4 Subscribe to a New Feed

If you want to subscribe to a new feed when you're in the **Your subscriptions** area, click the **Add a feed** link. Then search for a feed as described in **85 Subscribe to Feeds**.

5 Import Feeds

You can import a feed or group of feeds by choosing **Import Subscriptions** from the **More Actions** drop-down list box at the top of the **Your subscriptions** page. When you import a feed or group of feeds, you're importing the links to the subscriptions, not links to each individual post in each feed. Importing a feed is the equivalent of creating a new feed by yourself.

Why import a feed or group of feeds? If someone has a list of feeds she thinks you would be interested in, she can send you that list in a special format. When you import them in **Google Reader**, you have a large group of feeds without having to create each of them individually.

You import feeds using what's called the OPML format, a file format used for many things, including importing and exporting feeds. Someone has to send you the file (its filename ends in an **.opml** extension). Save the file on your computer. After it's saved, choose **Import Subscriptions** from the **More Actions** drop-down list box. You get a notification at the top of your screen that the subscriptions are being imported. When they're imported, you use them as you do any other subscriptions.

88

▶ NOTE

Unless you're technically sophisticated and are extremely familiar with the OPML format and how to create OPML files, don't try to export your subscriptions by choosing **Import subscriptions** from the **More Actions** drop-down list. You need a significant amount of expertise to properly create OPML files.

14

Managing and Sharing Pictures with Google's Picasa

IN THIS CHAPTER:

One of Google's least-known tools is an excellent photo- and picture-handling program called **Picasa**. It's not a full-blown photo editor, but instead is designed to enable you to do basic photo cleanup and add special effects—and then use those photos in many ways. You are able to create slideshows, screensavers, CDs, collage, prints, and more. So if you use photos at all, **Picasa** is well worth the download—it's free.

To get started, go to http://picasa.google.com/download/index.html to download the software and then install it. (For details about downloading and installing software, see Chapter 1, "Start Here.") When **Picasa** first runs, it asks whether it should scan your computer for pictures. Choose the **Completely scan my computer for pictures** option. **Picasa** then scans your entire computer for picture files. After it does that, you're ready to get started.

---

89   Organize Your Pictures

✔ **SEE ALSO**
──────────────────────────────
94 Create Slideshows

89

Picasa makes it extremely easy to view and organize your pictures. It scans all the folders on your hard disk for pictures, shows you what image files you have, and then enables you to move and organize them in several ways, as you'll see in this task.

1 Browse Through Your Pictures

To run **Picasa**, double-click its desktop icon, or click the **Start** button and choose it from the **All Programs** menu. After you install **Picasa** and ask it to scan your computer for pictures, it creates a list in chronological order of all the folders that contain pictures. The folders are displayed on the left side of the **Picasa** screen; on the right side of the screen are thumbnail images of the pictures in each folder. Click a picture, and it appears in the bottom-left corner of the screen in the picture tray.

2 Move a Picture to Another Folder

To move a picture to another folder, drag the image thumbnail from the right side of the screen to the folder in the list on the left side of the screen to which you want to move it. Note that you can also drag an image file from a folder on the right side of the screen to another folder on the right side of the screen.

1 Browse Through Your Pictures

List of Folders Containing Pictures **Thumbnails of Images in Each Folder** **3 Change the Order of Your Pictures**

Picture Tray

2 Move a Picture to Another Folder

4 Organize Pictures by Labels

5 Add New Folders

89

▶ **TIP**

You can select multiple pictures and move them all at the same time. Hold down the **Ctrl** key as you click the image thumbnails to select multiple individual pictures. Hold down the **Shift** key as you click two image thumbnails to select all contiguous pictures between (and including) the two images you click.

3 Change the Order of Your Pictures

To change the order in which your pictures appear in a folder, drag the image thumbnails around within the folder on the right side of the screen. Drag single or multiple pictures from one position to another within the folder.

4 Organize Pictures by Labels

Picasa allows you to create *labels*, which enable you to view pictures from different folders in a single location. For example, you might have pictures of Hawaii in several folders on your computer; to see all the photos, you would normally have to go to multiple folders or move all the photos to a single folder. Labels allow you to keep the pictures in their existing folders, but also allow you to view them all by filtering your photos based on the label.

89

▶ **KEY TERM**

Label (Picasa)—A method of organizing pictures in **Picasa** that enables you to view, in a single location, pictures from different folders.

To create a new label, select the picture(s) to which you want to apply the label, and then choose **File, New Label** from the menu bar. (You can also press **Ctrl+N**, or click the **Label** button at the bottom of the screen.) In the form that appears, type the label's name, select a date for it (if you don't want to use the current date), enter the name of the place where the photos were taken (this information is optional), and type any caption text for the label (the caption applies to all the pictures). Then click **OK** to create the label. For example, if you have gone on vacation to Hawaii, you could create a label called **Hawaii**; for the group caption, you might use **Spring Vacation, 2004**.

The label appears on top of your **Folder List** on the left side of the screen. Click the label to see the list of pictures with that label. To add more pictures to the label, drag pictures to the label in the **Folder List**. The pictures you drag to the label still exist in their original folders.

5 **Add New Folders**

When you create a new folder on your PC, **Picasa** does not automatically look through it to find pictures and display them in **Picasa**. You must tell **Picasa** that the new folder exists so **Picasa** can then scan the folder and keep the folder updated with pictures. To tell **Picasa** to scan a folder, select **File**, **Add Folder to Picasa** from the menu bar. In the **Folder Manager** dialog box that appears, select the folder you want to add to **Picasa**'s scan list and then select one of the following options:

- **Scan Once**—Select this option if you want **Picasa** to scan for pictures only this one time. Any new pictures you add to the folder are not added to **Picasa**.

- **Scan Always**—Select this option if you want **Picasa** to constantly scan the folder and add any new pictures it finds. When you select this option, the folder you select is added to the **Watched Folders** list in the bottom-right corner of the dialog box.

- **Remove from Picasa**—Select a folder in the **Folder List** on the left side of the dialog box and choose this option to delete the folder from **Picasa**'s scan list. The folder is not actually deleted from your hard disk.

90

90 **Touch up Photographs**

✔ BEFORE YOU BEGIN	→ SEE ALSO
89 Organize Your Pictures	**91** Add Visual Effects and Captions
	92 About Advanced Editing Tools

Picasa does more than just display photos—it also offers an easy-to-use set of photo-editing tools that enable you to perform basic photo-editing tasks, such as cropping, straightening, adjusting contrast, and fixing redeye. Here's how to do it.

1 **Select a Photo to Edit**

To select a photo to edit, double-click its thumbnail on the right side of the **Picasa** screen. You come to a screen that contains numerous editing tools. You can use the slider bar of image thumbnails above the large photo on the right side of the screen to edit the next photo or the previous photo in the current **Picasa** folder.

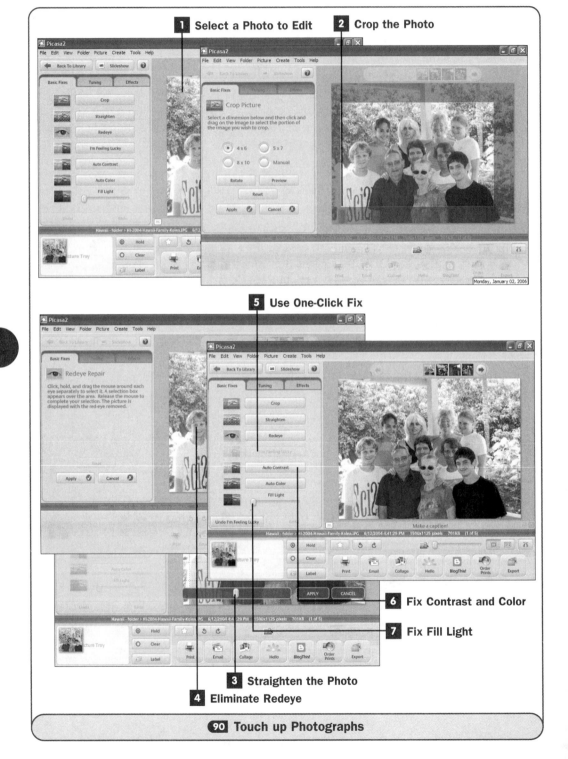

1 Select a Photo to Edit **2 Crop the Photo**

5 Use One-Click Fix

6 Fix Contrast and Color

7 Fix Fill Light

3 Straighten the Photo

4 Eliminate Redeye

90 Touch up Photographs

2 Crop the Photo

If you want to resize the picture to a common photo size or to a custom size, click the **Crop** button on the left side of the screen. (If you don't see the **Crop** button, click the **Basic Fixes** tab to display a list of basic photo-editing options.) From the pane that opens on the left side of the screen, choose the desired photo size. Then use your mouse to drag the bright rectangle to define the portion of the picture you want cropped. The bright portion of the photo is resized to the standard photo size you chose. If you choose the **Manual** option, you can drag the edges of the bright crop area to encompass all of the picture that you want to include; the darker areas will be cropped away (discarded). Click **Apply** when you've made your choices.

▶ **TIP**

Use the **Rotate, Preview,** and **Reset** buttons to help you better crop a photo. The **Rotate** button rotates the dimensions of the cropping area you've chosen. So, for example, if you choose **5 X 7** and you click **Rotate,** the cropping area changes to 7×5. Clicking the **Preview** button enables you to preview what the photo will look like after it's been cropped. And the **Reset** button undoes the cropping you've done.

3 Straighten the Photo

Photos at times are taken at an angle, and you can easily straighten them in **Picasa.** Click the **Straighten** button in the **Basic Fixes** tab on the left side of the screen. A grid of straight horizontal and vertical lines appears over the selected photo. You can use these gridlines as guides for straightening your photo. Move the slider that appears in the lower-left corner of the image to the left to rotate the photo to the left; drag the slider to the right to rotate the photo to the right. When it is straight in comparison with the gridlines, click the **Apply** button. The image zooms in after you straighten it to eliminate the blank areas that would otherwise be pulled into the photo.

▶ **TIP**

When you edit a photo with **Picasa,** the changes aren't made to the original photo. Instead, the edits you make are in effect only when you are viewing or working with the photos in **Picasa.** If you want to use the edited pictures with other programs, export the edited picture by clicking the **Export** button at the bottom-right corner of the screen, and following the directions for saving the picture.

4 Eliminate Redeye

Redeye is the bugaboo of photographers everywhere, and no matter how advanced the camera, it always seems to manage to creep its way into photos. (Redeye refers to someone's eyes being red in a photo because they have reflected the flash from a camera.) To eliminate redeye in the selected photo, click the **Redeye** button in the **Basic Fixes** tab on the left side of the screen. You then come to a screen in which you need to drag a selection box around each red eye you want to fix. Then click **Apply** to fix the redeye problem.

5 Use One-Click Fix

If you don't want to have to clean up the selected photo manually, click the **I'm Feeling Lucky** button in the **Basic Fixes** tab on the left side of the screen. The photo is automatically cleaned up—redeye is eliminated, the photo is straightened, and contrast and color are adjusted. If you want to undo the changes, click the **Undo I'm Feeling Lucky** button at the bottom of the **Basic Fixes** pane.

6 Fix Contrast and Color

If you think the contrast in the displayed photo could use some adjustment, click the **Auto Contrast** button, and the contrast is automatically optimized. If you want to undo the automatic fix, click the **Undo Auto Contrast** button at the bottom of the **Basic Fixes** pane. To fix the color, click the **Auto Color** button. If you want to undo the automatic fix, click the **Undo Auto Color** button at the bottom of the **Basic Fixes** pane.

7 Fix Fill Light

The *fill light* of a picture, according to **Picasa**, is how light or dark the picture is overall. To change the fill light, move the **Fill Light** slider on the **Basic Fixes** tab on the left side of the screen. The further you move the slider to the right, the lighter the picture becomes. To undo your changes, click the **Undo Fill Light** button at the bottom of the **Basic Fixes** pane.

91 Add Visual Effects and Captions

✔ BEFORE YOU BEGIN	→ SEE ALSO
90 Touch up Photographs	92 About Advanced Editing Tools

If you're a fan of special effects, such as adding sepia tones to make a photo look old-fashioned or adding a soft focus to the photo, you'll find **Picasa** to be a great program. You can add special effects to the selected image with a single click.

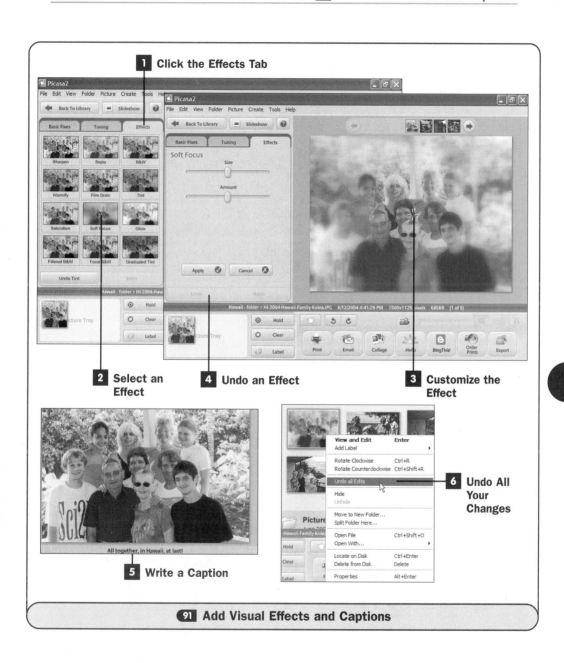

1 Click the Effects Tab

2 Select an Effect

4 Undo an Effect

3 Customize the Effect

5 Write a Caption

6 Undo All Your Changes

91

91 Add Visual Effects and Captions

1 Click the Effects Tab

After double-clicking a photo in the folder lists to open it in **Picasa**'s photo-editing mode, click the **Effects** tab on the left side of the screen. You see a list of thumbnails showing all the effects you can apply to the photo.

2 Select an Effect

To add an effect, click it. In some instances, such as when turning a color photograph into a black-and-white photograph or adding sepia tones, the changes take effect immediately.

3 Customize the Effect

In some instances, such as when adding the **Soft Focus** effect to a photograph, you need to make choices about how to apply the effect. For the **Soft Focus** effect, for example, a portion of the photograph remains in focus, but the rest of the photo blurs slightly. When you click to select the **Soft Focus** effect, you come to a screen that enables you to select the size of the area you want to remain in focus and the amount of blur you want to appear for the soft focus effect. Click in the photo on the right side of the screen to establish the center point of the sharp focus area. Make your changes and click **Apply**.

4 Undo an Effect

To undo an effect, click the **Undo** button in the lower-left corner of the effect pane.

5 Write a Caption

To write a caption, click the **Make a caption!** text just underneath the photograph, and type the text of your caption. Note that you must have completed the application of any special effects and be back at the main **Effects** tab (click **Apply** or **Cancel** for any effect to return to the main **Effects** tab).

6 Undo All Your Changes

If you make multiple changes to a photo and then decide you don't like any of the changes, it can be difficult to undo them all. For the quickest way to undo all your changes, go back to **Picasa**'s main screen by clicking the **Back to Library** button above the tabs on the left side of the screen, right-click the photo in the folder lists, and choose **Undo all Edits** from the context menu.

---

92 **About Advanced Editing Tools**

✔ **BEFORE YOU BEGIN**

90 Touch up Photographs
91 Add Visual Effects and Captions

If you are comfortable with photo editing, you should use **Picasa**'s **Tuning** tab when editing a photograph. As a group, the controls on this tab give you much finer control over your photos than the **Basic Fixes** tab. Here's what you can do with this tab:

- **Fill Light slider**—This option functions exactly like the same slider on the **Basic Fixes** tab.

- **Highlights slider**—This slider enables you to add to or reduce the highlights in your picture. In the **Picasa** world, *highlights* refers to the overall brightness of a picture.

- **Shadows slider**—This slider enables you to add more shadows to your photo. In the **Picasa** world, *shadows* refers to the overall dimness of a picture.

- **Color Temperature slider**—This slider enables you to make your picture warmer (move the slider to the right and you add more yellow tones) or cooler (move the slider to the left and you add more blue tones).

- **Neutral Color Picker**—This option enables you to tell **Picasa** which part of your picture should be considered absolute middle gray or absolute white. After you identify the white or gray point, the program color balances the colors in the photo, making adjustments based on the selection you made.

93

93 Share Pictures with Email

✔ BEFORE YOU BEGIN	→ SEE ALSO
89 Organize Your Pictures	**57** Set Up a Gmail Account

What good are pictures—especially photographs—if you can't share them with others? **Picasa** recognizes that and makes it easy to send pictures to your friends and relations using email. You are able to use your own email program or **Gmail** to send them, and you are able to send any picture in **Picasa**, including pictures you've edited. Here's how to do it.

1 Select the Picture You Want to Send

From **Picasa**'s main screen, click the picture you want to send as an email attachment to a friend or relative. The selected image appears in the picture tray in the lower-left corner of the screen.

1 Select the Picture You Want to Send

2 Click the Email Button

3 Select Your Email Method

4 Send from Your Email Program

5 Send Using Gmail

93 Share Pictures with Email

2 Click the Email Button

Click the **Email** button at the bottom of the main **Picasa** screen. When you click it, a **Select Email** dialog box appears, asking how you want to send your photos.

3 Select Your Email Method

You can choose to send the photo by email using your **Gmail** account, if you have one, or using your default email program (for example, Outlook). Click the method you want to use to email the selected photograph.

▶ **NOTE**

One of the choices for sending a photo is using **Picasa Mail**. But in fact, **Picasa Mail** is not a mail program—it's an instant messaging program called **Hello**. You need to install the **Hello** instant messenger software and sign up for an account if you want to send a picture using **Hello**. Note that you can send **Hello** instant messages only to other people who also use a **Hello** account. In my opinion, you're better off using email or AOL Instant Messenger (AIM) or a similar instant messaging program that's in widespread use.

4 Send from Your Email Program

93

If you select your own default email program (such as Outlook), a new email message is created, and the picture you selected in step 1 is included as an attachment. You won't have to first launch your email program in order to do this. Fill out the address of the recipient, change the default subject line (which is **a picture for you**), add any text of your own, and click **Send** to send the message.

5 Send Using Gmail

If you choose to send the selected picture using your **Gmail** account, you come to a login screen. Enter your **Gmail** username and password and click **Sign In**. If you want **Picasa** to remember your username and password so you don't have to enter them again when you want to email a picture using **Gmail**, check the box next to **Remember my password**.

A new **Gmail** message is created with some boilerplate text and the picture attached. Fill out the address of the recipient, change the default subject line (which is **a picture for you**), add any text of your own, and send the message.

94 Create Slideshows

✔ BEFORE YOU BEGIN	→ SEE ALSO
89 Organize Your Pictures	**98** Create Screensavers and Windows Wallpaper

One of **Picasa**'s nicer features is its capability to play a slideshow on your PC of pictures and photos. You can even have music of your choosing accompany the show. All the pictures you want to show in a slideshow must be in the same folder; if you want to use music with your slideshow, you can use only MP3 files.

94

1 Select a Folder or Label

In the **Picasa** main screen, click a folder or label in the **Folders on Disk** list on the left side of the screen. All the pictures contained in that folder or label are displayed in the slideshow. If you want to create a slideshow from pictures in several folders, create a new label, and then copy all the pictures into that label. For details about how to create a label, see **89** **Organize Your Pictures**.

2 Click Slideshow

Click the **Slideshow** button at the top of the screen to begin playing your slideshow. The slideshow displays each picture in the folder or label for three seconds before moving on to the next picture. After all the photos have been displayed once, the slideshow stops, and you are sent back to **Picasa**'s main screen.

3 Use Slideshow Controls

You can control several aspects of the slideshow using onscreen controls. To make the controls appear, move your mouse anywhere on the screen. The forward and backward arrows enable you to move forward or backward through the slideshow. The **Play** button resumes play of the slideshow. The two circular arrows rotate the current picture in the direction of the arrow.

To change the amount of time each picture should display, select a number under the **Display Time** label on the far right end of the control bar by using the plus or minus signs.

▶ NOTE

Can you solve the mystery of the pointless icon? The slideshow controls contain a button that enable you check or uncheck the current picture. But that button does not appear to serve a purpose. What does it do? Enquiring minds want to know.

1 Select a Folder or Label

2 Click Slideshow

3 Use Slideshow Controls

4 Customize the Slideshow

94 Create Slideshows

4 Customize the Slideshow

If you'd like, you can add music to your slideshow, and change other slideshow options. To do this, select **Tools**, **Options** from the menu bar; in the **Options** dialog box that opens, click the **Slideshow** tab. You have these options:

- **Loop slideshow**—If you select this option, the slideshow plays continually. Rather than exit the slideshow after the last photo in the folder or label is displayed, the slideshow starts back at the beginning.

- **Play MP3 tracks during slideshow**—Enable this option to play music in MP3 format during the slideshow. The option plays all the MP3 files in a folder that you select. To select the folder, click the **Browse** button next to the **Select Folder of MP3 Tracks** text box and select the folder.

- **Do full-resolution slideshow**—This option displays photos at their normal resolution, even if they are very high resolution. Displaying high-resolution images in a slideshow format can take up a significant amount of memory and system resources, so select this option only if you have a fast processor with at least 512MB of RAM. If you don't select this option, the photos display at a consistent resolution that is lower than that of the original images.

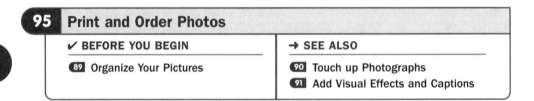

Almost anyone who takes photos wants to see them not just on the computer screen, but in print as well—and **Picasa** realizes that. The program makes it very easy to print photos on your own printer or to order them online, as you'll see in this task.

1 Select Your Photos

From **Picasa**'s main screen, select the photos you want to print or order. To select multiple individual photos within the same folder, press the **Ctrl** key while you click. To select a group of contiguous photos within the same folder, press the **Shift** key and click two photos; all the photos between (and including) the two you clicked are selected.

You can also select the photos by dragging them to the picture tray in the bottom-left corner of the screen. In fact, if you're selecting photos from different folders, you *have* to drag photos to the picture tray. Holding the **Ctrl** or **Shift** key and clicking from different folders doesn't work; that only works in the same folder.

1 Select Your Photos

2 Click Print

4 Click Order Prints

3 Print Your Photos

5 Create an Account or Log On to the Provider's Site

Choose a Provider

6 Finalize Your Order

2 Click Print

Click the **Print** button located at the bottom of the screen to display a dialog box that enables you to select your print options. In the **Print Layout** section, choose the size at which you want to print all the photos. If you've chosen a size that is smaller than some of your photos, you have to choose how to shrink your photos: Choose **Shrink to Fit** if you want the entirety of each picture in the print, but shrunk, and choose **Crop to Fit** if you want the photos to instead be cropped to fit the trim size. (You cannot adjust the crop for individual photos; it might be that Fluffy's paws or Grandpa's left elbow is cropped out of the finished print.)

In the **Printer Settings** section of the dialog box, choose your printer and printer options. Select the number of copies of each picture you want to make. To make standard adjustments to the printer setup, click the **Printer Setup** button.

3 Print Your Photos

Click the **Print** button to print your photos. Before printing, you can review all the photos you're planning to print by clicking the **Review** button and reviewing your photos in the **Review for Printing** dialog box. When you click the **Review** button, a small screen pops up, showing thumbnails of all your photos. These thumbnails show the pictures themselves, not how they will appear when they print. Remove any pictures you don't want to print, click **OK**, and then print the photos.

If you want to preview how the photos will look when they are printed, you should instead click the Forward and Back buttons at the bottom of the screen to review the photos.

▶ TIP

Low-resolution photos don't look particularly good when printed. You can have **Picasa** automatically remove any low-resolution photos from your selection. In the **Review for Printing** dialog box, choose the **Remove low quality pictures** option, click **OK**, and then print as you would normally.

4 Click Order Prints

If you want to order commercial prints for the selected photos rather than print them on your local printer, click the **Order Prints** button at the bottom of the main **Picasa** screen. You are brought to a page that lists many sites from which you can order. Click the **Choose** button under the site from which you want to order. (You have to be online to order the prints, so make sure you're online before doing this.)

To find more information about a provider, such as the cost per print, delivery charges (if they apply), and the kinds of services offered, click the **Learn more** link at the end of the paragraph describing the service.

5 Create an Account or Log On to the Provider's Site

After you select the provider of print services, you come to an upload screen that contains login information for the site from which you plan to order. If you haven't yet registered at that site, click the **Create an Account** link and sign up for that provider before proceeding. If you have already registered, type your login information.

6 Finalize Your Order

The way in which you finalize your order and upload the photos varies from site to site. When you upload photos, they are transferred over the Internet from your computer to the photo site. Follow the instructions for ordering photos after you upload them.

96

---

96 Burn Photo CDs and DVDs

✔ BEFORE YOU BEGIN	→ SEE ALSO
89 Organize Your Pictures	**94** Create Slideshows

The days of showing slides of your most recent vacation using a slide projector in a darkened room are thankfully long behind us. But sharing photos is more popular than ever. A great way to share them is to create a CD full of photos and give the CD to a friend or relative, as you'll see in this task.

1 Insert a CD or DVD

Before burning a CD or DVD, insert a blank disc into the CD or DVD drive.

▶ NOTE

Make sure you have a drive capable of burning CDs or DVDs, and not one capable of just reading them.

1 Insert a CD or DVD

2 Create a Gift CD

6 Click Burn Disc

3 Add New Pictures

4 Choose Your Settings

5 Name the CD

Progress Bar for Writing to CD

7 View the CD

8 Eject the CD

96 Burn Photo CDs and DVDs

2 Create a Gift CD

Click the **Gift CD** button at the top of the main **Picasa** screen. A **Create Gift CD** dialog box appears. **Picasa** selects all the photos in the current folder or label to be put onto the CD. You can choose only entire folders or labels, not individual photos. All the pictures in the current folder or label are included. If you want to create a CD with photos from different folders, create a new label as explained in **89 Organize Your Pictures**, and then choose that label for the CD.

3 Add New Pictures

You can add other folders or labels to the CD. Click the **Add More** button in the bottom-left corner of the **Create a Gift CD** dialog box, and you see a list of all the folders and labels on your hard disk. Enable the check box next to any labels or folders you want to include on the CD.

4 Choose Your Settings

In the **Selection and Settings** section in the bottom-left corner of the dialog box, choose the size you want the pictures to be by clicking the arrow next to the **Picture Size** box and making your selection. If you want all the pictures on the CD to be shown as a giant slideshow, check the box next to **Include Slideshow**. If you don't enable this option, you can look at the photos on the CD by browsing through the disc using Windows Explorer.

5 Name the CD

In the **Name the Gift CD** section in the bottom center of the dialog box, type a name for the CD. If you want **Picasa** to be included on the CD so that whomever you're giving the CD to can install it (the person viewing the slideshow needs **Picasa** to view the slideshow), enable the **Include Picasa** check box.

6 Click Burn Disc

Click the **Burn Disc** button on the right side of the dialog box. When you do this, **Picasa** burns the pictures onto the disc you inserted in the CD or DVD drive. It tells you the progress as it burns the disc. After several minutes, **Picasa** tells you that the disc is complete.

7 View the CD

When **Picasa** is finished burning the CD or DVD, it asks whether you want to view the disk or eject it. If you want to view it before ejecting it, click the

Show button. If you choose **Show** and you opted to include a slideshow, you see the same slideshow of all the pictures on the disc that whomever you give the CD to will see. To escape from the slideshow, press the **Esc** key.

8 Eject the CD

In the **CD Done** dialog box, click **Eject the CD**, and **Picasa** ejects it from the drive. You can now give it to friends or family.

---

97 Make Posters and Collages

✔ BEFORE YOU BEGIN	→ SEE ALSO
89 Organize Your Pictures	90 Touch up Photographs
91 Add Visual Effects and Captions	
95 Print and Order Photos	
96 Burn Photo CDs and DVDs	

97

Picasa makes it simple to turn photos or pictures into posters and collages. When making a poster, **Picasa** takes a picture and divides it into four parts. You then print each individual part on standard-sized paper and tape or glue the four pieces together to make a poster. When you create a collage, you have a choice of several preformatted collage designs you can use. Creating one takes only a few clicks.

1 Select a Picture

In **Picasa**'s main screen, click to select the photo you want to turn into a poster.

2 Start the Poster

Choose **Create, Make a Poster** from the menu bar. The **Poster Settings** dialog box appears. From the **Poster size** drop-down box, choose the size for your poster. From the **Paper size** drop-down box, choose how large you want the picture to print on the paper—either 4"×6" inches, or 8.5"×11". Select the **Overlap tiles** check box if you want there to be some overlap among the separate pictures so you can more easily align the pictures when you paste the poster together. Click **OK** after you make your selection.

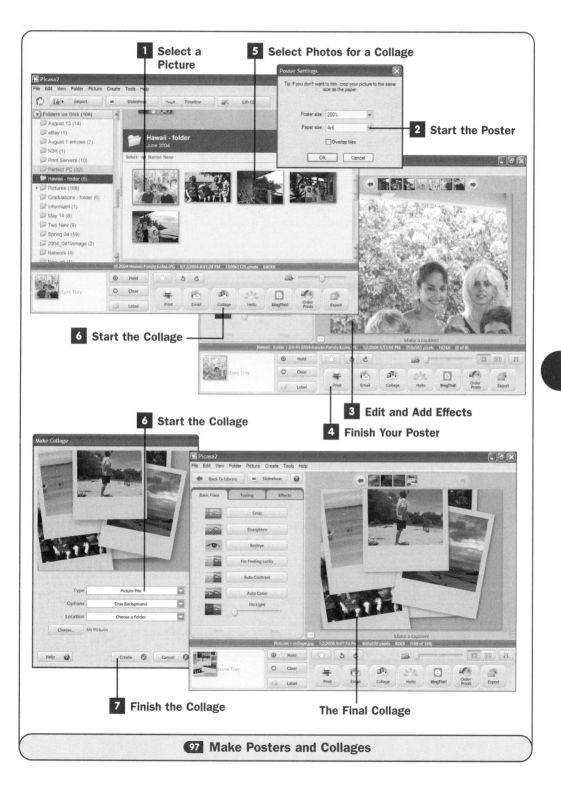

1 Select a Picture

5 Select Photos for a Collage

2 Start the Poster

6 Start the Collage

6 Start the Collage

3 Edit and Add Effects

4 Finish Your Poster

7 Finish the Collage

The Final Collage

97

Be careful when choosing the **Poster size** option because it dramatically affects how many pieces you have to put together for your poster. For example, with a picture of 1500×1125 pixels in resolution, if you choose 200% for the poster size and a 4×6 paper size, you end up with four printouts to put together for your poster. If you instead choose 400% for the poster size and keep the paper size the same, you end up with 16 pieces. For best results, experiment with different sizes.

▶ **NOTE**

The 200% size is the best size for printing a poster. You often print four separate pages, each containing a quarter of the original photo, and tape or glue them to make the poster. If you choose larger sizes, you often have to print and glue more pages.

3 **Edit and Add Effects**

Picasa take the photo you've chosen and breaks it into separate pieces. It opens them up in the photo-editing screen. (For details on how to use the photo-editing mode, see **91** **Add Visual Effects and Captions**.) Note that it's a better idea to edit the photo before you turn it into a poster, rather than adding the effects to the separate pieces of the poster. It can very difficult to get the effects exactly the same on all pieces of the poster.

97

4 **Finish Your Poster**

Print your poster pictures and glue or tape them together.

5 **Select Photos for a Collage**

Select multiple photos that you want to use for your collage, as outlined in **96** **Burn Photo CDs and DVDs**. Perhaps the simplest way to select photos is to drag them to the picture tray in the lower-left corner of the screen. You can drag them there from any folder.

6 **Start the Collage**

Click the **Collage** button at the bottom of the main **Picasa** screen; the **Make Collage** dialog box appears. From the **Type** drop-down box, choose the style of collage you want to make—as you choose it, just above that box, you see a preview of how the final will look, so preview several styles before making a final choice.

Next, choose the color of your collage's background by making a choice from the **Options** drop-down box. From the **Location** dialog box, choose where you want to save the collage. If you select the **Choose a Folder** option, click the **Choose** button and select a folder. You can save it in the current folder, choose a different folder, or use the default folder **Picasa** uses to create screensavers. If you choose to put it in that default folder, it becomes part of whatever screensaver you create with **Picasa**.

7 Finish the Collage

Click the **Create** button at the bottom of the **Make Collage** dialog box; **Picasa** creates the collage in the manner and in the folder you specified. The file containing the collage is named **collage.jpg**. If you create a second collage in the same location, the second creation overwrites the original collage. You can view it in **Picasa** or another graphics program, and use it in the same way you would use any other graphic.

---

98 **Create Screensavers and Windows Wallpaper**

✔ BEFORE YOU BEGIN	→ SEE ALSO
89 Organize Your Pictures	**94** Create Slideshows
90 Touch up Photographs	

98

What better way to personalize your PC than with your own photos and pictures? **Picasa** enables you to take any picture or photo on your PC and turn it into your wallpaper, also called the desktop background. And you can create your own slideshow-like screensaver using a selection of your photos as well.

1 Select a Picture for Wallpaper

In the **Picasa** main screen, select the picture you want to be your Windows wallpaper. Note that **Picasa** refers to the Windows wallpaper as the desktop.

2 Make It Your Wallpaper

From the **Create** menu, select **Set as Desktop**. A **Confirm** dialog box appears, asking whether you want to use the picture as your desktop background. Click **Yes**, and the picture appears as your wallpaper.

98

1 Select a Picture for Wallpaper

2 Make It Your Wallpaper

Image As Wallpaper

3 Select Pictures for a Screensaver

4 Create Your Screensaver

5 Edit Your Screensaver

98 Create Screensavers and Windows Wallpaper

▶ NOTE

Using **Picasa** isn't the only way to change your wallpaper. You can also do it yourself. In Windows XP, you change your desktop background in the **Desktop Display Properties** dialog box. Get there by right-clicking a blank area of the desktop, choosing **Properties** from the context menu to open the dialog box, and then selecting the **Desktop** tab. The background you've created using **Picasa** is listed at **picasabackground**, so if you choose a different desktop wallpaper and want to at some point go back to the background you've just created in **Picasa**, select **picasabackground** as your desktop. However, if you create a new background with **Picasa**, that new background appears when you choose **picasabackground** (**Picasa** overwrites the original image file with whatever you later select to be the wallpaper image).

3 Select Pictures for a Screensaver

From **Picasa**'s main screen, select the photos you want in your screensaver. To select multiple individual photos, press the **Ctrl** key while you click. To select contiguous photos, press the **Shift** key and click the starting and ending pictures; all the photos between (and including) the two photos you clicked are now selected. If you want to select pictures from different folders, create a label for those photos and then select them in the label as explained in **89 Organize Your Photos**. The screensaver you create looks like an automatic slideshow.

4 Create Your Screensaver

Select **Create, Screensaver** from the menu bar. The screensaver is created, and the Windows **Display Properties** dialog box opens to the **Screen Saver** tab. To preview your screensaver, click the **Preview** button. To change how long each photo should be displayed, click the **Settings** button and select the number of seconds. When you're done, click the **OK** button to finalize your screensaver.

After your computer remains idle for the amount of time specified in the **Wait** box in the **Display Properties** dialog box, the **Picasa** screensaver launches and begins showing the images you selected.

5 Edit Your Screensaver

When **Picasa** creates a screensaver, it creates a **Screensaver** folder and places the pictures you selected in that folder. By deleting pictures from that folder or adding pictures to it, you can change the pictures the screensaver uses. In the **Picasa** main screen, look for the **Screensaver** folder in the **Folders on Disk** area on the left side of the screen. Drag pictures into this folder to add them to the screensaver; drag pictures from this folder to remove them from the screensaver. When you remove pictures from the **Screensaver** folder, they still appear in their original location in **Picasa** and on your hard disk.

15

Chatting and Talking with Google Talk

IN THIS CHAPTER:

Most of the time when you use a Google tool or service, it's a one-way conversation. You ask for information and get it, but there's no talking back.

With **Google Talk**, that all changes. **Google Talk** is an instant messaging program that allows you to communicate in real time with other **Google Talk** users. You type messages on your keyboard, and they are instantly sent to the person with whom you're communicating—and she can type messages and send them to you as well. In addition. **Google Talk** enables you to voice chat—that is, hold voice conversations with other **Google Talk** users using your computer.

This chapter tells you everything you need to set up **Google Talk** and start talking.

▶ **TIP**

If you use a personal firewall, such as Norton Personal Firewall, McAfee Personal Firewall, or ZoneAlarm, you might not be able to connect to **Google Talk** because the firewall blocks access. If that happens, you need to change some settings on your firewall. For details on how to do this, go to www.google.com/support/talk/bin/answer.py?answer=24962.

99

99	**Create a Google Talk Account**

✔ **BEFORE YOU BEGIN**	→ **SEE ALSO**
57 Set Up a Gmail Account	**105** About Browsing and Reading Gmail from Google Talk
	106 Set Google Talk Options

The first step in using **Google Talk** is setting up an account. As you'll see in this task, it's quite simple, and should only take you a few minutes to get started.

1 **Create a Gmail Account**

Only people who have **Gmail** accounts can sign up for **Google Talk**, so if you don't have a **Gmail** account yet, you have to set up one. Go to http://mail.google.com and refer to **57** Set Up a Gmail Account for more details.

2 **Download and Install Google Talk**

You have to download and install the **Google Talk** software to use **Google Talk**. Get it at www.google.com/talk. For details on how to download and install software, see Chapter 1, "Start Here." After the **Google Talk** application installs, you find a desktop icon you can double-click to launch the program.

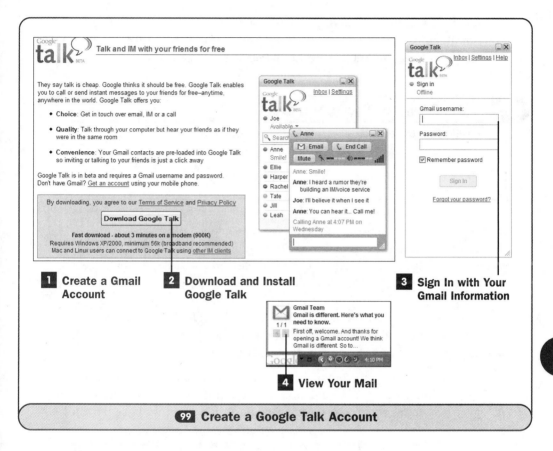

1 Create a Gmail Account

2 Download and Install Google Talk

3 Sign In with Your Gmail Information

4 View Your Mail

99 Create a Google Talk Account

3 Sign In with Your Gmail Information

After you install **Google Talk**, double-click the desktop icon to launch it. Then sign in. Use your **Gmail** username and password, and then click the **Sign In** button to sign into **Google Talk**.

▶ NOTE

When you run **Google Talk**, even when you're not using the program, it runs in the background so you can receive notifications that other people are trying to get in touch with you. To see whether it's running, look in the System Tray in the lower-right corner of your Windows desktop. You see a small icon of a talk balloon, like those you see in comic strips.

4 View Your Mail

Google Talk is integrated with **Gmail**, and it includes a mail notifier that alerts you when you have new email messages. Messages pop up out of the system tray at the bottom of your screen, alerting you to any mail in your **Gmail** inbox. For details on how to use **Gmail** and **Google Talk** together, see **105** **About Browsing and Reading Gmail from Google Talk**.

---

100 **Add a Friend to Your Contacts**

✔ BEFORE YOU BEGIN	→ SEE ALSO
99 Create a Google Talk Account	**101** Send and Receive Instant Messages
	102 Voice Chat with Others

100

Before you can communicate with others using **Google Talk**, you need to add them to your *contact list*. Your **Google Talk** contact list is separate from your **Gmail** contact list. Adding someone is as simple as a few clicks, as you'll see in this task. By the way, you should realize that the only people with whom you can communicate using **Google Talk** are other people who have installed the software. But as part of a business deal between Google and America Online, **Google Talk** users will eventually be able to communicate with users of America Online's instant messaging program, AOL Instant Messenger (AIM).

You can put people in your contact list who don't use **Google Talk**. But you won't be able to communicate with them until they install the **Google Talk** software. So if you try to send them a message using **Google Talk** before they have the software installed, you instead send them an email with the **Gmail** program, which invites them to download and install the **Google Talk** software.

Finally, your contact list is always visible in **Google Talk**—it's what takes up most of the screen.

▶ **KEY TERM**

Contact list—A list of people in **Google Talk** with whom you correspond.

1 **Click Add Friend**

Launch **Google Talk** by double-clicking the icon and signing in. To add a friend to your **Google Talk** contact list, click the **Add friend** link at the bottom of the **Google Talk** screen.

2 **Invite a Friend**

After you click the **Add friend** link, you are brought to a screen that asks if you want to invite a friend to **Google Talk**. This is a slightly confusing screen because it implies that all you're doing is inviting them to download and install the **Google Talk** software. In fact, though, you're adding the person to your list of **Google Talk** friends in your contact list.

To add someone, type his email address into the **Add** box, and click **Next**. If you want to invite someone from your list of **Gmail** contacts, click the **Choose from my contacts** button. From the screen that appears, enable the check boxes next to the people you want to invite to join you on **Google Talk**, and click **OK**.

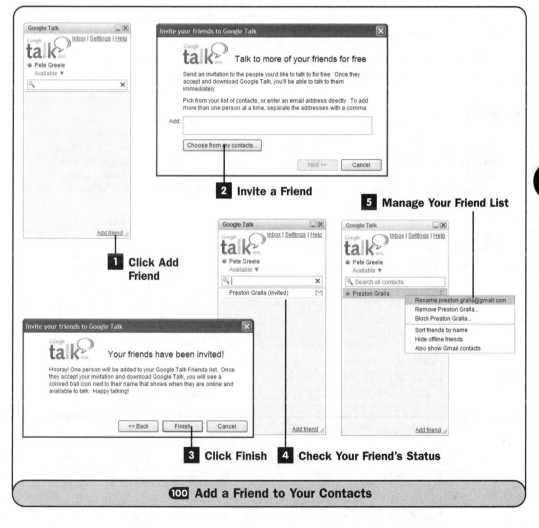

100

2 Invite a Friend

5 Manage Your Friend List

1 Click Add Friend

3 Click Finish   **4** Check Your Friend's Status

100 Add a Friend to Your Contacts

3 Click Finish

To complete the procedure for adding a friend to your contact list—and inviting him to download and install the **Google Talk** software so he can exchange instant messages with you—click the **Finish** button.

4 Check Your Friend's Status

At first, your friend shows up on your contact list (the list in the main **Google Talk** screen), but with the word **invited** after his name. If he has not yet downloaded and installed **Google Talk**, the **invited** status stays there. After he installs **Google Talk** and registers it, the **invited** status disappears and he is permanently added to your contact list.

Similarly, if you've invited someone who already has a **Google Talk** account, the **invited** status disappears after a time.

▶ NOTE

The various instant messaging clients, such as **Google Talk**, Yahoo! Messenger, MSN Messenger, and AOL Instant Messenger (AIM), do not speak to one another. So if you're a **Google Talk** user, you can't, for example, send an instant message to someone who uses Yahoo! Messenger. As of this writing, however, Google and America Online have announced that they will cooperate to enable users of **Google Talk** and AIM to send messages to one another.

100

5 Manage Your Friend List

When you've put friends on your contact list, you can manage how to display the list, and you can take action on the friends listed in it. Right-click a friend on the contact list to display a context menu of options. You have the following choices:

- **Rename**—You can rename the friend's entry in your contact list. For example, if the friend's name appears in your contact list as a nickname that is hard to decipher (such as Joe43XC3), you can rename the entry so it appears as his real name. Or if the entry appears as your friend's real name, you can rename the entry to display a nickname or something descriptive.

- **Remove**—If you no longer want the person listed in your contact list, select this option to remove the entry.

- **Block**—If you don't want to receive messages from the person or allow **Google Talk** to let this person know when you're online, select this option to block him.

▶ **NOTE**

If you've sent a contact an invitation and he has yet to respond to you, two additional options show up on this screen: **Invite Again** and **Withdraw Invitation**. Those options do exactly what they say—they enable you to send another invitation or to withdraw the one you've already sent.

- **Sort friends by name**—This option arranges the entries in your contact list in alphabetical order, rather than in the order in which you added them to your list.

- **Hide offline friends**—This option hides the names of people in your contact list who are not currently online. This option is useful if you have a long list of friends. If you hide offline friends, it is easy for you to see at a glance who is online and determine with whom you can communicate.

- **Also show Gmail contacts**—You can display the names of all the people in your **Gmail** contact list. For any contacts who are not also on your **Google Talk** friends list, highlight the name, click the **Invite** button that appears, and go through the process described in steps 2–4.

▶ **NOTE**

You can have your entire **Gmail** contact list automatically show up on your **Google Talk** friends list. To do that, at the bottom of the **Google Talk** screen, click the **Show all xxx** link, where **xxx** is the total number of your **Gmail** contacts.

101

---

101 **Send and Receive Instant Messages**

✔ BEFORE YOU BEGIN	→ SEE ALSO
100 Add a Friend to Your Contacts	**58** Compose and Send Mail
	102 Voice Chat with Others

After you've added friends to your contact list, it's time to start chatting. You need to be logged in to **Google Talk** (which, in turn, actives your Internet connection, if it isn't already active), and have a friend who is also logged into **Google Talk**. Follow these steps to chat.

1 **Check Your Friend's Status**

To chat with a friend, he needs to be online, so first check his status in your **Google Talk** contact list (launch and sign in to **Google Talk** to see the contact list screen). If your friend is offline and not available, the ball to the left of his name is grey, and an **M** icon appears to the right of his name. If the friend is online, the ball to the left of his name is green, and there is an icon of a green phone, rather than an **M**.

To confirm the status of your friend, hover your mouse over the ball to the left of his name in the contact list; **Google Talk** displays his status—**Offline** or **Available**.

2 Click the Green Phone Icon

To initiate a conversation, click the green phone icon to the right of your friend's name in the contact list or double-click his name, and then click the **Call** button. You hear a dial tone sound, notifying you that you're contacting your friend.

3 Wait for the Connection

If your friend accepts the call by clicking **Accept**, the dial tone sound notification stops. At the top of the screen, you see your friend's name, and a **hi** message from him. That means he has accepted the call.

If he doesn't accept the call or he ignores it (by clicking **Ignore**), you get a notification that the call wasn't answered.

101

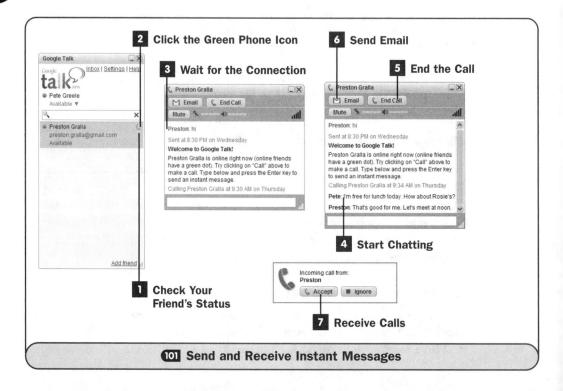

101 Send and Receive Instant Messages

4 Start Chatting

After the connection is made, type your message in the input box at the bottom of the screen and press **Enter**. The message is sent to your friend. When he responds with a message, it shows up just above the input box. You are able to see all your messages and his responses just above the input box. You can use the scroll bar on the right side of the screen to review the entire conversation.

▶ **NOTES**

Sometimes a person shows up on your **Google Talk** friends list without you adding them. This isn't voodoo, but a feature of **Google Talk** and **Gmail**. Every time you send a **Gmail** message, the recipient's email address is added automatically to your **Gmail** contact list. Exchange a lot of email with that person, and he is automatically added to your **Google Talk** friends list.

If you want to chat with more than one person at a time, just open another **Google Talk** window.

5 End the Call

To end the call, click the **End Call** button at the top of the **Google Talk** screen. If you don't end the call with this friend, the communication link between the two of you stays open, and you can start exchanging messages with this person again at any time.

6 Send Email

If you don't want to chat with your friend and instead want to send an email message, double-click the friend's name and then click the **Email** button that appears at the top of the screen; a new message to him is opened in **Gmail**. Complete the message as you would normally in **Gmail** (see **58 Compose and Send Mail**).

7 Receive Calls

If you're online and someone wants to initiate a call with you, a pop-up window appears at the bottom of your desktop, just above the System Tray. To accept the call, click the **Accept** button. To ignore the incoming call, click **Ignore**. From the point at which you click **Accept**, sending and receiving messages is the same as if you initiated the call.

101

102 | Voice Chat with Others

✔ **BEFORE YOU BEGIN**

101 Send and Receive Instant Messages

There's a good reason that Google's instant messaging client is called **Google Talk**—it enables you to literally talk with your friends, not just send them typed messages. You need the right hardware to do it—a microphone and speakers, or a headset—but after you get all the hardware in place, it's simple to talk. Using **Google Talk** this way is a free way to talk to others across the country or across the world. When you talk, the communication is instantaneous, as if you were on a telephone, although sometimes the voice quality can break up on one or both ends.

102

1 Install a Microphone

To talk with friends using **Google Talk**, you need to install a microphone into your computer. You can buy microphones at any store or website that sells computer equipment. Plug it into the microphone jack, usually located on the back of your computer. Some microphones instead work with a USB port, in which case you would plug it into an available USB port on your computer (as shown in the example). You can also buy a headset, which includes a microphone as well as headphones.

▶ TIP

Some computers, especially notebooks, come with a built-in microphone, and you might be tempted to use that instead of a separate microphone that you buy. Built-in microphones aren't of a good-enough quality for voice chat, so you really should buy an external microphone to install on your computer.

2 Open the Sound Controls

Before starting your voice-chat session, you should make sure that your PC's sound controls are working properly. Double-click the small speaker icon in the system tray in the bottom-right corner of your Windows desktop to open the Windows **Volume Control** dialog box. If the speaker icon isn't there, open the Windows **Control Panel**, click the **Sounds, Speech, and Audio Devices** icon and then click **Advanced Volume Controls**.

3 Make Sure the Sound Is On

Make sure that the **Mute** box isn't checked on your microphone controls or volume controls. If it is, disable the check box and exit the dialog box.

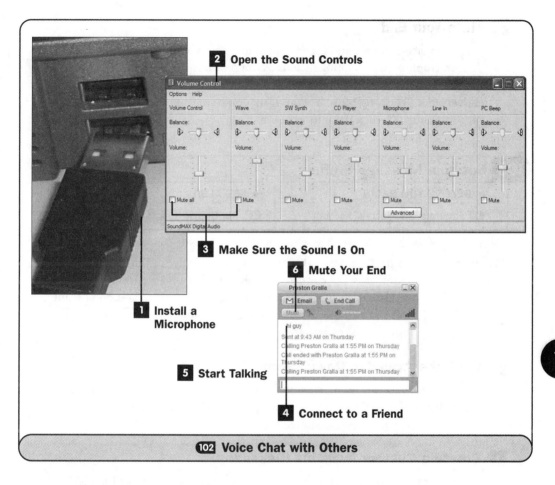

2 Open the Sound Controls

3 Make Sure the Sound Is On

6 Mute Your End

1 Install a Microphone

5 Start Talking

4 Connect to a Friend

102 Voice Chat with Others

4 Connect to a Friend

Invite a friend to chat just as you would normally, as outlined in **101 Send and Receive Instant Messages**.

5 Start Talking

When your friend has accepted your call, you don't have to do anything special to talk—simply start talking into the microphone. Your friend is able to hear your voice on her speakers or headset (if she is using one). And you, in return, are able to hear her when she speaks.

▶ NOTE

Although you can send typed instant messages while you are voice chatting, you cannot send text messages to the same person with whom you are voice chatting.

6 Mute Your End

If you're voice-chatting and it's your turn to listen, you might want to mute your microphone so no ambient sounds are sent from your PC to your friend's speakers or headphones while she's talking. To mute your end of the conversation, click the **Mute** button at the top of the **Google Talk** screen. To turn the mute off, click the button again.

---

103 Set Your Message Status

✔ BEFORE YOU BEGIN	→ SEE ALSO
99 Create a Google Talk Account	106 Set Google Talk Options

103

When you run **Google Talk**, your friends can automatically see that you're available to talk (as long as they are connected to the Internet and are also running **Google Talk**). If you like, you can change your status to tell them you don't want to be disturbed. And you can also set a customized message for when you're available and another message for when you're away.

1 Click the Available Down Arrow

In the **Google Talk** window, click the down arrow next to the **Available** status under your name. When you do this, you display a menu that enables you to change your message status.

2 Create a Custom Available Message

If you want to create a customized message that appears on your friends' screens when you are available, click the **Custom message** option next to the green ball and type the message you want to appear when you are available. The new custom message appears just under your name. When your friends run **Google Talk** and you are available, that message appears next to your name on their screens.

The custom message also appears as a choice whenever you click the **Available** down arrow. You can select it, or create a new message, as explained in this step.

3 Set Your Status to Busy

If you don't want to be disturbed, select **Busy** from the menu. Your friends see a **Busy** status next to your name in their **Google Talk** windows. If they try to invite you to a conversation, they receive a busy message, and the invitation is not sent.

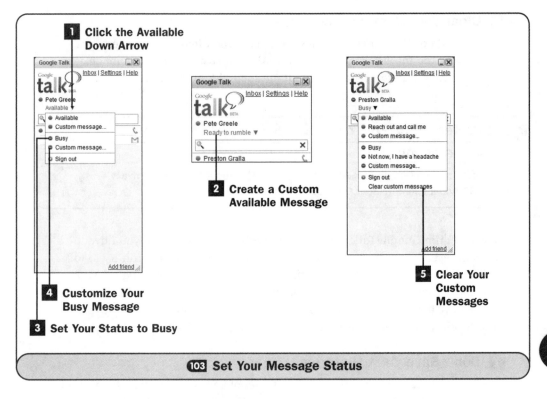

1 Click the Available Down Arrow

2 Create a Custom Available Message

4 Customize Your Busy Message

3 Set Your Status to Busy

5 Clear Your Custom Messages

103 Set Your Message Status

4 Customize Your Busy Message

You can create a new **Busy** message in the same way you created a new **Available** message in step 2: Click the **Custom message** option next to the red ball in the status drop-down list and type the message you want to appear when you are busy. This message appears just under your name in the **Google Talk** contacts list. When your friends run **Google Talk** and you are busy, that message appears next to your name on their **Google Talk** windows.

The customized **Busy** message also appears as a choice whenever you click the status down arrow to display the list of status options. You can select it, or create a new message.

▶ **NOTE**

You can create multiple customized **Busy** messages and multiple customized **Available** messages. Whenever you create a new one, it is added to the list.

5 **Clear Your Custom Messages**

To get rid of all your custom messages, select the **Clear custom messages** option from the status drop-down list. All your custom messages are deleted. There is no way to delete individual messages; it's all or none.

---

104 **Protect Your Privacy**

✔ BEFORE YOU BEGIN	→ SEE ALSO
99 Create a Google Talk Account	**67** About Gmail and Privacy
100 Add a Friend to Your Contacts	

104

When you run **Google Talk**, you're open to talk to the world. But you have to confront several privacy issues. First is that anyone who wants to can try to talk to you, whether you want to talk to them or not. Second is that Google saves your chat histories, and so anyone who uses your computer can see the conversations you've been having with others. If you want, however, there are ways to protect your privacy when you use **Google Talk**, as you'll see in this step.

1 **Don't Save Chat Histories**

Google Talk saves the 20 most recent lines of each conversation you've had with your friends. Those lines are visible when you click a friend's name in your contact list—the previous conversations you had with him appear on the screen. You can, however, tell Google not to save chat histories so that whenever you open a new conversation with a friend, the screen appears empty. From the options in the upper-right corner of the **Google Talk** window, choose **Settings** to open the **Settings** dialog box. From the left column of options, select **Privacy**. Then disable the **Save recent chat history** check box and click **OK**.

2 **Block a Contact**

To stop someone from contacting you, right-click his name in your contact list and choose **Block *Contact Name*** from the context menu, where ***Contact Name*** is the name of the person you want to block. That person's entry is removed from your friends list. When that person logs on to **Google Talk** on his own computer, he won't be able to see that you are online. He also cannot send you an invitation to chat, and there is no way he can contact you. Obviously, you cannot block someone from contacting you unless you know that person's contact name.

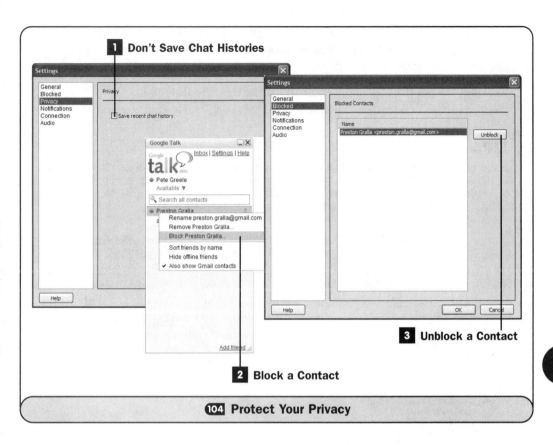

1 Don't Save Chat Histories

3 Unblock a Contact

2 Block a Contact

104 Protect Your Privacy

105

---

3 Unblock a Contact

If you've blocked someone and no longer want to block him from communicating with you, click the **Settings** link in the upper-right corner of the **Google Talk** window to open the **Settings** dialog box. Select the **Blocked** option from the list on the left. Highlight the person's name you want to unblock from the list on the right, click **Unblock**, and then click **OK**. That person now returns to your normal friends list and can contact you as usual.

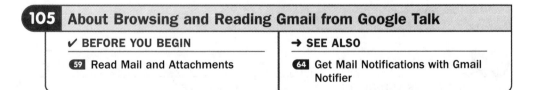

105 About Browsing and Reading Gmail from Google Talk

✔ BEFORE YOU BEGIN	→ SEE ALSO
59 Read Mail and Attachments	**64** Get Mail Notifications with Gmail Notifier

If you're a **Gmail** user, you'll appreciate **Google Talk**'s integration with that email program. As described in ⓾ **Send and Receive Instant Messages**, it's easy to send mail to someone directly from inside **Google Talk**.

But **Google Talk** features another useful feature as well—it notifies you whenever you have mail in your **Gmail** account, and then enables you to read the mail.

► **TIP**

If you don't use **Google Talk** or if you use it only sometimes, you can still get **Gmail** notifications. The free Google **Gmail Notifier** program monitors your **Gmail** account and alerts you when you have new mail, in the same way that **Google Talk** does. To get it, go to http://toolbar.google.com/gmail-helper.

You don't need to do anything special to tell **Google Talk** to check your **Gmail** account; it does it automatically.

When you receive new mail in **Gmail**, you receive a notification just above the **Google Talk** icon in the system tray. The notification shows you the first sentence or so of the message. If you have multiple messages, you can browse through them by clicking the arrows at the bottom of the notification window.

106

A notification from **Google Talk** *that mail is waiting in* **Gmail**.

To read any message, highlight the envelope in the upper-left corner of the notification. The envelope icon turns red. Click it, and your browser brings you to the message, from inside **Gmail**.

If at any time you want **Google Talk** to immediately check for **Gmail**, right-click the **Google Talk** icon (the speech bubble) in the system tray and choose **Check Mail Now** from the context menu. If you want to turn off future notification, right-click the **Google Talk** icon in the system tray and choose **Disable All Notifications**.

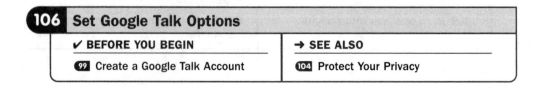

106 Set Google Talk Options	
✔ **BEFORE YOU BEGIN**	→ **SEE ALSO**
⓽ Create a Google Talk Account	⓾ Protect Your Privacy

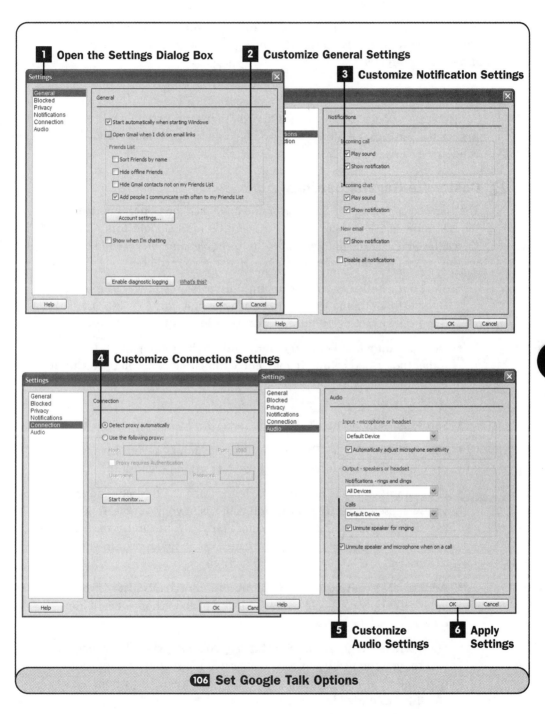

1 Open the Settings Dialog Box

2 Customize General Settings

3 Customize Notification Settings

4 Customize Connection Settings

5 Customize Audio Settings

6 Apply Settings

Don't like the way **Google Talk** works? No problem—you can customize it. You can change how your friends list is sorted, how you're notified that someone wants to chat, and more.

▮ Open the Settings Dialog Box

To customize **Google Talk**, you need to open the **Settings** dialog box. To open it, click the **Settings** link in the upper-right corner of the **Google Talk** window.

▮ Customize General Settings

The **General** section of the **Settings** dialog box (click the **General** option in the list on the left side of the dialog box) controls most **Google Talk** settings. Check the boxes for the options you want to enable, and uncheck the boxes for the options you don't want to enable. Here are your choices:

106

- **Start automatically when starting Windows**—If you select this option, **Google Talk** automatically starts whenever you start your PC. Disable the check box, and you have to start **Google Talk** manually instead.

- **Open Gmail when I click on email links**—This setting affects **Gmail**, rather than **Google Talk**. If you enable this check box, you open **Gmail** rather than an email program such as Outlook when you click an email link in a website.

- **Sort Friends by name**—This option sorts your friends list alphabetically.

- **Hide offline Friends**—This option hides the names of your friends who are offline; it's most useful if you have a very long friends list.

- **Hide Gmail contacts not on my Friends List**—Use this setting only if you've chosen to list all your **Gmail** contacts in your **Google Talk** friends list. When you make this choice, any of your **Gmail** contacts you have not already put on your friends list do not appear in your friends list.

- **Add people I communicate with often to my Friends List**—If you enable this option, people with whom you often exchange email are added to your friends list.

- **Show when I'm chatting**—Select this option, and when you're engaged in a conversation with someone (either text messaging or voice chatting), the word **Talking** shows up on anyone's friends list whom has you listed as a friend.

▶ **NOTE**

The **Account settings** button has nothing specifically to do with **Google Talk**. Instead, it brings you to your overall Google account settings. For details, see Chapter 1, "Start Here."

- **Enable diagnostic logging**—Click this button to turn on this option only if you've having problems with **Google Talk**, and a **Google Talk** technician has specifically told you to turn it on. This option is only used for troubleshooting.

3 Customize Notification Settings

The **Notifications** section of the **Settings** dialog box (click the **Notifications** option in the list on the left side of the dialog box) controls how you're notified about calls, events, and emails. For both incoming calls and incoming chats, you have two choices:

- **Play sound**—Enable this option to play a sound (a kind of repeating chime) when you have an incoming call or an incoming chat.

- **Show notification**—Enable this option to display a notification when you have an incoming call or incoming chat; a pop-up window appears just above the **Google Talk** icon in the system tray.

106

For new email, you also have a choice of whether to show a notification. For more details, see **105** **About Browsing and Reading Gmail from Google Talk**. You can also disable all notifications by choosing the **Disable all notifications** option at the bottom of the screen.

▶ **NOTE**

For information about the **Blocked** and **Privacy** settings located in the list on the left side of the screen, see **104** **Protect Your Privacy**.

4 Customize Connection Settings

The **Connection** section (click the **Connection** option in the list on the left side of the dialog box) enables you to use what's called a *proxy server*. You'll likely need to use this option only if your company requires the use of a proxy server. Ask your company's technical support department for proxy server settings, ask if you're required to use them, and then fill in the fields in the **Use the following proxy** section.

▶ **KEY TERM**

Proxy server—A server that provides Internet security by shielding you from direct connections over the Internet. Your PC makes a connection to a proxy server, which then makes the connection to the Internet.

The **Start monitor** button launches a monitor that watches and tracks Internet use. The monitor does not offer any text reports, but you can watch it on screen in its own window. The monitor watches only your **Google Talk** use, not any other kind of Internet use. The monitors technical things—protocols used, IP addresses, and more.

5 Customize Audio Settings

The **Audio** settings (click the **Audio** option in the list on the left side of the dialog box) control how **Google Talk** handles audio. You have these choices:

- **Input - microphone or headset**—The drop-down list in this section enables you to choose your system's default device for your microphone or headset (this is recommended), or you can instead choose a different one. You can choose from only those options on the list. In this section, you can also choose whether to have **Google Talk** automatically adjust the sensitivity of your microphone to match your voice level.

- **Output - speakers or headset**—The options in this section enable you to choose which devices should be used for notifications of incoming calls and the sounds for outgoing calls. You can choose your system's default device for your microphone or headset (this is recommended), or you can instead choose a different one. For example, you might have several audio devices installed on your system—a headphone as well as separate speakers—and the headphone might be set as the default. If you want, you can choose to make the speakers the default device. You can choose from only those options on the list.

- **Unmute speaker and microphone when on a call**—This option ensures that your microphone and speaker are not on mute when you're making a call using **Google Talk**.

6 Apply Settings

When you are done adjusting the settings for **Google Talk**, click **OK** to apply them to your current **Google Talk** session. You do not have to reset your computer or close and relaunch the application for the new settings to take effect.

106

Google Tools and Services

Google isn't a single site; it's a family of tools and services. Here's a quick list of its most important services and tools and where to find them.

Service	What It Is	URL
Apple-specific search	Search for anything related to Apple products	www.google.com/mac
Blogger	Google's blogging service	www.blogger.com
BSD-specific search	Search for anything to do with Berkeley Software Distribution (BSD), a version of the Unix operating system	www.google.com/bsd
Froogle	Find bargains online	www.froogle.com
Gmail	Google's email service	www.gmail.com
Google Alerts	Get news and search results via email	www.google.com/alerts
Google Answers	For-pay service for getting answers to questions	http://answers.google.com/answers
Google Blog Search	Search through blogs	http://blogsearch.google.com

Service	What It Is	URL
Google Book Search	Search through the contents of books	http://books.google.com or http://print.google.com
Google Catalogs	Online versions of shopping catalogs	http://catalogs.google.com
Google Desktop	Use the power of Google to search your PC	http://desktop.google.com
Google Directory	Browse the Web by category	www.google.com/dirhp
Google Earth	Travel in 3D around the world	http://earth.google.com
Google Groups	Search through discussion boards, called *newsgroups*, and set up newsgroups of your own	http://groups.google.com
Google Help Center	Page with links to dozens of specialized Google search sites	www.google.com/help/ features.html
Google Image Search	Search for images	http://images.google.com
Google Labs	Services and features Google is working on	http://labs.google.com
Google Language Tools	Translate web pages and text between languages	www.google.com/language_tools
Google Local	Get maps, directions, and local information	http://maps.google.com
Google News	News-tracking site	http://news.google.com
Google Reader	Google's RSS reader	www.google.com/reader
Google Scholar	Search through scholarly journals	http://scholar.google.com
Google Software Downloads	Central location for downloading Google tools	www.google.com/downloads
Google Talk	Google's instant messaging program	www.google.com/talk
Google Toolbar	Puts Google features on your browser's toolbar	http://toolbar.google.com
Google University Search	Search through university websites	www.google.com/options/ universities.html
Google Video	Search and display news and other videos	http://video.google.com

Service	What It Is	URL
Google Zeitgeist	List of most popular Google search terms	www.google.com/zeitgeist
Linux-specific search	Search for anything to do with Linux	www.google.com/linux
Microsoft-specific search	Search for anything related to Microsoft products	www.google.com/microsoft
Picasa	Google's downloadable image-management software	www.picasa.com

► **TIP**

Google Labs has a new feature called Google Suggest. Go to http://www.google.com/webhp?complete=1&hl=en and start typing a search term. As you type, Google pops up a list of suggested matches from which you can choose. Note that at press time, this feature was in Google Labs, so it might or might not be available long term.

Google Search Operators

Google allows you to search using *search operators*, special words and symbols that make it easy to get search results that match as closely as possible the information for which you're looking. You combine search operators with search terms to form a query, like this:

zeppelin –"Led Zeppelin"

That search would bring back pages that had the word *zeppelin* on them, but did not have the term *Led Zeppelin* on them.

Here are the common operators you can use with Google:

Operator	Description
AND	You don't need to use this operator because Google adds it by default to searches in which you use multiple terms. It returns results that contain all the terms in the search. So a search of **cow collagen** would return only those pages in which both **cow** *and* **collagen** appear.
OR	When you add this operator, Google returns pages on which *any* of the words are found. So a search of **cow OR collagen** returns pages in which **cow** appears and those pages on which **collagen** appears. So an **OR** search returns many more results than an **AND** search.

Operator	Description
–	The minus sign is called the *exclusion operator*, and it functions like the **NOT** operator. You combine it with other operators and terms and use it to exclude certain words from the search results. So the search **cow –collagen** returns pages on which the word **cow** appears and on which the word **collagen** does not appear. The operator has to go next to the word (or the phrase within quotes) that you want to exclude; there can be no spaces between them.
+	The plus sign is called the *inclusion operator* and serves an interesting purpose—it tells Google to use a word in a search that it normally ignores, or a stop word. So if you want to make sure that Google includes the word **to** in a search, you put it in the search as **+to**. As with the exclusion operator, the inclusion operator has to go next to the word you want to include; there can be no spaces between them.
*	The asterisk is called a *wildcard*. For those who are familiar with searches on a computer, you use it similarly to a computer wildcard search. It must be used in a quoted phrase, like this: **"I * New York"**. The operator returns pages that have any words in place of the * on them. So an **"I * New York"** search would return pages with **I Love New York**, **I Hate New York**, and so on, on them.
~	The tilde is called the *fuzzy operator* or *synonym operator*; it searches for pages that contain the specified term as well as synonyms for the term. So, for example, a search of **~generous** would return pages on which the word *generous* appears, as well as pages on which the word *unselfish* appears.

▶ **NOTE**

Google does not recognize the **NOT** operator, which is why you need to use – in its place.

Searching Strategies

Everyone has her own strategies for better searching, so it's always a good idea to ask others for their ideas. But here are a few hints that should help you with Google searches:

- **Be specific**—The Web is an enormous place, containing literally billions of pages. Almost any search you do brings back far too much information. So make sure that your search is as specific as possible. If you're looking for a history of the making of the album *Blonde on Blonde*, by Bob Dylan, don't just search for **"Blonde on Blonde"**. Try **history "Blonde on Blonde"** and you get better results.

- **Be brief**—More is not always better when it comes to searching. Be as precise as possible with the terms you search for, and you get the best possible results. A short, precise search is much more effective than a rambling, imprecise one.

- **Vary the order of search terms**—When you do a search, Google looks not only at the search terms themselves, but at the order in which you type them. It applies more weight to the first terms than to the later terms. So use more important terms first. It's also worth trying to do a search with the same search terms, but with the order varied; that often returns the results you want.

Search by Numbers Feature

You can type many numbers into Google to find information. Here's a list:

- Type a product's UPC code, and you are sent to the UPC Database, which gives you manufacturer information about any product.

- Type a Federal Express tracking number, and you are sent to a FedEx page that supplies tracking information.

- Type an U.S. Postal Service tracking number, and you are sent to a page with tracking information. You can only do it on packages that you can also track through the U.S. Postal Service site, which means this search works only for letters or packages you've sent using a method that allows tracking. For example, if you simply have a USPS number from shipping a package, but didn't pay for a service that offers tracking, such as registered mail or certified mail, the search doesn't work.

- Type the flight number of an airplane, including the airline, such as **Delta 1098**, and you get a list of pages from which you can track the status of a particular flight.

- Type the tail number of an airplane, and you see the full registration form for the plane.

- Type **Patent** and then a patent number, such as **"patent 5123123"**, to get patent information about any patent.

Index

Symbols

A

B

D

L

M

N

O

P

Q-R

S

T

U-V

W-X-Y-Z

Key Terms   Du 7/06

Don't let unfamiliar terms discourage you from learning all you can about Google tools. If you don't completely understand what one of these words means, flip to the indicated page, read the full definition there, and find techniques related to that term.

Algorithm
A set of rules for performing a task. In Google's case, algorithms are what determines what pages it says match your search requests.   **Page 6**

Archive
A list of messages in a group that are more than 30 days old. You do not have to do anything special to search or read through archives. But you cannot reply to a message that is more than 30 days old.   **73**

AutoFill
A feature of the Google Toolbar that fills in web forms with text you define.   **173**

AutoLink
A feature of the Google Toolbar that automatically creates links on pages you visit so that you can delve deeper into the information presented on the page.   **176**

Backlinks
A method of keeping track of other blogs and pages on the Web that link to your blog.   **254**

Blog
An online journal or column, typically written by a single person, which is often personal or political in nature.   **94**

Cached
A copy of something, such as a web page, that is stored locally or on a server. If the page is changed, the cached version stores the old version of the page.   **23**

Contact list
A list of people in Google Talk with whom you correspond.   **310**

Cookie
A small bit of data put on a computer that identifies a person and can store personal preferences and other information.   **12**

Driver
Software that hardware (such as printers, scanners, and digital cameras) needs in order to work with your computer.   **86**

Filters
A rule that is applied to incoming mail—for example, to move it to a certain label.   **Page 203**

Gmail
Google's email service, which you use by going to the Google Gmail page.   **184**

Google Toolbar
A toolbar for your browser that enables you to search Google no matter where you are on the Internet.   **168**

Header
Information about a newsgroup message or email message that includes information such as the Internet Service Provider, where the message originated, the servers the message traversed, and more.   **63**

IP address
A unique number, such as 233.23.234.22, that identifies each computer that uses the Internet. The IP address of your computer is typically assigned by your ISP when you connect to the Internet. Your ISP changes your IP address each time you connect, and if you have an always-on connection (such as with a cable modem or DSL modem), your ISP also changes the IP address occasionally.   **12**

Label (Gmail)
A way to organize your mail in Gmail. Labels function much like folders in email programs.   **203**

Label (Picasa)
A method of organizing pictures in Picasa that enables you to view, in a single location, pictures from different folders.   **282**

Newsgroup
An Internet-based discussion board. There are thousands of newsgroups available, and you can read them using Google Groups.   **52**

PageRank
A Google feature that ranks the importance of the page you're currently visiting on a 1–10 point basis, with 10 as the top choice.   **178**